ROMANS

Hope of the Nations

A COMMENTARY BY

PRACTICAL CHRISTIANITY FOUNDATION

L. L. SPEER, FOUNDER

GREEN KEY BOOKS

HOLIDAY, FLORIDA

ROMANS: HOPE OF THE NATIONS

International Standard Book Number: 1932587624

Cover Art: The Resource Agency, Franklin, Tennessee

Printed in the United States of America

For information:
Green Key Books
2514 Aloha Place
Holiday, Florida 34691
www.greenkeybooks.com

Library of Congress Cataloging-in-Publication Data available on request.

CONTENTS

PREFACE

From the conception of the Practical Christianity Foundation (PCF), it has been the goal of the organization to convey the truth in Scripture through verse-by-verse devotional studies such as this one. As part of that goal, we agree in an attempt neither to prove nor to disprove any traditional or alternative interpretations, beliefs, or doctrines but rather to allow the Holy Spirit to reveal the truth contained within the Scriptures. Any interpretations relating to ambiguous passages that are not directly and specifically verifiable by other scriptural references are simply presented in what we believe to be the most likely intention of the message based on those things that we are specifically told. In those instances, our conclusions are noted as interpretive, and such analyses should not be understood as doctrinal positions that we are attempting to champion.

This study is divided into sections, usually between six and eight verses, and each section concludes with a "Notes/Applications" passage, which draws practical insight from the related verses that can be applied to contemporary Christian living. The intent is that the reader will complete one section per day, will gain a greater understanding of the verses within that passage, and will daily be challenged toward a deeper commitment to our Lord and Savior

Jesus Christ. Also included at certain points within the text are "Dig Deeper" boxes, which are intended to assist readers who desire to invest additional time to study topics that relate to the section in which these boxes appear. Our prayer is that this study will impact the lives of all believers, regardless of age, ethnicity, or education.

Each of PCF's original projects is a collaborative effort of many writers, content editors, grammatical editors, transcribers, researchers, readers, and other contributors, and as such, we present them only as products of the Practical Christianity Foundation as a whole. These works are not for the recognition or acclamation of any particular individual but are written simply as a means to uphold and fulfill the greater purpose of our Mission Statement, which is "to exalt the holy name of God Almighty by declaring the redemptive message of His Son, the Lord Jesus Christ, to the lost global community and equipping the greater Christian community through the communication of the holy Word of God in its entirety through every appropriate means available."

Practical Christianity Foundation Value Statements

1. We value the Holy Name of God and will strive to exalt Him through godly living, committed service, and effective communication. "*As long as you live, you, your children, and your grandchildren must fear the Lord your God. All of you must obey all his laws and commands that I'm giving you, and you will live a long time*" (Deuteronomy 6:2).
2. We value the redemptive work of the Lord Jesus Christ for a lost world and will strive to communicate His redemptive message to the global community. "*Then Jesus said to them, 'So wherever you go in the world, tell everyone the Good News'*" (Mark 16:15).
3. We value the Holy Word of God and will strive to communicate it in its entirety. "[16]*Every Scripture passage is inspired by God. All of them are useful for teaching, pointing out errors, correcting people, and training them for a life that has God's approval.* [17]*They equip God's servants so that they are completely prepared to do good things*" (2 Timothy 3:16–17).
4. We value spiritual growth in God's people and will strive to enhance that process through the effective communication of God's Holy Word, encouraging them to be lovers of the truth. "*But grow in the good will and knowledge of our Lord and Savior Jesus Christ. Glory belongs to him now and for that eternal day! Amen*" (2 Peter 3:18).
5. We value the equipping ministry of the church of the Lord Jesus Christ and will strive to provide resources for that ministry by the communication of God's Holy Word through every appropriate means available. "[11]*He also gave apostles, prophets, missionaries, as well as pastors and teachers as gifts to his church.* [12]*Their purpose is to prepare God's people to serve and to build up the body of Christ*" (Ephesians 4:11–12).

INTRODUCTION

The book of Romans is a masterpiece of Christian doctrine in which the apostle Paul explained and defined many fundamental articles of the Christian faith. Doctrine is defined as "a body of principles presented for acceptance or belief, as by a religious, political, or philosophic group."[1] This letter contains the basic principles of God's teachings for His followers and provides clearly defined precepts that all Christians should adopt as their guideline for belief and practice.

Paul's authorship of this epistle should never be questioned. It has the unbroken testimony of the early church writers and has even survived the investigations of modern criticism.[2]

Throughout this letter, Paul, a servant of Jesus Christ (*Romans 1:1*), explains the doctrine of sin—humanity's fallen condition, and the doctrine of salvation—God's sovereign provision for redemption. Throughout the entire treatise, Paul inexorably demolishes humanity's alibis, pretenses, and self-justification. His logic carefully and thoroughly dismantles every argument that people can muster against Almighty God's truth.

Paul's letters and the book of Acts provide some information concerning his background and education. From these writings, we learn that Paul was a Pharisee and the son of a Pharisee (*Acts 23:6*); he was a Jew from the tribe of Benjamin (*Philippians 3:5*); he was a citizen of Rome, born in Tarsus, a thriving city of Cilicia (*Acts 22:3, 28*); he was educated in Jerusalem at the feet of Gamaliel, a highly respected expert in Moses' teachings (*Acts 5:34; 22:3*).

As a Pharisee, Paul devoutly adhered to the law and sought to maintain the purity of his religious belief by persecuting Christians (*Acts 9:1–2; 22:20*). When traveling to Damascus to continue his harassment of the Christian community, he was confronted by the risen Christ and his life was never the same. He became the Apostle to the Gentiles, using every faculty of his background and education to convince people of the truth of Christ's gospel (*Romans 11:13; 1 Corinthians 9:21–22*).

Paul wrote this letter to the Romans from the city of Corinth. The chronology of Acts chapter twenty leads scholars to conclude that it was written in late winter or early spring of A.D. 57–58. When completed, Paul sent the letter along with a woman named Phoebe who was sailing for Rome (*Romans 16:1–2*).

The purpose of Paul's letter to the believers in Rome was "to leave on file, in the capital of the world, a written explanation of the Nature of the Gospel of Christ."[3] Since there is no record of any apostolic mission to the city of Rome, how was the church there formed? Where did the gospel come from? Who was the messenger? How long did the church in Rome exist before Paul wrote this letter? The answer is relatively simple: "The nucleus of the Roman church probably had been formed by the Romans who were at Jerusalem on the Day of Pentecost."[4] This conclusion is supported by what we read in Acts 2:10, "We're Jewish people, converts to Judaism, and visitors from Rome."

Because of persecution, Paul was not sure that he would ever leave Corinth alive, but he deeply desired to visit Rome because it was the capital of the Gentile world, and his primary ministry was directed toward non-Jews (*Romans 11:13*). Three years after writing this letter, he would finally arrive in Rome, although under trying circumstances. At that time, Paul would be arrested in Jerusalem and would come to Rome as a prisoner, taking his appeal as a Roman citizen to Caesar.

Ultimately, the apostle Paul, servant of the Lord Jesus Christ and ambassador to the Gentiles, was beheaded for his faith in Jesus Christ about eight years after he wrote this letter. Through this servant, God has given us as readers a glimpse into His heart. In this letter, we are reminded that people are not out of God's reach and that "man's justification before God rests fundamentally, not on the Law of Moses, but on the mercy of Christ. It is not a matter of Law at all, because man, on account of his sinful nature, cannot fully live up to God's Law, which is an expression of God's holiness. But it is wholly because Christ, out of the goodness of His heart, forgives men's sins."[5]

As we study this letter to the believers in Rome, may we be humbled by the divine work of the Almighty God to draw the lost unto Himself, and may we consider the import of this question: To whom do we owe our salvation?

ROMANS 1

Romans 1:1–7

1:1 ***From Paul, a servant of Jesus Christ, called to be an apostle and appointed to spread the Good News of God.***

This letter from Paul begins with his calling and credentials as a servant of Jesus Christ. He presented himself first as *a servant*, which comes from a Greek word commonly used for "bondslave," or "a person who was owned by someone else."[1] When God called him, Paul became the Lord's willing servant. *"Our message is not about ourselves. It is about Jesus Christ as the Lord. We are your servants for his sake" (2 Corinthians 4:5).*

Paul was called to be an apostle, a term used for Jesus' original twelve disciples. Why then was Paul called an apostle since he was not among the Twelve? *"He appointed twelve whom he called apostles" (Mark 3:14). Apostle* comes from the transliteration of a Greek word literally meaning "one sent" or "an ambassador."[2] Paul acknowledged this high sacred calling yet always recognized his own unworthiness. *"I'm the least of the apostles. I'm not even fit to be called an apostle because I persecuted God's church" (1 Corinthians 15:9).*

As a servant and apostle of Jesus Christ, Paul was appointed by God to spread the gospel *(Galatians 1:15–16)*. God chose Paul to preach and teach the good news that His Son, Jesus Christ, came to the earth, died on the cross, was buried, arose from the dead, and ascended to the Father in heaven.

1:2 *(God had already promised this Good News through his prophets in the Holy Scriptures.*

The Old Testament repeatedly pointed to the coming of messiah, God's Anointed One. Every animal sacrifice given as atonement for sin on the altar in the tabernacle or temple foreshadowed God's giving of His Son, the Christ (Messiah) as the final atonement for all sin.

> *[25]Then Jesus said to them, "How foolish you are! You're so slow to believe everything the prophets said! [26]Didn't the Messiah have to suffer these things and enter into his glory?" [27]Then he began with Moses' Teachings and the Prophets to explain to them what was said about him throughout the Scriptures. (Luke 24:25–27)*

The tabernacle in the wilderness and the temple in Jerusalem symbolized Christ's coming. The New Testament accounts of Jesus' life, death, and resurrection thoroughly fulfilled the Old Testament prophecies. No passage more explicitly foretells the suffering Messiah than Isaiah 53:3–5:

> *[3]He was despised and rejected by people.*
> *He was a man of sorrows, familiar with suffering.*
> *He was despised like one from whom people turn their faces,*
> *and we didn't consider him to be worth anything.*
> *[4]He certainly has taken upon himself our suffering*
> *and carried our sorrows,*
> *but we thought that God had wounded him,*
> *beat him, and punished him.*

> [5]*He was wounded for our rebellious acts.*
> *He was crushed for our sins.*
> *He was punished so that we could have peace,*
> *and we received healing from his wounds.*

1:3 ***This Good News is about his Son, our Lord Jesus Christ. In his human nature he was a descendant of David.***

Jesus Christ is God's Son Who came to earth from His Father's throne. As a man, He descended from King David.

Matthew's gospel presents Jesus as the promised descendant of David by tracing Jesus' genealogy from Abraham through David to Joseph (although Matthew 1:16 specifically identifies Joseph as the husband of Mary, not the father of Jesus). Luke's gospel presents Jesus' humanity by tracing His ancestry backward from Mary through David to Adam and ultimately to God through Creation. The angel Gabriel informed Mary of Jesus' unique person:

> [30]*The angel told her,*
> *"Don't be afraid, Mary. You have found favor with God.*
> [31]*You will become pregnant, give birth to a son,*
> *and name him Jesus.*
> [32]*He will be a great man*
> *and will be called the Son of the Most High.*
> *The Lord God will give him*
> *the throne of his ancestor David."* (Luke 1:30–32)

Therefore, through the miraculous virgin birth, God sent His Son into the world as the perfect, sinless God-Man. Donald Grey Barnhouse, a noted preacher and teacher on the book of Romans, notes, "If Jesus had been the son of Joseph, He would have been, just like every other man, accursed and could never have been Messiah."[3]

1:4 ***In his spiritual, holy nature he was declared the Son of God. This was shown in a powerful way when he came back to life.***

Jesus Christ was not only born the Son of God, but He has always been the Son of God. Jesus was, in fact, God indwelling human flesh.

> *[1]In the beginning the Word already existed. The Word was with God, and the Word was God. [2]He was already with God in the beginning . . . [14]The Word became human and lived among us. We saw his glory. It was the glory that the Father shares with his only Son, a glory full of kindness and truth. (John 1:1–2, 14)*

The New Testament affirms Christ's deity. For example, in announcing Jesus' birth to Mary, the angel said: "The Holy Spirit will come to you, and the power of the Most High will overshadow you. Therefore, the holy child developing inside you will be called the Son of God" *(Luke 1:35)*. God the Father identified Jesus Christ as His Son. "*[16]After Jesus was baptized, he immediately came up from the water. Suddenly, the heavens were opened, and he saw the Spirit of God coming down as a dove to him. [17]Then a voice from heaven said, 'This is my Son, whom I love—my Son with whom I am pleased'" (Matthew 3:16–17)*. When Jesus died, the Roman officer declared, "Certainly, this man was the Son of God!" *(Mark 15:39)*. After His resurrection and ascension, the apostles affirmed this fact in their preaching:

> *God has fulfilled the promise for us, their descendants, by bringing Jesus back to life. This is what Scripture says in the second psalm:*
>
> *"You are my Son.*
> *Today I have become your Father." (Acts 13:33)*

In this verse, the apostle Paul declared this truth as confirmed by Jesus' resurrection.

1:5–6 ***[5]Through him we have received God's kindness and the privilege of being apostles who bring people from every nation to the obedience that is associated with faith. This is for the honor of his name. [6]You are among those who have been called to belong to Jesus Christ.)***

Jesus Christ, the eternal Son, conveys God's kindness through both salvation and service.

> *[8]God saved you through faith as an act of kindness. You had nothing to do with it. Being saved is a gift from God. [9]It's not the result of anything you've done, so no one can brag about it. [10]God has made us what we are. He has created us in Christ Jesus to live lives filled with good works that he has prepared for us to do. (Ephesians 2:8–10)*

Kindness as used here is often translated as "grace," meaning "undeserved favor."[4] No one merits this gift, so we receive it only through believing in Christ and receiving His sacrifice on our behalf. "*[12]However, he gave the right to become God's children to everyone who believed in him. [13]These people didn't become God's children in a physical way—from a human impulse or from a husband's desire to have a child. They were born from God" (John 1:12–13).*

Paul confessed his utter dependence on this gift. "*But God's kindness made me what I am, and that kindness was not wasted on me. Instead, I worked harder than all the others. It was not I who did it, but God's kindness was with me" (1 Corinthians 15:10)*. Paul's dramatic conversion described in Acts chapter nine was accompanied by a clear calling to be named one of the apostles. "*From Paul—an apostle chosen not by any group or individual but by Jesus Christ and God the Father who brought him back to life" (Galatians 1:1)*. His calling, and ours, is solely for the honor of His name.

Furthermore, our calling to be God's children and followers is no less special than Paul's was. "*God saved us and called us to be holy, not because of what we had done, but because of his own plan and kindness" (2 Timothy 1:9)*. We rest in God's sovereign purpose. Experiencing

His electing love should move us to thanksgiving that we are included in His plan of redemption.

1:7 ***To everyone in Rome whom God loves and has called to be his holy people. Good will and peace from God our Father and the Lord Jesus Christ are yours!***

In his salutation to the believers in Rome, Paul pronounced his blessing on this young church. Although he would spend his final years with them (*Acts 28*), he had not yet met them and longed to visit them. This letter was written not to everyone in Rome but only to God's "holy people."[5] Believers are God's holy people only by His sovereign will and work:

> *[9]However, you are chosen people, a royal priesthood, a holy nation, people who belong to God. You were chosen to tell about the excellent qualities of God, who called you out of darkness into his marvelous light. [10]Once you were not God's people, but now you are. Once you were not shown mercy, but now you have been shown mercy. (1 Peter 2:9–10)*

Notes/Applications

Although directed originally to the Christians at Rome, this letter is a part of God's holy Word, intended for all believers in every age. "*[16]Every Scripture passage is inspired by God. All of them are useful for teaching, pointing out errors, correcting people, and training them for a life that has God's approval. [17]They equip God's servants so that they are completely prepared to do good things" (2 Timothy 3:16–17)*.

With this in mind, let us apply ourselves to this study of Romans with due diligence, awed by this masterpiece of Scripture and determined not only to hear it but also to obey it. "*Do your best to present yourself to God as a tried-and-true worker who isn't ashamed to teach the word of truth correctly" (2 Timothy 2:15)*. Paul is a prime example of God's amazing love and almighty power. Barnhouse made this astute observation:

> If God could stoop to pick out the man who had been His greatest enemy and call him, equipping him to be His greatest messenger, then no one need feel that he may not be reached of God. God works through grace, not according to man's deserts. Grace is the secret of salvation and grace is the secret of the calling of God.[6]

Humbled by his past treachery in persecuting Christians, Paul was driven by a divine desire to serve His Lord faithfully. "[6]My *life is coming to an end, and it is now time for me to be poured out as a sacrifice to God. I have fought the good fight.* [7]*I have completed the race. I have kept the faith*" *(2 Timothy 4:6–7)*.

As believers, we are to be humbled by our past without being enslaved to it. We do not live under the burden of guilt for our sins because God has forgiven us. Therefore, like Paul, we can serve God with confidence.

Romans 1:8–13

1:8 ***First, I thank my God through Jesus Christ for every one of you because the news of your faith is spreading throughout the whole world.***

Paul rejoiced that the faith of Roman believers was becoming known everywhere. His expression of thanks is typical of his attitude toward the Christians to whom he wrote. For example, to the believers in Ephesus, Paul wrote, "[15]I, too, have heard about your faith in the Lord Jesus and your love for all of God's people. For this reason [16]I never stop thanking God for you. I always remember you in my prayers" *(Ephesians 1:15–16)*.

Paul commended the Christians in Rome for their faithful witness for Christ, which had made a deep impression throughout the world. *"Everyone has heard about your obedience and this makes me happy for you" (Romans 16:19)*.

1:9–10 ***[9]I serve God by spreading the Good News about his Son. God is my witness that I always mention you [10]every time I pray. I ask that somehow God will now at last make it possible for me to visit you.***

It is evident here and in his other letters that Paul prayed faithfully for his fellow believers. His specific request expressed his great desire to see them. *"[23]For many years I have wanted to visit you. [24]Now I am on my way to Spain, so I hope to see you when I come your way… [32]Also pray that by the will of God I may come to you with joy and be refreshed when I am with you" (Romans 15:23–24, 32)*. As strongly as he wished to see them, it was always "Lord willing," acknowledging that God's will would be done. How interesting that God was pleased to answer his request when, before Festus in Acts chapter twenty-five, Paul challenged the allegations against him and demanded an audience with the Roman emperor! *"If I am guilty and have done something wrong for which I deserve the death penalty, I don't reject the idea of dying. But if their accusations are untrue, no one can hand me over to them as a favor. I appeal my case to the emperor!"* (Acts 25:11). His trip to Rome was long and treacherous, but he arrived safely and had a rich ministry there for two years. "[30]*Paul rented a place to live for two full years and welcomed everyone who came to him.* [31]*He spread the message of God's kingdom and taught very boldly about the Lord Jesus Christ. No one stopped him"* (Acts 28:30–31).

1:11–12 ***[11]I long to see you to share a spiritual blessing with you so that you will be strengthened. [12]What I mean is that we may be encouraged by each other's faith.***

Paul had a deep longing to share with these Roman believers so that they might be *strengthened*, meaning "to put or place something firmly in a location—'to cause to be fixed, to establish in a place.'"[7] While he could commend them for their evident faith and witness, he also knew the importance of spiritual nurture, which God was pleased to give through him.

Then, as if in an afterthought, he expressed his desire for mutual encouragement. The pastor-teacher is called and equipped to build up the saints in God's Word but also needs to be refreshed by them. "*The person who is taught God's word should share all good things with his teacher"* (Galatians 6:6). As believers in the Lord Jesus Christ, we are a united body whether we live close together or far apart. Paul says that we are all one. We are all essential to the body of Christ, each with his or her appointed gifts and tasks. We are called to help and support one another.

1:13 ***I want you to know, brothers and sisters, that I often planned to visit you. However, until now I have been kept from doing so. What I want is to enjoy some of the results of working among you as I have also enjoyed the results of working among the rest of the nations.***

Paul explained to these believers that even though he had wanted to visit them, God had other plans, so Paul had been unable to have his heart's desire. In this case, God had consistently answered Paul's prayers with a firm, "No." Does this mean that Paul's motives were not right or his prayers were not in God's will? Not at all! It simply indicates that Paul sincerely sought this opportunity. Nevertheless, despite his personal wishes, he submitted to the will of God as noted in verse ten above. Paul followed the example of his Lord, Jesus Christ, the Son of God, Who submitted to the Father's will *(John 4:34)*. Eventually, according to the timing of His sovereign will, God granted Paul's request.

God answers prayer in His own time and not according to our shortsighted wisdom or desires. His timing is an essential aspect of His will. While we are invited to pray for our daily needs, and even for our desires, it must always be with the plea, "Let your will be done on earth as it is done in heaven" *(Matthew 6:10)*.

The Roman believers must have felt Paul's true, godly love for them even though they had not yet met him. Without doubt, they also desired to meet Paul and enjoy his ministry among them. He effectively communicated his love for them and assurance that he would visit them, Lord willing.

Paul's motives for visiting them were honorable: He wanted to enjoy some of the results of working among them. His great desire was to see spiritual fruit in these believers, the kind of fruit that he had been privileged to see in others to whom he had ministered. Although Paul had planted many churches, he had not planted the church in Rome, yet he longed to spend time with and nurture these Roman believers. Glad that the church already had been planted by other believers, Paul wanted to be a part of the process, a part of their spiritual growth.

Paul clearly understood the value of all the people in the process—those who plant and those who nurture. In writing to the Corinthian church, Paul clearly stated that he had been just a part of God's working among them.

> [6]*I planted, and Apollos watered, but God made it grow.* [7]*So neither the one who plants nor the one who waters is important because only God makes it grow.* [8]*The one who plants and the one who waters have the same goal, and each will receive a reward for his own work.* [9]*We are God's coworkers. You are God's field.*
> *(1 Corinthians 3:6–9)*

This expressed his godly attitude in serving Christ, a good model to all who minister in His name.

We are to desire the fruit of the Spirit in our lives and in those to whom we minister—those are the "results" for which we strive. "*For the fruit of the Spirit is in all goodness, righteousness, and truth*" *(Ephesians 5:9, NKJV)*. In contrast we are to reject the unfruitful works of the world. "*Have nothing to do with the useless works that darkness produces. Instead, expose them for what they are*" *(Ephesians 5:11)*.

Notes/Applications

The apostle Paul's godly attitude and motivations are evident in these verses. He genuinely loved these Roman believers even though he had not yet met them. He often prayed for the opportunity to visit them, and he continued to ask for this while always undergirding his requests with "Lord willing." He desired first "a spiritual blessing" for them (*verse eleven*) and then the privilege to participate in cultivating the "results" of their faith—that is, the growth of the fruit of the Spirit in their lives. In contrast, some of his fellow preachers brought dishonor to Christ through ungodly motives:

> [15]*Some people tell the message about Christ because of their jealousy and envy. Others tell the message about him because of their good will.* [16]*Those who tell the message of Christ out of love know that God has put me here to defend the Good News.* [17]*But the others are insincere. They tell the message about Christ out of selfish ambition in order to stir up trouble for me while I'm in prison.*

> [18]*But what does it matter? Nothing matters except that, in one way or another, people are told the message about Christ, whether with honest or dishonest motives, and I'm happy about that. (Philippians 1:15–18)*

What an example of genuine humility and trust in God! Paul was interested in communicating God's truth, love, and grace but not in who received the credit. Whoever or whatever method God used was fine with Paul. In his communication with these Roman believers, we see a true Christian relationship that transcends time and space. The communication between them was energized by the Holy Spirit. When God finally allowed Paul to travel to Rome and meet these believers, they were like old friends.

God is not limited by geography. Christians are as united to other believers on the other side of the world as they are to those in their local churches.

Romans 1:14–17

1:14 *I have an obligation to those who are civilized and those who aren't, to those who are wise and those who aren't.*

Why did Paul have this obligation? Was it from the people or from God? The answer is clear from his testimony to the Corinthians: "If I spread the Good News, I have nothing to brag about because I have an obligation to do this. How horrible it will be for me if I don't spread the Good News!" *(1 Corinthians 9:16)*. In a sense, Paul acknowledged his debt to these people; however, even more, his debt was to the Lord, for he was a condemned sinner saved by God's grace.

Truly, this good news is for everyone, not just for a few or for a certain group. Paul clarified that this message was for all people, regardless of ethnic or racial background. It is both for the educated and the uneducated, the wise and the ignorant. This message is not restricted, for God is no respecter of persons. "*God loved the world this way: He gave his only Son so that everyone who believes in him will not die but will have eternal life*" (*John 3:16*). "[34]*Then Peter said: 'Now I understand that God doesn't play favorites.* [35]*Rather, whoever respects God and does what is right is acceptable to him in any nation*'" (Acts *10:34–35*). This is the good news that Paul was obligated to God to tell every person.

1:15 *That's why I'm eager to tell you who live in Rome the Good News also.*

Paul was more than "obligated" to share the good news of Jesus Christ. He was eager to proclaim it. Paul's ministry was the fulfillment of the final phase of Jesus' Great Commission to the Twelve just before His ascension. "*But you will receive power when the Holy Spirit comes to you. Then you will be my witnesses to testify about me in Jerusalem, throughout Judea and Samaria, and to the ends of the earth*" *(Acts 1:8)*.

As the capital of the Roman empire, Rome was the power center of the world. As God's appointed Apostle to the Gentiles, Paul was eager to take on this great assignment.

> [19]*Also pray that God will give me the right words to say. Then I will speak boldly when I reveal the mystery of the Good News.* [20]*Because I have already been doing this as Christ's representative, I am in prison. So pray that I speak about this Good News as boldly as I have to. (Ephesians 6:19–20).*

1:16 ***I'm not ashamed of the Good News. It is God's power to save everyone who believes, Jews first and Greeks as well.***

Certain of his divine mandate and filled with the Holy Spirit, Paul was bold in his witness of the gospel. Such boldness was a public mark of the apostles in the book of Acts *(4:13, 29–31)*. Paul was unafraid to speak with anyone about this gospel that had so radically changed his life, many times despite suffering ridicule, beatings, and imprisonment. Even the threat of death could not shame him into silence.

Paul proclaimed the good news of Christ as the only hope for eternal salvation to lost people. All who believe in Christ, who trust in Him alone for salvation, will have eternal life. He did so without regard for a person's ethnic background. Since he was a Jew, he went first to the synagogues *(Acts 18:4)*. However, he considered himself God's apostle to the Gentiles.

The phrase "Jews first and Greeks as well" does not mean that the Jew is better than the Greek (or non-Jew). "First" describes the chronology by which the good news was delivered to humanity, not the preference of one over the other. The Scriptures tell how God chose Israel as His people through whom He would bring salvation to everyone, both Jew and Greek *(Deuteronomy 7:7–9)*. This entire letter presents the fullness of God's message proclaimed throughout the redemptive history of the Hebrew people and then to all nations.

1:17 ***God's approval is revealed in this Good News. This approval begins and ends with faith as Scripture says, "The person who has God's approval will live by faith."***

Under the law, God's standard of approval is perfection. Because no one is perfect, we all stand guilty before Him (*Romans 3:10–12*).

The "Good News" belongs to Christ, and it is revealed through Him as God's power and righteousness to anyone who believes. The very faith of Jesus Christ is revived in the spirit of the newly reborn and will instill God's power and righteousness in their lives. Paul is asserting not only that the gospel is true but that it is evidenced in the lives of those who believe. Therefore, he is not ashamed to preach the gospel even if it may appear foolish to the unregenerate. After all, "the person who has God's approval will live by faith." Faith, then, is not only the manner through which Christ offers rescue for His creation's hopeless condition, but it is also the means by which we continually receive our spiritual subsistence.

Notes/Applications

Verses fourteen to seventeen provide a "springboard" for the coming chapters, which are filled with a profound and reasoned presentation of God's grand design to redeem humanity from its helpless and hopeless condition.

Sinking in sin, we cannot save ourselves. Only the outside influence of God's grace and forgiveness rescues us from this condition of despair. God used this passage to bring the light of the good news to Martin Luther.[8] When Luther awoke to the truth that salvation is the gift of God, provided freely for humankind's sins and granted through faith in Christ, his life was transformed. This set off the great Reformation movement that reestablished the Scriptures as the only source of absolute truth and faith in Christ as the only basis of salvation.

Luther testified to the divine origin and power of God's Word in verse four of his beloved hymn entitled, "A Mighty Fortress Is Our God":

That Word above all earthly powers, no thanks to them, abideth;
The Spirit and the gifts are ours through Him Who with us sideth:
Let goods and kindred go, this mortal life also;
The body they may kill: God's truth abideth still,
His kingdom is forever.[9]

The only way we can come to God is through faith, and yet even that faith is God's gift. "[8]*God saved you through faith as an act of kindness. You had nothing to do with it. Being saved is a gift from God.* [9]*It's not the result of anything you've done, so no one can brag about it*" *(Ephesians 2:8–9)*. This truth reflects God's eternal character. He is both loving and just, holding us accountable for our sins but providing a way of salvation through His Son. What a wonderful gift for all who believe!

Romans 1:18–25

1:18 *God's anger is revealed from heaven against every ungodly and immoral thing people do as they try to suppress the truth by their immoral living.*

Having briefly announced the good news by which we may receive God's approval, Paul now begins a profound description of the ungodliness and immorality of all people who do not believe in Him. Whereas God's approval is upon those who believe, His anger is with all who reject His truth and salvation.

God's righteous anger is directed against every ungodly and immoral act because by those very immoral actions, people are attempting to suppress God's truth. It is as if they are pushing the truth away by their immoral living.

This judgment is already upon those who reject the good news of Jesus Christ. *"Whoever believes in the Son has eternal life, but whoever rejects the Son will not see life. Instead, he will see God's constant anger"* (*John 3:36*). God always has the last word, and all who refuse His truth will be without excuse.

1:19 *What can be known about God is clear to them because he has made it clear to them.*

God the Creator has revealed to all people that He exists:

> [14]*For example, whenever non-Jews who don't have laws from God do by nature the things that Moses' Teachings contain, they are a law to themselves even though they don't have any laws from God.* [15]*They show that some requirements found in Moses' Teachings are written in their hearts. Their consciences speak to them. Their hearts accuse them on one occasion and defend them on another.*
>
> [16]*This happens as they face the day when God, through Christ Jesus, will judge people's secret thoughts. He will use the Good News that I am spreading to make that judgment.* (*Romans 2:14–16*)

Therefore, whether Jew or non-Jew, each of us is accountable for this general revelation. Our consciences bear witness to this truth.

1:20 ***From the creation of the world, God's invisible qualities, his eternal power and divine nature, have been clearly observed in what he made. As a result, people have no excuse.***

While the created universe does not fully unveil God's revelation in Jesus Christ, it provides sufficient evidence to hold people accountable. God's invisible qualities, specifically His eternal power and divine nature, are "made visible, or made clear" leaving us without excuse.[10] God's glory, power, and providence are clearly visible in His creation if people look closely. Psalm nineteen beautifully expresses this:

> [1]*The heavens declare the glory of God,*
> *and the sky displays what his hands have made.*
> [2]*One day tells a story to the next.*
> *One night shares knowledge with the next*
> [3]*without talking,*
> *without words,*
> *without their voices being heard.*
> [4]*Yet, their sound has gone out into the entire world,*
> *their message to the ends of the earth.*
> *He has set up a tent in the heavens for the sun,*
> [5]*which comes out of its chamber like a bridegroom.*
> *Like a champion, it is eager to run its course.*
> [6]*It rises from one end of the heavens.*
> *It circles around to the other.*
> *Nothing is hidden from its heat. (Psalm 19:1–6)*

As people everywhere see the marvelous works of creation, they should also be able to see the sustaining power of the sovereign God:

> [24]*The God who made the universe and everything in it is the Lord of heaven and earth. He doesn't live in shrines made by humans,* [25]*and he isn't served by humans as if he needed anything. He gives everyone life, breath, and everything they have.* [26]*From one man he has made every nation of humanity to live all over the earth. He has given them the seasons of the year and the boundaries within which to live.* [27]*He has done this so that they would look for God, somehow reach for him, and find him. In fact, he is never far from any one of us.* (Acts 17:24–27)

The apostle Paul spoke these words to the Greeks in Athens who suppressed the truth through their man-made philosophies. In like manner, modern people continue to reject this revelation through false religions and philosophies. God has clearly revealed Himself in creation. In the final judgment, people will be speechless and without excuse, regardless of their sophistication or their ignorance.

1:21 *They knew God but did not praise and thank him for being God. Instead, their thoughts were pointless, and their misguided minds were plunged into darkness.*

Humans were created in God's image. "*Then God said, 'Let us make humans in our image, in our likeness. Let them rule the fish in the sea, the birds in the sky, the domestic animals all over the earth, and all the animals that crawl on the earth'*" (*Genesis 1:26*). Therefore, every person has some awareness of God. Still, people desire to make their own gods or to make themselves to be gods. They see no reason to praise and thank the true God revealed through this marvelous world and magnificent universe. They take for granted the very power and blessings of God and do not even acknowledge God's existence.

This ingratitude leads to sin. As people reject God's clear revelation in creation and do not thank Him, their thoughts are so distorted that they become nonsense. The Greek word for *pointless* actually is used to convey that which is "foolish, wicked, or idolatrous."[11] This foolishness leads to misguided minds and spiritual darkness. "*Godless fools say in their hearts, 'There is no God'*" (*Psalm 14:1*).

The hearts and minds of believers have been transformed from this spiritual darkness, so we are warned not to think or live like these people:

> [17]*So I tell you and encourage you in the Lord's name not to live any longer like other people in the world. Their minds are set on worthless things.* [18]*They can't understand because they are in the dark. They are excluded from the life that God approves of because of their ignorance and stubbornness.* (Ephesians 4:17–18)

God is light, and as people reject this light, their minds become darker and darker. "[19]*The wisdom of this world is nonsense in God's sight. That's why Scripture says, 'God catches the wise in their cleverness.'* [20]*Again Scripture says, 'The Lord knows that the thoughts of the wise are pointless'*" (*1 Corinthians 3:19–20*).

1:22 *While claiming to be wise, they became fools.*

Earthly wisdom, which rejects God's truth, is vain and foolish. Those people who merely speak of God but do not glorify Him are subject to His judgment.

> [13]*The Lord says,*
>
> *"These people worship me with their mouths*
> *and honor me with their lips.*
> *But their hearts are far from me,*
> *and their worship of me is based on rules made by humans.*
> [14]*That is why I am going to do something completely amazing*
> *for these people once again.*
> *The wisdom of their wise people will disappear.*
> *The intelligence of their intelligent people will be hidden."*
> *(Isaiah 29:13–14)*

1:23 ***They exchanged the glory of the immortal God for statues that looked like mortal humans, birds, animals, and snakes.***

Truly, in our sinful nature, we reject the truth that God has created us in His image, and we seek instead to make God in our image. This directly violates the first two commandments. "[3]*Never have any other god.* [4]*Never make your own carved idols or statues that represent any creature in the sky, on the earth, or in the water*" (Exodus 20:3–4). The consequence of disobeying the sovereign Creator is that people will continually bear the fruit of unrighteousness. The prophet Habakkuk vividly described the contrast between those who disobey God's revelation and those who believe Him:

> [18]"*What benefit is there in a carved idol*
> *when its maker has carved it?*
> *What benefit is there in a molded statue, a teacher of lies,*
> *when its maker has molded it?*
> *The one who formed it trusts himself*
> *to make worthless idols that cannot speak.*
> [19]'*How horrible it will be for the one*
> *who says to a piece of wood, "Wake up!"*
> *and to a stone that cannot talk, "Get up!"*'
> *Can that thing teach anyone?*
> *Just look at it!*
> *It's covered with gold and silver,*
> *but there's absolutely no life in it.*"
>
> [20]*The LORD is in his holy temple.*
> *All the earth should be silent in his presence.* (Habakkuk 2:18–20)

Despite achieving marvelous advances in technology, modern humanity has generally rejected God's revelation. As a result, the world continues in spiritual darkness. Nevertheless, peering through this darkness, we see the light and hope that come to those who willingly receive the good news of salvation through the Lord Jesus Christ.

1:24 ***For this reason God allowed their lusts to control them. As a result, they dishonor their bodies by sexual perversion with each other.***

When people keep insisting on their own way and persist in idol worship of any kind, God will eventually, after exercising His patient restraint, release them to the consequences of their rebellion. "*So I let them go their own stubborn ways and follow their own advice*" *(Psalm 81:12)*. As people doggedly resist God's ways and disobey His rules, they dishonor their bodies and continue in a downward spiral into bondage and eventual destruction. "*Make no mistake about this: You can never make a fool out of God. Whatever you plant is what you'll harvest*" *(Galatians 6:7)*.

1:25 ***These people have exchanged God's truth for a lie. So they have become ungodly and serve what is created rather than the Creator, who is blessed forever. Amen!***

God's truth is absolute, but people think they can hide from Him in half-truths and lies, and eventually they adopt their perversion as "truth." Nevertheless, God is sovereign and will expose all falsehood. Those who continue to believe a lie instead of God's truth will eventually be unable to see truth. "[11]*That's why God will send them a powerful delusion so that they will believe a lie.* [12]*Then everyone who did not believe the truth, but was delighted with what God disapproves of, will be condemned*" *(2 Thessalonians 2:11–12)*.

In rejecting the light of God's natural revelation, people deny the Creator and worship the creation. In essence, they are saying, "Let us make God in our image," rejecting the truth in Genesis 1:26 when God said, "Let us make humans in our image." This perversion of the truth is pride—the root of all ungodliness—which will bring certain judgment. In essence, God said to these rebels, "If that is what you want, go ahead and be that way! But it will cost you!"

The Creator, however, is blessed forever. His truth and righteousness will prevail. "[3]*This is eternal life: to know you, the only true God, and Jesus Christ, whom you sent…* [17]*Use the truth to make them holy. Your words are truth"* (John 17:3, 17).

Notes/Applications

We recoil at this ugly picture of the condition of humankind in its rejection of God's revelation. Sadly, it reflects the nature and consequences of humanity's will in rebellion against God. In contrast, all believers, while fully aware that the world's lies are seeking to seduce them, are to be assured by God's promises on their behalf:

> [21]*I'm writing to you because you know the truth, not because you don't know the truth. You know that no lie ever comes from the truth.*
>
> [22]*Who is a liar? Who else but the person who rejects Jesus as the Messiah? The person who rejects the Father and the Son is an antichrist.* [23]*Everyone who rejects the Son doesn't have the Father either. The person who acknowledges the Son also has the Father.* [24]*Make sure that the message you heard from the beginning lives in you. If that message lives in you, you will also live in the Son and in the Father.* [25]*Christ has given us the promise of eternal life.*
>
> [26]*I'm writing to you about those who are trying to deceive you.* [27]*The anointing you received from Christ lives in you. You don't need anyone to teach you something else. Instead, Christ's anointing teaches you about everything. His anointing is true and contains no lie. So live in Christ as he taught you to do.* (1 John 2:21–27)

God promises that His children will know the truth because the Spirit of truth will indwell them, giving them the ability to discern between righteous and false teaching. However, with this truth comes the responsibility to live obediently.

May we be lovers of the truth as revealed by our faithful Creator, the Lord Jesus Christ. May we seek Him each day to empower us to reject the lies of the world, the flesh, and Satan.

Romans 1:26–32

1:26 ***For this reason God allowed their shameful passions to control them. Their women have exchanged natural sexual relations for unnatural ones.***

Women were not created to desire other women; this was not God's purpose in creation, nor is it found anywhere in nature *(Genesis 1:26–28)*. God created male and female to join in a sexual union. This is true throughout God's entire created order. Mankind, made in God's image, joins this union within the bonds of marriage *(Genesis 2:21–25)*. Two women cannot be united in this way. When people refuse the Creator's design, they become consumed by their passions.

1:27 ***Likewise, their men have given up natural sexual relations with women and burn with lust for each other. Men commit indecent acts with men, so they experience among themselves the punishment they deserve for their perversion.***

Likewise, homosexual behavior among men is also an abomination. God designed men and women for sexual union within marriage. Any other arrangement is disobedience and is, therefore, sin. "*Never have sexual intercourse with a man as with a woman. It is disgusting*" *(Leviticus 18:22)*.

"Burn with lust" means they were consumed by their desires, conveying a passion that becomes overwhelming and out of control. This sin is reprehensible even to many unbelievers because it defies not only God's moral code but also the most fundamental principle of His created order. Certainly, the sin of adultery is also condemned as violating God's law. Nevertheless, the clear teaching here is that those who practice this sin are perverted and will receive the temporal and eternal consequences of their sin. The eternal consequences can only be eradicated by the blood of Jesus Christ. The influence of our present culture makes this an unpopular view, but nonetheless, we must heed the warnings of the Word of God.

1:28 ***And because they thought it was worthless to acknowledge God, God allowed their own immoral minds to control them. So they do these indecent things.***

When people reject God's truth as revealed in His creation and His Word, they increasingly see no need to acknowledge Him at all. We can see this in people's dogmatic rejection of the biblical account of God, humanity, and the universe. This has robbed humankind of any basis for moral thinking and behavior, which leads to increasing chaos.

When people deny God and His truth, they invite all sorts of deceit and lies. When they refuse to be corrected, God allows "their own immoral minds to control them."

A reprobate mind is void of sound judgment because it cannot discern right and wrong. It does as it pleases and will not subject itself to any outside revelation.

How horrible it will be for those
who call evil good and good evil,
who turn darkness into light and light into darkness,
who turn what is bitter into something sweet
and what is sweet into something bitter. (Isaiah 5:20)

There are severe and frightful consequences when people abandon God and become their own authority. Without the Almighty's gracious intervention, the historical trend is a downward spiral into darkness, debauchery, and despair.

1:29–31 ***[29]Their lives are filled with all kinds of sexual sins, wickedness, and greed. They are mean. They are filled with envy, murder, quarreling, deceit, and viciousness. They are gossips, [30]slanderers, haters of God, haughty, arrogant, and boastful. They think up new ways to be cruel. They don't obey their parents, [31]don't have any sense, don't keep promises, and don't show love to their own families or mercy to others.***

What a sad and sordid description of the depths of depravity to which people can sink when their evil minds and hearts are unrestrained! While this might not describe any one person, it portrays a composite picture of humanity that has chosen not only to reject the good news revealed in Scripture but also to refuse the light of God's revelation in the created universe.

This is consistent with similar descriptions of humankind in the Old Testament. Early in history, God determined to judge the world, sparing only Noah and his family in the ark. "[5]*The* L*ORD saw how evil humans had become on the earth. All day long their deepest thoughts were nothing but evil . . .* [13]*God said to Noah, 'I have decided to put an end to all people because the earth is full of their violence. Now I'm going to destroy them along with the earth'*" (Genesis 6:5, 13). Likewise, in His long-suffering dealings with the chosen people of Israel, God told Moses to step aside so that His wrath could be visited upon them. "*I've seen these people, and they are impossible to deal with.* [14]*Leave me alone! I'll destroy them and wipe their name off the earth. Then I'll make you into a nation larger and stronger than they are*" *(Deuteronomy 9:13–14)*. Several centuries later, the Lord warned His people of impending judgment through the prophets with this indictment: "The human mind is the most deceitful of all things. It is incurable. No one can understand how deceitful it is" *(Jeremiah 17:9)*.

Jesus also exposed the evil nature of humankind, describing it as darkness:

> [19]*This is why people are condemned: The light came into the world. Yet, people loved the dark rather than the light because their actions were evil.* [20]*People who do what is wrong hate the light and don't come to the light. They don't want their actions to be exposed. (John 3:19–20)*

In several of his epistles, Paul spoke of the works of the flesh (a list similar to these verses) in contrast with the fruit of the Spirit. His exhortation to Timothy is a reminder of this diagnosis of the depth of corruption in human nature.

> [1]*You must understand this: In the last days there will be violent periods of time.* [2]*People will be selfish and love money. They will brag, be arrogant, and use abusive language. They will curse their parents, show no gratitude, have no respect for what is holy,* [3]*and lack normal affection for their families. They will refuse to make peace with anyone. They will be slanderous, lack self-control, be brutal, and have no love for what is good.* [4]*They will be traitors. They will be reckless and conceited. They will love pleasure rather than God.* [5]*They will appear to have a godly life, but they will not let its power change them. Stay away from such people. (2 Timothy 3:1–5)*

We might see this passage as a "divine x-ray" of the human inner being throughout history after Adam and Eve rebelled in the garden of Eden. What an ugly and hopeless picture of humankind apart from God's grace!

1:32 ***Although they know God's judgment that those who do such things deserve to die, they not only do these things but also approve of others who do them.***

All who commit these sins have God's law written in their conscience; they know their sins are evil and that they deserve death. "*They show that some requirements found in Moses' Teachings are written in their hearts. Their consciences speak to them. Their thoughts accuse them on one occasion and defend them on another*" (Romans 2:15). Although these people know their deeds are wrong, they encourage others to do them and applaud those who do. Those who seduce others into joining them in their depraved lifestyle will be held accountable.

Can anything be worse than committing such sins? In his commentary on Romans, John Calvin states, "It is the summit of all evils, when the sinner is so void of shame, that he is pleased with his own vices, and will not bear them to be reproved, and also cherishes them in others by his consent and approbation."[12] Such an attitude displays a depraved mind desiring to deny God's very existence and thus His rule over the universe. This arrogant attitude and blatant behavior will surely incur Almighty God's wrath.

Notes/Applications

These verses give us a panoramic view of the depraved state to which humanity has fallen since sin entered the world. We are reminded of sin's devastating consequences, both in this life and in eternity, and that without divine intervention a person's rebellion will receive God's ultimate denial. At His discretion, God will turn that individual over to his or her desires and allow perversion to consume and control. At that point, there is no further hope for redemption. This is the mystery of God's judgment which is exercised at His sole discretion. Nevertheless, no one, even the most persistent and rebellious of sinners, lives beyond the reach of God's limitless grace.

Even though all people have sinned, some have been redeemed from the cesspool of their rebellion. It is easy for those of us who have experienced the Holy Spirit's recreating power to become haughty and complacent in our salvation. We, therefore, need to reflect continually upon the love and mercy that Christ has shown us in drawing us up out of sin's miry clay and unto Himself. We need to be mindful that we, too, would be sharing their fate if not for the grace of God. Without God's intervention, we, too, would be held accountable for our wickedness, leading immoral lives filled with despair and emptiness. "*Because all people have sinned, they have fallen short of God's glory*" *(Romans 3:23)*. "*The payment for sin is death, but the gift that God freely gives is everlasting life found in Christ Jesus our Lord*" *(Romans 6:23)*.

What an awesome salvation! The Lord Jesus Christ has provided salvation to unrighteous, undeserving sinners. "*Christ died for us while we were still sinners. This demonstrates God's love for us*" *(Romans 5:8)*. True, God is love, but He is also holy and just. We must acknowledge the urgency of the matter and the seriousness of sin's destruction, and we must seek God's forgiveness. Praise God! He forgives all who repent and cleanses every sin from them *(1 John 1:8–9)*.

ROMANS 2

Romans 2:1–8

2:1 ***No matter who you are, if you judge anyone, you have no excuse. When you judge another person, you condemn yourself, since you, the judge, do the same things.***

People can be so quick to judge one another, and yet they are so very unqualified. Jesus' command on this matter is clear and challenging:

> *"[1]Stop judging so that you will not be judged. [2]Otherwise, you will be judged by the same standard you use to judge others. The standards you use for others will be applied to you. [3]So why do you see the piece of sawdust in another believer's eye and not notice the wooden beam in your own eye? [4]How can you say to another believer, 'Let me take the piece of sawdust out of your eye,' when you have a beam in your own eye? [5]You hypocrite! First remove the beam from your own eye. Then you will see clearly to remove the piece of sawdust from another believer's eye."* (Matthew 7:1–5)

By saying that we have "no excuse," Paul denounced the act of passing judgment as indefensible conduct.[1] Theologian John Calvin comments: "This reproof is directed against hypocrites, who dazzle the eyes of men by displays of outward sanctity, and even think themselves to be accepted before God, as though they had given him full satisfaction."[2] Such self-righteous people believe that they are superior to others and, therefore, are filled with a condescending attitude toward those who disagree with them. Their hypocrisy not only blinds them, it actually incriminates them.

God alone knows each of our thoughts and motives, and we can trust Him to judge everything in perfect righteousness.

2:2 ***We know that God's judgment is right when he condemns people for doing these things.***

God judges rightly and righteously both in this life and in the life to come. All of His judgments are true because He is truth. Those who practice sin will receive the just consequences of their actions from this righteous judge. "[7]*Make no mistake about this: You can never make a fool out of God. Whatever you plant is what you'll harvest.* [8]*If you plant in the soil of your corrupt nature, you will harvest destruction. But if you plant in the soil of your spiritual nature, you will harvest everlasting life"* *(Galatians 6:7–8)*. To deceive ourselves into believing that we have done nothing to incur judgment is foolishness. When we judge others, we live as if we are in a self-righteous position. We may fool ourselves, but the truth is that God will hold each of us accountable.

2:3 ***When you judge people for doing these things but then do them yourself, do you think you will escape God's judgment?***

By this rhetorical question, Paul revealed a deeper understanding of human nature. In presuming a right to judge others "for doing these things" while actually practicing the same, how can a person possibly evade God's judgment? This indictment is primarily for those with a "holier-than-thou" attitude who do not live out their faith. God is perfect and all-knowing, so there is no escaping His righteous correction:

> [30]*We know the God who said,*
>
> *"I alone have the right to take revenge.*
> *I will pay back."*
>
> *God also said,*
>
> *"The Lord will judge his people."*
>
> [31]*Falling into the hands of the living God is a terrifying thing.*
> *(Hebrews 10:30–31)*

If God's discipline does not immediately follow our actions, we may think that God has forgotten, that our behavior doesn't matter, or that we have "gotten away with it." While God is patient and merciful, His chastisement is certain. "*When I choose the right time, I will judge fairly*" *(Psalm 75:2)*. Our actions matter.

2:4 ***Do you have contempt for God, who is very kind to you, puts up with you, and deals patiently with you? Don't you realize that it is God's kindness that is trying to lead you to him and change the way you think and act?***

Paul continued to address hypocrites with two more rhetorical questions. The first addresses the irony that God's mercy and patience lead many to take Him for granted and therefore despise His gifts! He provides not because people deserve it but out of His concern for humanity. "*He makes his sun rise on people whether they are good or evil. He lets rain fall on them whether they are just or unjust*" *(Matthew 5:45)*. The very air we breathe, our health, the beauty of creation and life itself—all these demonstrate God's gifts to the human race. Every blessing in life comes because of God's grace. We deserve nothing. He cares for His creation while providing opportunities for repentance as He patiently waits. "*The Lord isn't slow to do what he promised, as some people think. Rather, he is patient for your sake. He doesn't want to destroy anyone but wants all people to have an opportunity to turn to him and change the way they think and act"* (2 Peter 3:9).

The second question addresses the purpose for God's kindness. It is provided to lead individuals to repent of their sins and receive His salvation.

> [30]*God overlooked the times when people didn't know any better. But now he commands everyone everywhere to turn to him and change the way they think and act.* [31]*He has set a day when he is going to judge the world with justice, and he will use a man he has appointed to do this. God has given proof to everyone that he will do this by bringing that man back to life.* (Acts 17:30–31)

God's goodness and patience are not based on people's worthiness but on His mercy. In view of our tendency to go our own way, taking for granted God's grace, we would do well to heed the warnings put into place for our benefit. "*So how will we escape punishment if we reject the important message, the message that God saved us? First, the Lord told this saving message. Then those who heard him confirmed that message*" (Hebrews 2:3).

2:5 ***Since you are stubborn and don't want to change the way you think and act, you are adding to the anger that God will have against you on that day when God vents his anger. At that time God will reveal that his decisions are fair.***

The Old Testament prophets warned Israel of the coming "day of the LORD." Zephaniah 1:14–18 describes this as a day of wrath, of trouble and distress, of devastation and desolation, of darkness and gloom, of clouds and overcast skies, and of battle cries against fortified cities. When this day comes, all opportunity to repent will be gone, and God's revelation will be vindicated. The voice of wisdom calls out through the writer of Proverbs:

> [24]*I called, and you refused to listen.*
> *I stretched out my hands to you, and no one paid attention.*
> [25]*You ignored all my advice.*

You did not want me to warn you.
[26]*I will laugh at your calamity.*
I will make fun of you
when panic strikes you,
[27]*when panic strikes you like a violent storm,*
when calamity strikes you like a wind storm,
when trouble and anguish come to you.

[28]*They will call to me at that time, but I will not answer.*
They will look for me, but they will not find me,
[29]*because they hated knowledge*
and did not choose the fear of the LORD. (Proverbs 1:24–29)

As people reject God's Word, their hearts harden over a period of time. As individuals turn away from God's ways, their disobedience leads to increasing darkness. Stephen, a leader in the early New Testament church, pointed this out as he defended himself before the Jewish council. In his statement *(Acts 7)*, he accused Israel's leadership of this kind of rebellion against God. Their response? They stoned him to death.

At Stephen's stoning, in an ironic historical twist, those who executed him "left their coats with a young man named Saul" who approved of their behavior *(Acts 7:58; 8:1)*. Because Saul was present (the Saul who soon after was transformed into the apostle Paul, writer of Romans), he heard these last climactic words from Stephen:

> [51]*How stubborn can you be? How can you be so heartless and disobedient? You're just like your ancestors. They always opposed the Holy Spirit, and so do you!* [52]*Was there ever a prophet your ancestors didn't persecute? They killed those who predicted that a man with God's approval would come. You have now become the people who betrayed and murdered that man.* [53]*You are the people who received Moses' Teachings, which were put into effect by angels. But you haven't obeyed those teachings.* (Acts 7:51–53)

2:6 *He will pay all people back for what they have done.*

When that day of judgment comes, no one will have any excuse. Truth will triumph, and God's justice will be executed *(1 Corinthians 3:12–15)*. Almighty God keeps a perfect account of every work *(Revelation 20:12–13)*.

All people will appear before Christ, the righteous judge *(2 Corinthians 5:10)*. When they do, they will give an account for the lives they have lived and the decisions they have made. Believers, however, will not face eternal judgment for their disobedience because Christ's blood has washed them of all unrighteousness.

2:7–8 *[7]He will give everlasting life to those who search for glory, honor, and immortality by persisting in doing what is good. But he will bring [8]anger and fury on those who, in selfish pride, refuse to believe the truth and who follow what is wrong.*

Eternal life is the gift of God's grace rather than something we work to earn. Nevertheless, genuine believers express their faith by their actions. "*God has made us what we are. He has created us in Christ Jesus to live lives filled with good works that he has prepared for us to do*" *(Ephesians 2:10)*. Our lives should be marked by a desire to bring glory and honor to God. "*But first, be concerned about his kingdom and what has his approval. Then all these things will be provided for you*" *(Matthew 6:33)*.

In contrast, those who go their own way and disobey God's way bring judgment on themselves. God is actually angry with those who refuse to believe Him and live for themselves. *Fury* is translated from a Greek word that implies an anger born of passion.[3] God revealed in Himself a passionate love when He sent His Son to bring salvation. Here He also reveals a passionate anger and fury against those who refuse His love. Just as He is merciful to all who seek Him, He is angry with all who reject His truth. "*God is a fair judge, a God who is angered by injustice every day*" *(Psalm 7:11)*. Almighty God is not quick to judge, but there will be the predetermined day of judgment when His justice will be dispensed.

Notes/Applications

Paul vehemently warned of the hypocrisy of judging others. He exhorted us that when we pass judgment upon others we are, in fact, inviting God's judgment upon ourselves because we are just as guilty as those we seek to indict.

Passing judgment upon others is ultimately a distraction ploy. We seek to validate ourselves by averting the attention off of ourselves and onto another. *"Look at him! His life is a wreck,"* or, *"I can't believe she did that. How could anyone do that?"*

Perhaps, we believe that the Heavenly Father is somehow swayed by our poker faces. But He is not. Just like He knows the sins of the most hardened criminal, He, too, knows the sins of the one who appears to be the most virtuous saint. Even more sobering is the fact that in His eyes no sin is more or less sinful than another.

So where is the line between standing against sin and passing judgment? Much of the answer to that question is found in our own attitudes and beliefs. What happens when we assert ourselves and our own opinions concerning the wrong in others' lives all the while ignoring the sin in our own lives? We place ourselves in the role of judge. We ignore the fact that left to our human inclinations we would very well be guilty of committing the same indiscretions that we condemn. When we see ourselves as the ultimate communicator and dispenser of punishment and correction, we place ourselves in the role of judge.

When we reach for the gavel of correction in rendering that another is beyond God's forgiveness, we have truly crossed the line. It does not matter whether we verbalize such a verdict or not if we, nevertheless, believe it to be true. Sometimes we even hope that such is the case. Bestselling author and beloved minister Max Lucado explains:

> Anyone who filters God's grace through his own opinion. Anyone who dilutes God's mercy with his own prejudice. He is the prodigal son's elder brother who wouldn't attend the party (see Luke 15:11–32). He is the ten-hour worker, upset because the one-hour worker got the same wage (see Matt.20:1–16)...Not only are we ignorant about yesterday, we are ignorant about tomorrow. Dare we judge a book while chapters are yet unwritten? Should we pass a verdict on a painting while the artist still holds the brush? How can you dismiss a soul until God's work is complete? "God began doing a good work in you, and I am sure he will continue it until it is finished when Jesus Christ comes again." (Phil.1:6).[4]

There are several reasons why we must not assume the role of judge, but they all boil down to one eternal truth: God is God, and we are not. We are not perfect, and we are not without sin; therefore, we cannot render righteous decisions. We are not all-knowing; therefore, we cannot decipher others' motives and perceptions. We are not all-powerful; therefore, we do not have the authority to forgive sin.

How different would it be if we, as humans, held the fate of the guilty in our hands! Thankfully, such is not the case. The Heavenly Father is the just and loving judge Who meets each of us in His courtroom of justice and rules with absolute truth, mercy, and righteousness. *"Mercy belongs to you, O Lord. You reward a person based on what he has done" (Psalm 62:12).*

Romans 2:9–16

2:9 ***There will be suffering and distress for every person who does evil, for Jews first and Greeks as well.***

The natural fruits of evil are suffering and distress. "*If you plant in the soil of your corrupt nature, you will harvest destruction*" (*Galatians 6:8*). Whoever disobeys God's ways feels the pressure of sin. This comes in various forms: pressure on the conscience, lack of peace, conflicts with others, and so forth.

Those who practice evil will have inner stress and outer conflict. They will desire to run from themselves without hope of escape. They will face external conflict in their relationships and the world around them with no lasting solution.

Sin's ramifications affect all people in all walks of life. Jews and non-Jews alike will stand before God's bar of justice, the Jews first because they were especially entrusted with God's written revelation.

2:10 ***But there will be glory, honor, and peace for every person who does what is good, for Jews first and Greeks as well.***

The fruits of good works are glory, honor, and peace. What a contrast to the suffering and distress that come from practicing evil! "*Dear friend, never imitate evil, but imitate good. The person who does good is from God. The person who does evil has never seen God*" (*3 John 11*). Only what is done to please God is truly good. Doing deeds to please oneself is not acceptable to God, even if the deeds themselves seem to be good. The emphasis is on working hard to do good in order to ultimately please God, not just performing good deeds.[5] The Scriptures instruct us to walk in obedience to the Lord, motivated by a delight in pleasing Him and following His teachings (*Psalm 1:1–3*).

As with the results of doing evil, as a matter of order but not preference, the blessings of obedience are given to the Jew first and then to the non-Jew.

2:11 *God does not play favorites.*

This is the pivotal statement of the first three chapters of Romans: all people, Jews and non-Jews alike, stand before God as sinners and are saved only by His grace through Christ Jesus. History reveals humanity's tendency to justify its own sinful ways while holding God accountable for all that is wrong in the world.

Moses taught the people in Deuteronomy 10:17: "The LORD your God is God of gods and Lord of lords, the great, powerful, and awe-inspiring God. He never plays favorites and never takes a bribe." In spite of this clear teaching, mankind has still sought to justify itself and blame God for injustice.

DIG DEEPER: *God Does Not Show Partiality*

Two additional passages teach us about this profound truth concerning God's character—that He does not "play favorites": Peter's testimony about his experience in the house of Cornelius *(Acts 10:34–43)* and James' teaching about the sin of "favoring one person over another" *(James 2:1–9)*.

2:12 *Here's the reason: Whoever sins without having laws from God will still be condemned to destruction. And whoever has laws from God and sins will still be judged by them.*

Regardless of whether or not they are cognizant of God's laws, all are accountable for their sins if they continue to reject the grace of God through Jesus Christ. They will be condemned because they have sinned against God in the light of the revelation in His creation. The issue is sinning against a holy God, and all are guilty before His throne.

2:13 ***People who merely listen to laws from God don't have God's approval. Rather, people who do what those laws demand will have God's approval.***

The fundamental framework of God's approval is predicated upon a person's obedience of the law regardless of whether or not there is an awareness of the law. However, the standard of righteousness required by God is perfection as reflected by absolute obedience, and the impossibility of attaining perfection through keeping the law is clearly stated in James 2:10: "If someone obeys all of God's laws except one, that person is guilty of breaking all of them."

2:14–15 ***[14]For example, whenever non-Jews who don't have laws from God do by nature the things that Moses' Teachings contain, they are a law to themselves even though they don't have any laws from God. [15]They show that some requirements found in Moses' Teachings are written in their hearts. Their consciences speak to them. Their thoughts accuse them on one occasion and defend them on another.***

God handed down His written law to the children of Israel through Moses. However, the manner in which the law was declared to Israel was not the only manner by which the law existed and functioned.

The law is eternal, was with God from the beginning, and has been imparted to mankind as the guiding conscience of an individual's judgment and conduct. Accordingly, the people who observe the provision of the law by nature show the evidence of the law and its presence in the very essence of who they are even if they have not received the written law through Moses. Their conscious awareness of the law is fundamentally tantamount to having the written law. Their conscience becomes the intrinsic tablet upon which the law is inscribed.

As the bearers of their own conscience, all people are "a law to themselves." Therefore, those who received the written law and those within whose conscience the law operates possess the same knowledge of the law and are commanded to equally live in subjection to its provisions.

Just as the written law affirms either compliance or violation, the law inscribed upon the conscience also bears witness of the good and the right while convicting the same person of the bad and the wrong. It commends obedience while condemning rebellion. It encourages observance while restrains the inclination toward evil.

2:16 ***This happens as they face the day when God, through Christ Jesus, will judge people's secret thoughts. He will use the Good News that I am spreading to make that judgment.***

The consequences of obedience or disobedience will ultimately be revealed when Christ will judge everyone. At His appointed time, all will be revealed *(1 Corinthians 4:5; Mark 4:22; Ecclesiastes 12:14)*. No action escapes His scrutiny and people will be held responsible for everything they have done.

However, the criterion for this ultimate judgment has nothing to do with obedience or disobedience to this law. There is a distinct shift in Paul's emphasis at this point in his argument. He begins to unveil the answer to the dilemma of a person's ability to obey the law that God has placed within them. The measuring stick of a person's approval by God will be based on the Good News that Paul and the other apostles are declaring to everyone.

Notes/Applications

Although God is just and demands perfect obedience to His Word, He is also concerned for His people. The good news that Paul was called to proclaim offers hope to all who recognize their failure to meet God's standard of perfection. Only through Christ's perfect obedience to the law, His sacrificial death on the cross, and His triumphant resurrection from the dead can we receive assurance of forgiveness from sin and the promise of eternal life.

Thank God for such profound words as found in verse eleven: "God does not play favorites." The message of these first two chapters is that every individual is guilty before Him. Chapter three describes the universal sinfulness of mankind with this verdict: "[22]There is no difference between people. [23]Because all people have sinned, they have fallen short of God's glory" *(Romans 3:22–23)*.

Thank God, this is not the end of the story! God has not left us without hope for He has provided a way, the only way, to reconciliation with Him. Romans 3:24 proclaims this good news: "They receive God's approval freely by an act of his kindness through the price Christ Jesus paid to set us free from sin."

Therefore, as the classic hymn "Come, Ye Souls by Sin Afflicted" entreats us, let us praise Jesus for the grace and mercy that He has extended to us:

Come, ye souls by sin afflicted
Bowed with fruitless sorrow down;
By the broken law convicted,
Through the cross behold the crown;
Look to Jesus; mercy flows through Him alone.[6]

Romans 2:17–24

2:17–18 ***[17]You call yourself a Jew, rely on the laws in Moses' Teachings, brag about your God, [18]know what he wants, and distinguish right from wrong because you have been taught Moses' Teachings.***

Paul addressed those who were trusting in their Jewish heritage and laws for salvation. During Jesus' ministry, He addressed the Pharisees in much the same way (John 8:33–42).

The Jewish people, in general, boasted about being God's chosen people while rejecting the truth that salvation could only come through faith in God's sacrifice for their sins (not by merely keeping the law). They thought they knew God's will and could tell right from wrong because of their knowledge of the law. Ultimately, they claimed to be taught by God's holy law but were not humbled in the process.

2:19–20 ***[19]You are confident that you are a guide for the blind, a light to those in the dark, [20]an instructor of ignorant people, and a teacher of children because you have the full content of knowledge and truth in Moses' Teachings.***

The Jews, led by the Pharisees and scribes, were certain that they were the appointed teachers to others. In their minds, everyone else was spiritually blind. How ironic that the Jews had forgotten the purpose of Moses' teachings: to show their need for salvation.

These religious Jews were attempting to teach others—the spiritually ignorant and those young in the faith—while they themselves were unbelievers. They knew the full content of Moses' teachings, but they missed the true meaning. "*They will appear to have a godly life, but they will not let its power change them*" (*2 Timothy 3:5*). They were teaching religion based on the law rather than on a relationship with God, the lawgiver.

2:21–22 ***[21]As you teach others, are you failing to teach yourself? As you preach against stealing, are you stealing? [22]As you tell others not to commit adultery, are you committing adultery? As you treat idols with disgust, are you robbing temples?***

These Jews were not practicing what they preached. Instead, they instructed others to behave one way while they themselves behaved contrary to their own teachings. They forced heavy burdens upon others but would not lift a finger to help. They sought the praise of men in the form of loving titles and honors. While teaching "You shall not steal," they stole from widows.

They had not only profaned God's law as revealed through Moses, but they had also added human rules that distorted the very Word of God.

2:23–24 ***[23]As you brag about the laws in Moses' Teachings, are you dishonoring God by ignoring Moses' Teachings? [24]As Scripture says, "God's name is cursed among the nations because of you."***

Paul rendered a stinging indictment upon the Jews in Rome, who proudly claimed to be God's people. Barnhouse comments on this matter:

> They knew that God had called them and had made them the channels of His revelation. Instead of being driven by this stupendous fact to an extraordinary humility, they seized upon it as a flatterer for their human pride. They rested upon their possession of the law which had become a couch to them instead of a goad. They made their boast to God; that is to say, they had come to the place where they thought that they had a patent and copyright on God. There can be no doubt from Scripture that those whom God has chosen for His own have a right to say that God is their God. This we say today. The God of the Lord Jesus Christ, the God of the open tomb and the resurrection, the God of the Bible is indeed our God. But the knowledge must be very humbling. It must drive us to a humble

> walk with Him and a momentary seeking to acknowledge Him and do His will.[7]

These people were putting confidence in themselves rather than in God. Their laws were more important than His law and were a burden to common people. The effect, as prophesied, was that "God's name is cursed among the nations because of you":

> *So what do I find here? asks the LORD. My people are taken away for no reason. Their rulers are screaming, declares the LORD. And my name is cursed all day long (Isaiah 52:5).*
>
> *[20]But wherever they went among the nations, they dishonored my holy name. People said about them, 'These are the LORD's people, yet they had to leave his land.' [21]I became concerned about my holy name because my people dishonored it among the nations wherever they went (Ezekiel 36:20–21).*

God's people, chosen in love to honor His name and be a light to the nations, had become appalling obstacles to those around them.

Notes/Applications

What a stinging condemnation by God of the haughty, religious Jews of that day! They were proud of their heritage as His chosen people, claiming to be guides and teachers of the law while being hypocrites who were actually disobeying its teachings and demands. They had utterly failed to heed the Lord's admonition given through the prophet Micah: "You mortals, the LORD has told you what is good. This is what the LORD requires from you: to do what is right, to love mercy, and to live humbly with your God" *(Micah 6:8)*. According to all three requirements, they had utterly failed God's test, yet they arrogantly claimed to be righteous before Him.

It is easy to condemn their sins and hypocrisy while denying that these sins exist in our own lives. We profess to be saved by grace through faith as taught in Ephesians 2:8–9, but we often ignore verse ten, which states that God "has created us in Christ Jesus to live lives filled with good works that he has prepared for us to do." Faith in Christ will be followed by works that continually express the reality of the renewal that has taken place in our hearts.

The book of James confronts us with serious probing about the genuineness of our faith:

> [22]*Do what God's word says. Don't merely listen to it, or you will fool yourselves.* [23]*If someone listens to God's word but doesn't do what it says, he is like a person who looks at his face in a mirror,* [24]*studies his features, goes away, and immediately forgets what he looks like.* [25]*However, the person who continues to study God's perfect teachings that make people free and who remains committed to them will be blessed. People like that don't merely listen and forget; they actually do what God's teachings say. (James 1:22–25)*

We need to be honest with ourselves, asking the Holy Spirit to search our hearts and reveal to us the truth about ourselves.

> [23]*Examine me, O God, and know my mind.*
> *Test me, and know my thoughts.*
> [24]*See whether I am on an evil path.*
> *Then lead me on the everlasting path. (Psalm 139:23–24)*

Romans 2:25–29

2:25 ***For example, circumcision is valuable if you follow Moses' laws. If you don't follow those laws, your circumcision amounts to uncircumcision.***

Circumcision was the mark upon the Jewish males (and, accordingly, the nation) setting them apart by God to serve Him. God had given the requirement of circumcision as a sign of His covenant with Abraham *(Genesis 17:9–14)*.

Through twenty centuries after God's promise to Abraham, circumcision was associated with the law given through Moses:

> [16]*The promises were spoken to Abraham and to his descendant. Scripture doesn't say, "descendants," referring to many, but "your descendant," referring to one. That descendant is Christ.* [17]*This is what I mean: The laws given to Moses 430 years after God had already put his promise to Abraham into effect didn't cancel the promise to Abraham. (Galatians 3:16–17)*

Although Paul clarified in the book of Galatians the true intent of circumcision as a sign of the covenant promise, he spoke of circumcision here in Romans in terms of its perversion as a sign of keeping the law. Circumcision, as with any ritual, was supposed to function as a symbol of a commitment already present, not as a way to earn God's favor.

Now, addressing this false premise, Paul pressed upon his Jewish readers this logical application: If one is circumcised and does not obey the law, his circumcision means nothing. The rite of circumcision is meaningful only if the heart is first circumcised (set apart as God's). *"The LORD your God will circumcise your hearts and the hearts of your descendants. You will love the LORD your God with all your heart and with all your soul, and you will live" (Deuteronomy 30:6)*. If a person's heart is not circumcised, then he is uncircumcised.

2:26 ***So if a man does what Moses' Teachings demand, won't he be considered circumcised even if he is uncircumcised?***

Having established the premise that true circumcision must be evidenced by obedience to the law, Paul pressed this rhetorical question: If a person obeys Moses' teaching, even though that person may be physically uncircumcised, is he not circumcised according to its true meaning? The answer is clearly the affirmative. As the "circumcised" one who breaks the law is really uncircumcised, the "uncircumcised" one who obeys the law must really be circumcised, at least in God's eyes, where it matters most.

It is clear that circumcision and other religious rites are valid only as they are accompanied with regeneration and obedience to God's law. Obedience to God out of a trusting heart pleases Him most.

2:27 ***The uncircumcised man who carries out what Moses' Teachings say will condemn you for not following them. He will condemn you in spite of the fact that you are circumcised and have Moses' Teachings in writing.***

Paul continued to emphasize that the Pharisees' persistent submission to the law would not yield righteousness. He further implied that the crux of the matter remained with the individual's heart. The righteous in heart would rise up and judge those who only had an appearance of obedience. Therefore, those who were not Jews by physical birth but who were righteous in heart or spiritually circumcised would ultimately sit in judgment of those who were Jews by physical birth but who had not been reconciled with the Almighty God through faith in His Son, the Lord Jesus Christ.

In another New Testament reference, Jesus Himself gave a similar proclamation where Gentiles would one day judge the religious leaders of His day:

> *[41]The men of Nineveh will stand up with you at the time of judgment and will condemn you, because they turned to God and changed the way they thought and acted when Jonah spoke his message. But look, someone greater than Jonah is here! [42]The queen from the south will stand up at the time of judgment with you. She will condemn you, because she came from the ends of the earth to hear Solomon's wisdom. But look, someone greater than Solomon is here! (Matthew 12:41–42)*

2:28–29 ***[28]A person is not a Jew because of his appearance, nor is circumcision a matter of how the body looks. [29]Rather, a person is a Jew inwardly, and circumcision is something that happens in a person's heart. Circumcision is spiritual, not just a written rule. That person's praise will come from God, not from people.***

Compare this startling statement with Paul's self-portrait in Philippians, his personal testimony of the radical change in his conversion to become a follower of Jesus Christ:

> *[3]We are the true circumcised people of God because we serve God's Spirit and take pride in Christ Jesus. We don't place any confidence in physical things, [4]although I could have confidence in my physical qualifications. If anyone else thinks that he can trust in something physical, I can claim even more. [5]I was circumcised on the eighth day. I'm a descendant of Israel. I'm from the tribe of Benjamin. I'm a pure-blooded Hebrew. When it comes to living up to standards, I was a Pharisee. [6]When it comes to being enthusiastic, I was a persecutor of the church. When it comes to winning God's approval by keeping Jewish laws, I was perfect.*
>
> *[7]These things that I once considered valuable, I now consider worthless for Christ. (Philippians 3:3–7)*

Through his dramatic encounter with Jesus (*Acts 9*), Paul learned that being born Jewish does not make a person a Jew at heart, and ritual circumcision has no value without true circumcision of the heart. In expressing deep concern for his kindred in the flesh, he would identify more fully the biblical view of God's chosen ones:

> [3]*I wish I could be condemned and cut off from Christ for the sake of others who, like me, are Jewish by birth.* [4]*They are Israelites, God's adopted children. They have the Lord's glory, the pledges, Moses' Teachings, the true worship, and the promises.* [5]*The Messiah is descended from their ancestors according to his human nature. The Messiah is God over everything, forever blessed. Amen.*
>
> [6]*Now it is not as though God's word has failed. Clearly, not everyone descended from Israel is part of Israel* [7]*or a descendant of Abraham. However, as Scripture says, "Through Isaac your descendants will carry on your name."* [8]*This means that children born by natural descent from Abraham are not necessarily God's children. Instead, children born by the promise are considered Abraham's descendants. (Romans 9:3–8)*

This truth is basic to understanding the entire book of Romans and the entire revelation of Jesus Christ in the New Testament. It harmonizes with Jesus' teaching that He came to fulfill the law and with Paul's other letters, especially Galatians, Ephesians, Philippians, and Colossians. Here Paul declared that a true Jew is one inwardly and true circumcision is of the heart. The true Jew worships God with his whole being, physical and spiritual. True circumcision cuts away human pride and creates a sincere love for Almighty God. "*The* LORD *your God will circumcise your hearts and the hearts of your descendants. You will love the* LORD *your God with all your heart and with all your soul, and you will live*" *(Deuteronomy 30:6)*. The outward deed and appearances will naturally follow as the inward man loves and obeys Him.

True circumcision comes by the Lord Jesus Christ. "*In him you were also circumcised. It was not a circumcision performed by human hands. But it was a removal of the corrupt nature in the circumcision performed by Christ*" *(Colossians 2:11)*. He alone can cut around humanity's sinfulness and remove it. This spiritual circumcision creates a newness of life that is godly, holy, and righteous.

Praise from God will last forever; praise from people will last only a very short time. People's praise causes false pride; God's praise leads to humble gratitude. Praise from God brings growth in one's soul as His Word nourishes the whole being. Happy is the one who receives praises from the Lord and Savior!

Notes/Applications

This teaching about spiritual circumcision applies to everyone. Even as genuine believers, we must accept God's knife of circumcision upon our hearts and lives as He continually refines us. The surgeon's knife hurts, yet God is the Great Physician and knows how to cut deeply into our being, removing our selfish flesh and creating in us new hearts. In Psalm 51:10, King David cried out in the misery of his sin, "Create a clean heart in me, O God, and renew a faithful spirit within me."

In Christ, we have been freed from the empty ritual of physical circumcision or any other ritual that in itself cannot save us. Paul further informs us of this truth, exhorting us to live in the freedom Christ offers us by His death and resurrection:

> [1]*Christ has freed us so that we may enjoy the benefits of freedom. Therefore, be firm in this freedom, and don't become slaves again…* [6]*As far as our relationship to Christ Jesus is concerned, it doesn't matter whether we are circumcised or not. But what matters is a faith that expresses itself through love.* (Galatians 5:1, 6)

May our faithful Lord enable us to fulfill His admonition: "to do what is right, to love mercy, and to live humbly with [our] God" *(Micah 6:8)*.

ROMANS 3

Romans 3:1–8

3:1 ***Is there any advantage, then, in being a Jew? Or is there any value in being circumcised?***

Certain groups were teaching that in order to be a Christian a person first had to obey all the Jewish laws and men had to be circumcised. Essentially, one had to become a Jew before becoming a Christian. Paul contended that a person did not have to become a Jewish proselyte (that is, a convert to Judaism) or be physically circumcised before being able to become a Christian. So was there value in being Jewish or in circumcision? If, in light of the work of Christ, Jews and Gentiles stood on equal ground spiritually, were there any advantages to being Jewish?

3:2 ***There are all kinds of advantages. First of all, God entrusted them with his word.***

Paul responded to such questions with an emphatic affirmative answer. He reminded his readers that Moses, the leader of the Israelite nation, declared God's purpose for the Jewish people:

> *[6]You are a holy people, who belong to the LORD your God. He chose you to be his own special possession out of all the nations on earth. [7]The LORD set his heart on you and chose you, even though you didn't outnumber all the other people. You were the smallest of all nations. [8]You were chosen because the LORD loved you and kept the oath he swore to your ancestors. (Deuteronomy 7:6–8)*

As God's select people, the Israelites' primary role involved God's word—the written word, of course, and also, eventually, the incarnate Word, Jesus Christ. "*[4]But when the right time came, God sent his Son into the world. A woman gave birth to him, and he came under the control of God's laws. [5]God sent him to pay for the freedom of those who were controlled by these laws so that we would be adopted as his children" (Galatians 4:4–5)*.

What a privilege to be God's instrument to give His eternal Word, His beloved Son, to the entire world! The Jews were appointed this great treasure—an awesome heritage and responsibility. The hope of the Messiah had been a part of their shared history from the beginning. "*[4]They are Israelites, God's adopted children. They have the Lord's glory, the pledges, Moses' Teachings, the true worship, and the promises. [5]The Messiah is descended from their ancestors according to his human nature. The Messiah is God over everything, forever blessed. Amen" (Romans 9:4–5)*.

3:3 *What if some of them were unfaithful? Can their unfaithfulness cancel God's faithfulness?*

Would unfaithfulness among God's people nullify God's faithfulness? If this were possible, it would make His sovereign will dependent upon human will. Paul answered in the negative based upon God's character: "If we are unfaithful, he remains faithful because he cannot be untrue to himself" *(2 Timothy 2:13)*.

Would God truly be God if He depended upon humans in any way? Almighty God never depends upon the faithfulness or faithlessness of His creation to accomplish His sovereign will. God graciously allows people to participate in His divine plan, but God's faithfulness is dependent only upon God Himself.

3:4 ***That would be unthinkable! God is honest, and everyone else is a liar, as Scripture says, "So you hand down justice when you speak, and you win your case in court."***

The term *unthinkable* aptly describes the impossibility of God's will being undermined or subjected to anyone else's scrutiny. In His divine being, He alone is honest and true. Human unbelief cannot change that.

In stark contrast, every person is "a liar." This seems harsh and unfair until we realize how unreliable our word is even on a daily basis. The Bible is the authority for this accusation, but our own experience also affirms its validity.

When Almighty God judges, He speaks with absolute truth and authority. Paul here quoted from a psalm in which King David acknowledged God's flawless justice: "I have sinned against you, especially you. I have done what you consider evil. So you hand down justice when you speak, and you are blameless when you judge" *(Psalm 51:4)*.

3:5 ***But if what we do wrong shows that God is fair, what should we say? Is God unfair when he vents his anger on us? (I'm arguing the way humans would.)***

As Paul developed his argument, he posed a typical human response: If unrighteousness only magnifies God's justice and vindicates divine truth, why then would He punish people for making Him look good? Simply asked: Isn't it unfair for Him to vent His anger that way? Paul knew this was a silly argument—the kind humans would try because of their limited understanding of God. God alone knows the heart and motivation of every person, and He alone judges in absolute truth. Because He *is* righteous, His anger is justified. "*We know the God who said, 'I alone have the right to take revenge, I will pay back.' God also said, 'The Lord will judge his people'*" *(Hebrews 10:30)*.

3:6 ***That's unthinkable! Otherwise, how would God be able to judge the world?***

As in verse four, Paul answered, "Unthinkable!" Posing the question from a human viewpoint, he then gave a reply from God's perspective. How interesting that his answer is in the form of a question, implying that the alternative is inconceivable.

God, by His very being, is justified in judging those who sin and rebel against Him. In fact, according to the law, mankind's sinfulness demands the death penalty, but God's mercy has provided an alternative through the sacrifice of His Son, Jesus Christ. "The payment for sin is death, but the gift that God freely gives is everlasting life found in Christ Jesus our Lord" (Romans 6:23). Since Christ was offered to save us from God's wrath, He is our only hope for everlasting life. It is through Him that we escape condemnation.

> *[16]God loved the world this way: He gave his only Son so that everyone who believes in him will not die but will have eternal life. [17]God sent his Son into the world, not to condemn the world, but to save the world. [18]Those who believe in him won't be condemned. But those who don't believe are already condemned because they don't believe in God's only Son. (John 3:16–18)*

3:7 ***If my lie increases the glory that God receives by showing that God is truthful, why am I still judged as a sinner?***

Paul returned momentarily to the distorted logic reflected in verse five, that somehow humanity's sinfulness could increase God's glory. In fact, it's the other way around. God is all-knowing, all-powerful, holy, pure, righteous, true, and merciful, and these are only some of His divine attributes. These attributes are not affected by humanity's sinfulness. We can neither increase nor diminish His glory or any of His attributes by anything we do or say. Instead, when we begin to understand His character, we can better understand the depth of our own sinfulness and the necessity for His mercy. This conviction highlights for us the pathway that can guide us away from our human dilemma: God has made a way for us.

However, just because we are the recipients of His forgiveness still does not mean that sinning adds anything to His character or nature. God is advised by no one. Everything He does is motivated from the pure direction of His holy volition. God's gift of salvation does not give us liberty to sin but should always motivate us to glorify Him for the unmerited favor He has shown us.

3:8 ***Or can we say, "Let's do evil so that good will come from it"? Some slander us and claim that this is what we say. They are condemned, and that's what they deserve.***

Paul declared that he and other believers had been accused of teaching that people may continue in sin so that good will result. He, therefore, rebuked this as *slander,* which by its Greek definition means "to revile, to defame, to blaspheme."[1] In his rebuke, he used the most severe word possible, the very expression for defaming the name of God. Paul's word choice here made it clear that those who were spreading this lie deserved the judgment that would befall them.

When we receive God's grace, we are not given liberty to sin. *"Then what is the implication? Should we sin because we are not controlled by laws but by God's favor? That's unthinkable!" (Romans 6:15).* Once God's grace has been received, believers are released from that kind of life and have the power and the desire through the Holy Spirit to overcome sin. *"We know that the person we used to be was crucified with him to put an end to sin in our bodies. Because of this we are no longer slaves to sin" (Romans 6:6).*

Notes/Applications

Paul posed a logical question: What advantage was there in being a Jew? The advantage was that, in spite of unbelief and rebellion throughout the centuries, the Jews were still a favored people. God had chosen them to reveal His truth through Moses and the prophets and then to bring forth His Son, Who fully revealed God to the world.

The Jewish nation is not the only one afflicted with the maladies of unbelief and rebellion. All of humanity seeks to indulge in its own selfish pursuits, having a "what's-in-it-for-me" attitude. Rather than showing gratitude and humble obedience, we respond with self-centered demands and complaints. Still, people's sin and rebellion did not change God's faithfulness. He remained unchanged in His plan to give His Son for the lost.

Our calling, the ultimate purpose for our lives, is to experience reconciliation with the Almighty God through the sacrifice of His Son, to walk in obedience as we love the Lord with all our being, and to love our neighbors as ourselves. Any other indulgence will leave our souls continually weak and thirsty. All other pursuits will not satisfy.

As we partake in God's mercy and seek His power to walk in His ways, He will give us victory and abundant living. "[1]*I will sing forever about the evidence of your mercy, O* L*ORD. I will tell about your faithfulness to every generation.* [2]*I said, 'Your mercy will last forever. Your faithfulness stands firm in the heavens'*" *(Psalm 89:1–2).*

Romans 3:9–18

3:9 ***What, then, is the situation? Do we have any advantage? Not at all. We have already accused everyone (both Jews and Greeks) of being under the power of sin,***

Are the Jews better than the Greeks (meaning Gentiles—hence, anyone who is not Jewish)? No. All people are sinners unable to meet God's standard of righteousness. In verse two, Paul made the point that there are indeed certain advantages to being Jewish; here, however, he made it clear that in the end, all people are sinners in need of salvation.

Humanity has developed innumerable distinctions that are used wrongly to establish one person's superiority over another. There are leaders, and there are followers. There are strong nations, and there are weak nations. There are people of all races and cultures. Still, none of these distinctions mean anything to God. Everyone is on the same level—misguided and deceived in his or her sinfulness.

3:10–12 ***[10]as Scripture says, "Not one person has God's approval. [11]No one understands. No one searches for God. [12]Everyone has turned away. Together they have become rotten to the core. No one does anything good, not even one person.***

Verses ten through eighteen are quotations from the Old Testament. These first three verses come from Psalm fourteen:

> *[1]Godless fools say in their hearts,*
> *"There is no God."*
> *They are corrupt.*
> *They do disgusting things.*
> *There is no one who does good things.*
> *[2]The LORD looks down from heaven on Adam's descendants*
> *to see if there is anyone who acts wisely,*
> *if there is anyone who seeks help from God.*
> *[3]Everyone has turned away.*

> *Together they have become rotten to the core.*
> *No one, not even one person, does good things. (Psalm 14:1–3)*

On our own, we can never please God. In his earlier training as a Pharisee, Paul thought he had God's approval through keeping the law. After meeting Christ, he learned otherwise: "I didn't receive God's approval by obeying his laws. The opposite is true! I have God's approval through faith in Christ" *(Philippians 3:9)*.

Paul found that, despite the level he had attained of this world's knowledge, he would have no true understanding without God. "*The fear of the LORD is the beginning of wisdom. The knowledge of the Holy One is understanding*" *(Proverbs 9:10)*. Truly, human knowledge and understanding do not lead to God.

> *[20]Where is the wise person? Where is the scholar? Where is the persuasive speaker of our time? Hasn't God turned the wisdom of the world into nonsense? [21]The world with its wisdom was unable to recognize God in terms of his own wisdom. So God decided to use the nonsense of the Good News we speak to save those who believe. (1 Corinthians 1:20–21)*

Throughout Scripture, we are reminded that "we have all strayed like sheep. Each one of us has turned to go his own way, and the LORD has laid all our sins on him" *(Isaiah 53:6)*. Isaiah's words describe mankind's self-centeredness. Jesus, too, made it clear that individuals do not come to God of their own volition. "*People cannot come to me unless the Father who sent me brings them to me*" *(John 6:44)*. "*I am the way, the truth, and the life. No one goes to the Father except through me*" *(John 14:6)*. God sent Jesus, the Light of the World, to rescue us from darkness, but most people have rejected that Light. "*The light came into the world. Yet, people loved the dark rather than the light because their actions were evil*" *(John 3:19)*. This explains the history of the world and how, without the light of the good news and the uncommon grace of God, people inherently move toward darkness, chaos, and evildoing.

3:13 ***Their throats are open graves. Their tongues practice deception. Their lips hide the venom of poisonous snakes.***

People's sin nature manifests itself in the evils of speech. A thousand years before the birth of Jesus, King David recorded this observation: "Nothing in their mouths is truthful. Destruction comes from their hearts. Their throats are open graves. They flatter with their tongues" *(Psalm 5:9)*. Everyone speaks damaging lies to and about others at one time or another. The human tongue innately enjoys its engagement in deception and destruction. Out of the throat flow voices wielding much pain. Truly, more destruction is wrought through the human mouth than by instruments of war, for it can sometimes be easier to heal physically than emotionally.

Our tongues often spew out what is in our hearts, but at times, they may also hide our inner thoughts. David described both of these dangers in his psalm: "They make their tongues as sharp as a snake's fang. Their lips hide the venom of poisonous snakes" *(Psalm 140:3)*. Either way, whether we speak lies or cover them up, each of us is self-centered and wicked, hurting others with damaging words.

3:14 ***Their mouths are full of curses and bitter resentment.***

The human mouth is full of ugliness. Human depravity is revealed by spoken words. The common expression "two-faced" could as easily be "two-mouthed." In fact, it is this universal character flaw that too often warrants the common accusation of hypocrisy:

> *[9]With our tongues we praise our Lord and Father. Yet, with the same tongues we curse people, who were created in God's likeness. [10]Praise and curses come from the same mouth. My brothers and sisters, this should not happen! [11]Do clean and polluted water flow out of the same spring? (James 3:9–11)*

Similarly, bitterness is a venomous poison that will eventually destroy a person and often harm those around. "*[3]They sharpen their tongues like swords. They aim bitter words like arrows [4]to shoot at inno-*

cent people from their hiding places" *(Psalm 64:3–4)*. Speaking bitter words is the result of allowing resentment to take up residence in the heart.

3:15 *They run quickly to murder people.*

This verse illustrates how humanity has few second thoughts about committing sins against its fellow man. Sin starts in the heart. In humanity's sinful nature, no one is above committing any sin, even murder. How long did it take for murder to enter the human race? Cain, the firstborn son of Adam and Eve, killed his brother Abel because he envied his brother's goodness. Murder has been common to humanity ever since. "[7]*Their feet run to do evil. They hurry to shed innocent blood. Their plans are evil. Ruin and destruction are on their highways.* [8]*They don't know the way of peace.* [9]*There's no justice on their highways. They've made their paths crooked. Whoever walks on them will never know peace*" *(Isaiah 59:7–9)*.

3:16 *There is ruin and suffering wherever they go.*

Psalm one parallels this verse in expressing so clearly the contrast between the way of the righteous and the way of the wicked: "The LORD knows the way of righteous people, but the way of wicked people will end" *(Psalm 1:6)*. The ways of the unrighteous lead to ruin and suffering.

This principle is not as evident in our individual lives because each of us focuses upon the externals and strives to appear good to others. This is self-deceiving and destructive. "*There is a way that seems right to a person, but eventually it ends in death*" *(Proverbs 14:12)*. How important, then, is God's revelation of the truth!

3:17 *They have not learned to live in peace.*

As sinful creatures, humans are not peaceable. We prefer discord, conflict, and even war if necessary. We want our own way and will fight for it. This is evident even in a small child whose desires are threatened. Through the prophet Isaiah, God accused His people of their evil ways and described how this threatened their well being. The history of mankind is marked by hostilities and aggression, and only in Christ can there be lasting peace. *"I'm leaving you peace. I'm giving you my peace. I don't give you the kind of peace that the world gives"* (John 14:27).

3:18 *They are not terrified of God."*

John Calvin, a sixteenth-century French reformer and theologian, wrote, "Every wickedness flows from a disregard of God: for as the principal part of wisdom is the fear of God, when we depart from that, there remains in us nothing right or pure."[2] The greatest indictment against mankind is that its members do not fear God, the Creator, Redeemer, Sovereign, and Sustainer. *"Falling into the hands of the living God is a terrifying thing"* (Hebrews 10:31). Many times, people focus primarily on the love of God but little upon His holiness. This is dangerous because it is unbalanced and does not warn us of His righteous judgment.

Notes/Applications

This "spiritual X-ray" of mankind by God Himself is somber yet true. Our instinct is to deny its validity or to touch up the negatives. We know it is true of our hearts, but we have learned to cover it with good appearances and to accept one another's façades. For the good news to be effective, the bad news must be honest. In this early part of Romans, Paul revealed the real picture of humanity to show us our need of God's provision for our salvation.

Is this truth apparent in our Christian witness as we proclaim the good news? Are we not more inclined to affirm the "good" in others and present Jesus as a better way to happiness? We don't want to point out that people are hopeless sinners in need of a Savior. However, if a friend has a life-threatening disease, we know how important it is to face reality and seek a remedy. How much greater must be our willingness to face the real diagnosis of humanity's spiritual condition!

May we be eager to study and obey the word of God and to understand and accept His truth in all its fullness, fully appreciating that "Christ died for us while we were still sinners. This demonstrates God's love for us" *(Romans 5:8)*.

Romans 3:19–26

3:19 ***We know that whatever is in Moses' Teachings applies to everyone under their influence, and no one can say a thing. The whole world is brought under the judgment of God.***

The entire moral law that God gave through Moses applies to all people. "*They show that some requirements found in Moses' Teachings are written in their hearts. Their consciences speak to them. Their thoughts accuse them on one occasion and defend them on another*" *(Romans 2:15)*. The Jews are accountable since they received the written revelation of God. However, all others are guilty because this law is "written" in their consciences as well. The previous chapters show that God's revelation of this truth is clear and that all creation is under His judgment.

God's law is His standard. It is His high, pure, and holy way. To compare this standard with people's ways is like comparing light with darkness and the truth with a lie. No one can survive God's judgment based upon this righteous standard. The King James Version of Romans 3:19 states that the moral law was given so that "every mouth may be stopped" as it attempts to justify sinful actions. God's law stops short every rationale, argument, and self-justification. God pronounces humanity guilty. People's goodness is no match for God's holiness.

3:20 ***Not one person can have God's approval by following Moses' Teachings. Moses' Teachings show what sin is.***

Although individuals may perform deeds in obedience to God's law, they can never earn God's redemption. In fact, the law was given to bring the knowledge of sin but not to save from the penalty of sin. The law is like a mirror showing us our sin and how far short we fall of God's requirement of perfection. Its purpose is to teach us the truth about our sinful condition and God's provision for us. "*Before Christ came, Moses' laws served as our guardian. Christ came so that we could receive God's approval by faith"* (Galatians 3:24). *"Yet, we know that people don't receive God's approval because of their own efforts to live according to a set of standards, but only by believing in Jesus Christ"* (Galatians 2:16).

3:21 ***Now, the way to receive God's approval has been made plain in a way other than Moses' Teachings. Moses' Teachings and the Prophets tell us this.***

God's approval is not achieved by following Moses' teachings. Paul affirmed that even Moses and the prophets revealed that God's approval must be gained by some other means. All of these Scriptures were pointing to God's messiah and the sacrifice He would make in order to alleviate the penalty for our inability to obey the law perfectly.

In His Sermon on the Mount, Jesus explained that He came to fulfill the law and the prophecy: "Don't ever think that I came to set aside Moses' Teachings or the Prophets. I didn't come to set them aside but to make them come true" *(Matthew 5:17)*. The Lord Jesus Christ alone could obey the entire law because He is God. He became the perfect man and lived a sinless life, thereby fulfilling the letter of the law.

3:22 ***Everyone who believes has God's approval through faith in Jesus Christ. There is no difference between people.***

God's approval of us comes through Christ alone, and we receive it through faith alone. In having God's approval, we are declared righteous through trusting Jesus Christ as our sin-bearer. *"God had Christ, who was sinless, take our sin so that we might receive God's approval through him"* (2 Corinthians 5:21). This righteousness is never in us but only in Him. *"You are partners with Christ Jesus because of God. Jesus has become our wisdom sent from God, our righteousness, our holiness, and our ransom from sin"* (1 Corinthians 1:30).

This blessing of God's approval through faith in Christ is available to all people, Jews and Gentiles. In our sinful nature, we are all alike, alienated from God and under His judgment. In Christ, we are declared righteous through His death on our behalf, and we are reunited with God and bonded with one another.

3:23 ***Because all people have sinned, they have fallen short of God's glory.***

We have all sinned or "missed the mark."[3] Sin is universal, and no one is exempt from God's verdict of "guilty." Every human being since Adam and Eve has sinned. Jesus said that we must be perfect as our Father in heaven is perfect *(Matthew 5:48)*, and He alone lived up to that standard of righteousness.

People were created to glorify God but fall far short of His call to worship Him. Great people such as Adam, Eve, Abraham, Moses, David, the prophets, John, and Paul were all sinners, and so are we. As a result, we must all pay the inevitable penalty of sin, which is death. This is the truth of sin's consequence, a truth that everyone must honestly face.

3:24 ***They receive God's approval freely by an act of his kindness through the price Christ Jesus paid to set us free from sin.***

The good news is that God has provided the way for us to be accepted. His gift of salvation is offered to all through His perfect Son, Jesus Christ. While this is offered freely to us, it is given at the awful cost of Jesus Christ's perfect life. "[8]*Christ died for us while we were still sinners. This demonstrates God's love for us.* [9]*Since Christ's blood has now given us God's approval, we are even more certain that Christ will save us from God's anger" (Romans 5:8–9)*.

This salvation cannot be earned. It is the gift of God's mercy. We have God's unconditional pardon through His kindness, which is undeserved and unmerited. By giving His Son's life for us, we are set free or redeemed from sin's bondage and penalty. "*Through the blood of his Son, we are set free from our sins. God forgives our failures because of his overflowing kindness" (Ephesians 1:7)*.

At creation, God made people after His divine image, giving them the ability to choose within the parameters set by Him as the Creator. When Adam and Eve sinned in the garden, God pronounced the sentence of eternal death on them and their descendents. And yet, God loved His creation so much that He provided a way for people to receive eternal life through His Son, Who is called "the last Adam." "*This is what the Scripture says: 'The first man, Adam, became a living being.' The last Adam became a life-giving spirit*" (*1 Corinthians 15:45*). This is a love we cannot comprehend, but we can experience it through faith in Christ. "*God saved you through faith as an act of kindness. You had nothing to do with it. Being saved is a gift from God*" (*Ephesians 2:8*).

3:25–26 ***[25]God showed that Christ is the throne of mercy where God's approval is given through faith in Christ's blood. In his patience God waited to deal with sins committed in the past. [26]He waited so that he could display his approval at the present time. This shows that he is a God of justice, a God who approves of people who believe in Jesus.***

The Greek word translated as *showed*, *προέθετο* (proetheto), means "to formulate a future course of action—'to plan beforehand, to purpose, to intend.'"[4] God purposely established this plan before creation. "*[3]Praise the God and Father of our Lord Jesus Christ! Through Christ, God has blessed us with every spiritual blessing that heaven has to offer. [4]Before the creation of the world, he chose us through Christ to be holy and perfect in his presence*" (*Ephesians 1:3–4*).

The "throne of mercy" refers to the cover of the ark of the covenant, which sat in the innermost chamber of the tabernacle. Also called the "mercy seat," the throne of mercy foreshadowed God's gracious provision for the sins of His people. It represented the means by which sins would be forgiven.[5] Through His death, Christ fully atoned for our sins, satisfying God's just verdict of death and giving eternal life. "*This is love: not that we have loved God, but that he loved us and sent his Son to be the payment for our sins*" (*1 John 4:10*).

The blood comes between the violated law and the violators, the people. This sacrificial system offered a temporary reprieve and was repeated on an annual basis. The blood of Jesus was offered once and permanently satisfied the just requirements of God's holy law, which mankind broke. It paid the penalty for sin and thus removed that which had separated people from their Creator, restoring that broken relationship. It exonerated sinful humanity, removing its sin, its guilt, and its penalty.[6]

Jesus can declare an individual righteous because He is sinless and became that person's substitute on the cross. Isaiah the prophet foretold this seven centuries beforehand:

> [5]*He was wounded for our rebellious acts. He was crushed for our sins. He was punished so that we could have peace, and we received healing from his wounds.* [6]*We have all strayed like sheep. Each one of us has turned to go his own way, and the* LORD *has laid all our sins on him. (Isaiah 53:5–6)*

Paul stated this same truth: "God had Christ, who was sinless, take our sin so that we might receive God's approval through him" *(2 Corinthians 5:21)*.

In providing this profound remedy, God showed great patience concerning past sins. This form of the word *patience* demonstrates God's restraint in the outpouring of His wrath.[7] No human restrains God's actions. If God is going to show His patience, He must by His very nature restrain Himself. "*The Lord isn't slow to do what he promised, as some people think. Rather, he is patient for your sake. He doesn't want to destroy anyone but wants all people to have an opportunity to turn to him and change the way they think and act" (2 Peter 3:9)*. In Psalm 103:8, David praised the Lord, Who is "compassionate, merciful, patient, and always ready to forgive."

God's purpose for "waiting" was to reveal His righteousness at the right time. "*Look at it this way: At the right time, while we were still helpless, Christ died for ungodly people" (Romans 5:6)*. The amazing truth is that He planned redemption before creation. He previewed

His plan in Genesis 3:15 in the garden of Eden, designed it through His chosen people Israel, and fulfilled it through His Son.

> *He is the lamb who was known long ago before the world existed, but for your good he became publicly known in the last period of time. (1 Peter 1:20)*

> *[1]In the past God spoke to our ancestors at many different times and in many different ways through the prophets. [2]In these last days he has spoken to us through his Son. (Hebrews 1:1–2)*

God alone saves us and sustains us by His almighty power. He approves of people not because of their worth or work but through His worthy Son and His work at Calvary. The Lord Jesus Christ, in His death and resurrection, met the holy God's demands and fulfilled the promise of salvation to Jews and Gentiles who receive His gift of salvation. Our only fitting response must be to believe in Him and to obey His Word.

Notes/Applications

This passage may well be called the "watershed" of the good news proclaimed by Paul. Verses twenty-three through twenty-six express our helplessness and God's rescue. Romans 3:23 has been memorized by many Christians for its simple statement of everyone's sinfulness. Let's not forget verse twenty-four, which states that we are "justified freely by his grace" (KJV).

It is as if we were in a cave of total darkness with no way out, only to suddenly see light up ahead—that gives us hope! In fact, the apostle John's gospel account opens with the statement that Jesus, "the real light, which shines on everyone, was coming into the world" *(John 1:9)*. The good news is truly a message of hope because it proclaims the truth revealed by God Himself.

Our task as believers is to spread this light by proclaiming the truth delivered to us. God's work, however, is to open the eyes of the spiritually blind to see His light:

> [3]*So if the Good News that we tell others is covered with a veil, it is hidden from those who are dying.* [4]*The god of this world has blinded the minds of those who don't believe. As a result, they don't see the light of the Good News about Christ's glory. It is Christ who is God's image.*
>
> [5]*Our message is not about ourselves. It is about Jesus Christ as the Lord. We are your servants for his sake.* [6]*We are his servants because the same God who said that light should shine out of darkness has given us light. For that reason we bring to light the knowledge about God's glory which shines from Christ's face.*
> *(2 Corinthians 4:3–6)*

In the light of this truth, we can sing with conviction great hymns such as "When I Survey the Wondrous Cross" which proclaim "Love so amazing, so divine, demands my soul, my life, my all!"[8]

Romans 3:27–31

3:27 ***So, do we have anything to brag about? Bragging has been eliminated. On what basis was it eliminated? On the basis of our own efforts? No, indeed! Rather, it is eliminated on the basis of faith.***

This verse again emphasizes that no one can brag or take any credit for salvation. Even faith is God's gift, so no individual can take pride in contributing to his or her own redemption. "[8]*God saved you through faith as an act of kindness. You had nothing to do with it. Being saved is a gift from God.* [9]*It's not the result of anything you've done, so no one can brag about it"* (*Ephesians 2:8–9*).

No matter how hard we try, we can never keep the law perfectly and thereby achieve God's righteousness. In reality, we fall far short of perfection. "*We've all become unclean, and all our righteous acts are like permanently stained rags. All of us shrivel like leaves, and our sins carry us away like the wind*" (*Isaiah 64:6*). If anyone thinks that he is able to attain perfection, Scripture reminds that person of the sobering truth: "If someone obeys all of God's laws except one, that person is guilty of breaking all of them" (*James 2:10*).

We cannot brag about the good things we do because redemption is initiated, provided, and sustained by our Creator and purchased by the blood of Jesus Christ, our Redeemer.

3:28 ***We conclude that a person has God's approval by faith, not by his own efforts.***

This verse sums up the argument: No one can earn or merit God's approval. The only way to gain His favor is by faith in Christ, Who came to purchase our pardon on Calvary. "*Yet, we know that people don't receive God's approval because of their own efforts to live according to a set of standards, but only by believing in Jesus Christ*" (*Galatians 2:16*).

Obeying God's law is important, but it cannot save us from our sins. We may be good by the world's standards, but our best efforts fall far short of God's righteous standard. Our sin nature will never be able to meet those conditions that will permit us to survive or even approach the holy presence of God. The law was given not as a means of salvation but to show us our need for a Savior. *"Before Christ came, Moses' laws served as our guardian. Christ came so that we could receive God's approval by faith" (Galatians 3:24)*. Our salvation is a gift of God, which we receive by faith in His only Son, Who gave His life for us.

3:29–30 ***[29]Is God only the God of the Jews? Isn't he also the God of people who are not Jewish? Certainly, he is, [30]since it is the same God who approves circumcised people by faith and uncircumcised people through this same faith.***

Is Israel God's favorite nation? No, the Israelites are His "chosen people" through whom He sent the promised Messiah, His only Son. All believers in Christ, Jews and Gentiles, comprise His nation and His people:

> *[9]However, you are chosen people, a royal priesthood, a holy nation, people who belong to God. You were chosen to tell about the excellent qualities of God, who called you out of darkness into his marvelous light. [10]Once you were not God's people, but now you are. Once you were not shown mercy, but now you have been shown mercy. (1 Peter 2:9–10)*

Clearly, He is the God of the redeemed, whether Jew or Gentile, who together are united as the church, often identified as the body of Christ. He has justified them all through the gift of faith. Therefore, since there is one God and one means of salvation, all believers are united in Him, no matter what their nationality or heritage.

Circumcision was a physical mark God gave to Abraham as a sign and seal of His promise to raise up a nation through whom all the peoples of the earth would be blessed. This custom was given to confirm the covenant between God and His people. Unfortunately, it became associated with the law (rather than the promise) and, in the New Testament, was used by the unbelieving Jews to reject the Messiah and those who followed Him. The irony of this was that Jesus was sent to fulfill the law. In his letter to the Colossians, Paul addressed the issue head-on, teaching that both the circumcised and the uncircumcised must be "circumcised in heart" through faith:

> *[11]In him you were also circumcised. It was not a circumcision performed by human hands. But it was a removal of the corrupt nature in the circumcision performed by Christ. [12]This happened when you were placed in the tomb with Christ through baptism. In baptism you were also brought back to life with Christ through faith in the power of God, who brought him back to life.*
>
> *[13]You were once dead because of your failures and your uncircumcised corrupt nature. But God made you alive with Christ when he forgave all our failures. [14]He did this by erasing the charges that were brought against us by the written laws God had established. He took the charges away by nailing them to the cross. [15]He stripped the rulers and authorities of their power and made a public spectacle of them as he celebrated his victory in Christ. (Colossians 2:11–15)*

The Lord Jesus Christ in His death and resurrection met the just demands of the holy God. He fulfills the promise of salvation to Jews and Gentiles who receive His gift of eternal life.

3:31 *Are we abolishing Moses' Teachings by this faith? That's unthinkable! Rather, we are supporting Moses' Teachings.*

Human nature tends to go to extremes. For example, the Pharisees and religious teachers taught that people could only please God by keeping the letter of the law. At the opposite extreme is the person who receives the good news of salvation by faith in Jesus Christ and then views the law as no longer having any value. Jesus, however, declared emphatically in Matthew 5:17: "Don't ever think that I came to set aside Moses' Teachings or the Prophets. I didn't come to set them aside but to make them come true."

It is important to understand the law and its purpose. In verse twenty, Paul stated that God gave us the law to "show what sin is." Then at the appointed time He sent His Son to deliver us from the deadly consequences of our sinfulness. "[4]*But when the right time came, God sent his Son into the world. A woman gave birth to him, and he came under the control of God's laws.* [5]*God sent him to pay for the freedom of those who were controlled by these laws so that we would be adopted as his children*" *(Galatians 4:4–5)*. In Jesus Christ, the law is fulfilled and faith is established.

Notes/Applications

Simply stated, the Bible is the story of the creation, fall, and redemption of mankind, which is so clearly presented in Romans chapters one through three. The world, created in light and hope, was darkened by Satan's rebellion against God and humanity's fall into sin. Because of sin, all mankind falls under the judgment of God and is without hope. The good news is that God reaches out in love to call people to Himself and provide salvation through His Son, Jesus Christ.

In concluding this section, Paul raised a very human response. We are compelled by our sinfulness to brag about our achievements in order to establish some measure of our worth. However, such bragging gets us nowhere in the presence of God's holiness. Paul insisted that we cannot earn our salvation but that it is a gift of God that we receive through faith. This does not eliminate our tendency to brag, but it does provide strong motivation to repent and ask for God's forgiveness.

This salvation, so mercifully given, raises a serious dilemma. Does this salvation mean that God's law is no longer applicable to the redeemed? With Paul, we should answer emphatically, "That's unthinkable!" Jesus declared that He came to fulfill the law and the prophets. As the redeemed of God by His matchless grace, we are under the instruction of the law, not out of obligation or duty but because of the very grace that we have been given.

There is freedom in obedience to God's ways. We are His creation, made in His image, and should be obedient. The law provides the boundaries of behavior that God has given so that we may enjoy the fruits of His instruction. The law is the schoolmaster giving us guidance within God's boundaries.

As believers, we obtain a clear conscience and intimate fellowship with God by asking for forgiveness and then seeking to obey by the power of the Holy Spirit. This process never ends. It is the holy tension under which redeemed people live. We are never sinless; we are always in need of forgiveness:

> [7]*But if we live in the light in the same way that God is in the light, we have a relationship with each other. And the blood of his Son Jesus cleanses us from every sin.* [8]*If we say, "We aren't sinful" we are deceiving ourselves, and the truth is not in us.* [9]*God is faithful and reliable. If we confess our sins, he forgives them and cleanses us from everything we've done wrong.* [10]*If we say, "We have never sinned," we turn God into a liar and his Word is not in us. (1 John 1:7–10)*

In light of Paul's uncompromising analysis of our human condition, we should search the depths of our deceitful hearts, fall on our knees, repent, and ask the Lord to search our hearts, unveiling all of our hypocrisies.

ROMANS 4

Romans 4:1–8

4:1 ***What can we say that we have discovered about our ancestor Abraham?***

Did Abraham gain favor with God because of the good things he did? Were the people of the Old Testament made righteous before the holy God by their works?

Paul previously established that no one could be justified before God by good works. This was true for the Old Testament believers as well. Abraham was the highly esteemed father of the Jews. If it could be shown that even Abraham had to come to God by faith and not by works, then Paul could prove that a relationship with God is by faith alone.

Was Abraham justified by his obedience to God's law? Was he justified by his sacrifices? Was he justified by his circumcision? The answer is no. If Abraham, a great saint of God, was not justified by any of his works, then no one else can be either.

4:2 ***If Abraham had God's approval because of something he did, he would have had a reason to brag. But he could not brag to God about it.***

If anyone could boast about his good deeds, it would have been Abraham: "The Scripture passage came true. It says, 'Abraham believed God, and that faith was regarded by God to be his approval of Abraham.' So Abraham was called God's friend" *(James 2:23)*. Someone called "God's friend" obviously had God's approval. Nevertheless, regardless of everything that Abraham did, his deeds were worthless for gaining that approval.

4:3 ***What does Scripture say? "Abraham believed God, and that faith was regarded by God to be his approval of Abraham."***

In this verse, Paul quoted from Genesis fifteen to establish the scriptural basis for his contention that Abraham was justified by faith alone:

> [1]*Later the* LORD *spoke his word to Abram in a vision. He said,*
>
> *"Abram, don't be afraid.*
> *I am your shield.*
> *Your reward will be very great."*
>
> [2]*Abram asked, "Almighty* LORD, *what will you give me? Since I'm going to die without children, Eliezer of Damascus will inherit my household.* [3]*You have given me no children, so this member of my household will be my heir."*
>
> [4]*Suddenly, the* LORD *spoke his word to Abram again. He said, "This man will not be your heir. Your own son will be your heir."* [5]*He took Abram outside and said, "Now look up at the sky and count the stars, if you are able to count them." He also said to him, "That's how many descendants you will have!"*
>
> [6]***Then Abram believed the* LORD, *and the* LORD *regarded that faith to be his approval of Abram.***
> *(Genesis 15:1–6, emphasis added)*

The Scripture is clear: Abraham's faith was the basis for his right standing with God. His good works resulted from believing God's promise. In addition, the apostle Paul affirmed the same about his own salvation. "*This means that I didn't receive God's approval by obeying his laws. The opposite is true! I have God's approval through faith in Christ*" *(Philippians 3:9)*.

4:4 *When people work, their pay is not regarded as a gift but something they have earned.*

A person who works deserves payment for that work. "*Never oppress or rob your neighbor. Never keep the pay you owe a hired worker overnight*" *(Leviticus 19:13)*. If one has earned a wage, he may stand before a court and demand payment. If people were able by any means to earn their way to heaven, they would be able to stand before God and demand payment. However, Paul has already established that the deeds done in the flesh are worthless before God *(Romans 3:19–20)*. Our works do not make God indebted to us. God does not owe anything to anyone.

4:5 *However, when people don't work but believe God, the one who approves ungodly people, their faith is regarded as God's approval.*

God's approval comes by faith alone. Salvation is a gift, and a gift cannot be earned. "[8]*God saved you through faith as an act of kindness. You had nothing to do with it. Being saved is a gift from God.* [9]*It's not the result of anything you've done, so no one can brag about it*" *(Ephesians 2:8–9)*. The only work that can obtain God's stamp of approval is to believe on His Son and on the work He accomplished at Calvary. "[28]*The people asked Jesus, 'What does God want us to do?'* [29]*Jesus replied to them, 'God wants to do something for you so that you believe in the one whom he has sent'*" *(John 6:28–29)*.

No one can merit God's approval. Even moral, law-abiding people are not fit for His presence. They may be good and acceptable by the world's standards, but God demands absolute perfection. "[1]*The LORD spoke to Moses,* [2]*'Tell the whole congregation of Israel: Be holy because I, the LORD your God, am holy'" (Leviticus 19:1–2).* We are all sinners and fail to meet His holy standard.

The good news is that by faith we receive God's righteousness as a gift. All who believe will be blessed as Abraham was blessed.

> *[9]So people who believe are blessed together with Abraham, the man of faith.*
>
> *[10]Certainly, there is a curse on all who rely on their own efforts to live according to a set of standards because Scripture says, "Whoever doesn't obey everything that is written in Moses' Teachings is cursed." [11]No one receives God's approval by obeying the law's standards since, "The person who has God's approval will live by faith." [12]Laws have nothing to do with faith, but, "Whoever obeys laws will live because of the laws he obeys."*
>
> *[13]Christ paid the price to free us from the curse that God's laws bring by becoming cursed instead of us. Scripture says, "Everyone who is hung on a tree is cursed." [14]Christ paid the price so that the blessing promised to Abraham would come to all the people of the world through Jesus Christ and we would receive the promised Spirit through faith. (Galatians 3:9–14)*

It is vitally important to know that salvation is assured to all who believe in Christ and that no one will be saved through good works. "*[17]God sent his Son into the world, not to condemn the world, but to save the world. [18]Those who believe in him won't be condemned. But those who don't believe are already condemned because they don't believe in God's only Son" (John 3:17–18).*

4:6 *David says the same thing about those who are blessed: God approves of people without their earning it.*

A blessed person is one who is approved by his Maker. King David, a man after God's own heart, affirmed this in Psalm 146:5–6: "[5]Blessed are those who receive help from the God of Jacob. Their hope rests on the LORD their God, [6]who made heaven, earth, the sea, and everything in them. The LORD remains faithful forever." What an apt description of the believer, who trusts the Lord in everything! Our righteousness before God is by His grace through our faith and not our works. It is a great blessing from God to know that we have His approval through the work of His eternal Son and the Holy Spirit.

4:7–8 ***David said, [7]"Blessed are those whose disobedience is forgiven and whose sins are pardoned. [8]Blessed is the person whom the Lord no longer considers sinful."***

These verses were taken from Psalm 32:1–2, wherein King David expressed his gratitude for God's forgiveness of his grievous sins.

What is the difference between the words *disobedience* and *sins* as used in verse seven? The Greek word for *disobedience* as it is used here means "illegality, violation of the law."[1] The Greek word for *sins* means "missing the mark."[2] Everyone disobeys the law because everyone fundamentally "misses the mark" of God's perfection. Throughout our lives, both before we are saved and even afterward, we violate the law. We are sinners. That is who we are by our human nature. God's provision, however, is complete in Christ as promised in Isaiah 53:6: "We have all strayed like sheep. Each one of us has turned to go his own way, and the LORD has laid all our sins on him." He has forgiven our disobedience.

In the Lord Jesus Christ, God has laid aside our sins and covered them in the blood of His Son Jesus Christ. "*God is faithful and reliable. If we confess our sins, he forgives them and cleanses us from everything we've done wrong*" *(1 John 1:9)*. Verse eight teaches the amazing truth that in Christ we are no longer considered sinful. Compare what Paul wrote to the Corinthians: "God had Christ, who was sinless, take our sin so that we might receive God's approval through him" *(2 Corinthians 5:21)*. This means that when God receives us, our sins are laid on Christ, and His righteousness is laid on us.

Blessed is the person who believes this based on God's Word. That person is free from the penalty for his or her sin, cleansed by the blood of Christ, and clothed in His righteousness.

Notes/Applications

If Abraham, the revered father of the Jewish nation, could not merit salvation by anything he did, then neither can any of us. Charles Hadden Spurgeon, the great nineteenth-century preacher, candidly declared:

> I venture to say that a sinner justified by God stands on even a surer footing than a righteous man justified by his works, if there is such. We could never be sure that we had done enough works. Our conscience would always be uneasy for fear that, after all, we would fall short and only have the trembling verdict of a fallible judgment to rely on. But when God Himself justifies, and the Holy Spirit bears witness thereto by giving us peace with God, then we feel that the matter is sure and settled, and we enter into rest.
>
> No tongue can tell the depth of that calm which comes over the soul that has received the peace of God which passes all understanding.[3]

How comforting and freeing to know that our salvation is from God! He has enabled us to receive His gift through His Son, our Lord Jesus Christ. "*Christ paid the price so that the blessing promised to Abraham would come to all the people of the world through Jesus Christ and we would receive the promised Spirit through faith*" *(Galatians 3:14)*. Of all the religions throughout the world, only Christianity offers forgiveness for sin and promises eternal life based on God's approval alone. The Bible clearly teaches that salvation is by God's grace through faith, only through Christ and His sacrifice for our sins. Truly, "the Law is for the self-righteous, to humble their pride. The Gospel is for the lost, to remove their despair."[4]

A happy, contented person is one who has experienced genuine forgiveness and peace with God through Jesus Christ. Through faith that is demonstrated by obedience, we can live in harmony with God and with others.

Romans 4:9–17a

4:9 ***Are only the circumcised people blessed, or are uncircumcised people blessed as well? We say, "Abraham's faith was regarded as God's approval of him."***

Paul's question essentially asked: Is circumcision necessary to receiving God's blessing? The apostle did not answer this immediately but chose first to affirm his statement in verse three that "Abraham's faith was regarded as God's approval of him" (*see also Genesis 15:6*).

Later in this epistle, Paul clearly rejected any distinction between Jews and non-Jews. "[12]*There is no difference between Jews and Greeks. They all have the same Lord, who gives his riches to everyone who calls on him.* [13]*So then, 'Whoever calls on the name of the Lord will be saved'*" *(Romans 10:12–13)*. Everyone is saved in the same way.

4:10 ***How was his faith regarded as God's approval? Was he circumcised or was he uncircumcised at that time? He had not been circumcised.***

The two questions posed in this verse are actually one and the same. When did Abraham receive God's approval by faith? Was it after or before being circumcised? Genesis fifteen gives a full account of God's call and Abraham's response in faith, and this occurred before Abraham's circumcision. Years later, when Abraham was ninety-nine, he was circumcised as a sign of God's covenant with him:

> [1]*When Abram was 99 years old, the* LORD *appeared to him. He said to Abram, "I am God Almighty. Live in my presence with integrity.* [2]*I will give you my promise, and I will give you very many descendants."* [3]*Immediately, Abram bowed with his face touching the ground, and again God spoke to him,* [4]*"My promise is still with you. You will become the father of many nations.* [5]*So your name will no longer be Abram (Exalted Father), but Abraham (Father of Many) because I have made you a father of many nations"* . . .

> [9]*God also said to Abraham, "You and your descendants in generations to come are to be faithful to my promise.* [10]*This is how you are to be faithful to my promise: Every male among you is to be circumcised."* (Genesis 17:1–5, 9–10)

Abraham was circumcised years after receiving God's covenant. The Scriptures here tell us that righteousness was reckoned to Abraham before the rite of circumcision, which he received in obedience to God's command. "*As far as our relationship to Christ Jesus is concerned, it doesn't matter whether we are circumcised or not. But what matters is a faith that expresses itself through love*" (Galatians 5:6). "*Certainly, it doesn't matter whether a person is circumcised or not. Rather, what matters is being a new creation*" (Galatians 6:15).

4:11 ***Abraham's faith was regarded as God's approval while he was still uncircumcised. The mark of circumcision is the seal of that approval. Therefore, he is the father of every believer who is not circumcised, and their faith, too, is regarded as God's approval of them.***

Abraham received the mark of circumcision as a seal of the righteousness given by God's grace through his servant's faith. A sign is representative of something; it is a symbol. The sign of circumcision, therefore, signified the spiritual change that had already taken place when Abraham believed God.

The word for *seal,* σφραγῖδα (sphragida), means "an engraved object used to make a mark denoting ownership, approval, or closure of something (normally done by pressing into heated wax and usually attached to a document or letter)."[5] The seal was used to certify the genuineness of an agreement, usually the conclusion of a transaction in which ownership was transferred. Therefore, circumcision was the seal to prove what had taken place in Abraham's heart when he received God's approval. In the tragic development of Israel's history, the "letter" of law-keeping replaced the "spirit" of obedient faith. This spiritual meaning is also taught in the Old Testament.

"The LORD *your God will circumcise your hearts and the hearts of your descendants. You will love the* LORD *your God with all your heart and with all your soul, and you will live"* (Deuteronomy 30:6).

All believers are children of Abraham. "[7]*You must understand that people who have faith are Abraham's descendants . . .* [29]*If you belong to Christ, then you are Abraham's descendants and heirs, as God promised"* (Galatians 3:7, 29). We have been spiritually circumcised and are Abraham's spiritual heirs through our Savior Jesus Christ, Who was born of the seed of Abraham. "[15]*Certainly, it doesn't matter whether a person is circumcised or not. Rather, what matters is being a new creation.* [16]*Peace and mercy will come to rest on all those who conform to this principle. They are the Israel of God"* (Galatians 6:15–16).

4:12 ***He is also the father of those who not only are circumcised but also are following in the footsteps of his faith. Our father Abraham had that faith before he was circumcised.***

The good news was preached to the Jews first and then to the Gentiles. As a result, some of the Jews believed in Christ. Many of these were among the believing "remnant," that minority in each generation who believed God and received His approval in the footsteps of Abraham. It is good to recall that first great ingathering of God's people on the day of Pentecost, fifty days after Christ's resurrection:

> [5]*Devout Jewish men from every nation were living in Jerusalem.* [6]*They gathered when they heard the wind. Each person was startled to recognize his own dialect when the disciples spoke.*
>
> [7]*Stunned and amazed, the people in the crowd said, "All of these men who are speaking are Galileans.* [8]*Why do we hear them speaking in our native dialects?* [9]*We're Parthians, Medes, and Elamites. We're people from Mesopotamia, Judea, Cappadocia, Pontus, the province of Asia,* [10]*Phrygia, Pamphylia, Egypt, and the country near Cyrene in Libya. We're Jewish people, converts to Judaism, and visitors from Rome,* [11]*Crete, and Arabia. We hear*

these men in our own languages as they tell about the miracles that God has done." (Acts 2:5–11)

At this phenomenal moment in the church's history, the enormous crowd was described as "devout Jewish men from every nation." After the apostle Peter preached the good news, "those who accepted what Peter said were baptized. That day about three thousand people were added to the group" *(Acts 2:41)*. This implies strongly that this first mass conversion was of Jewish men, including "proselytes" who had become Jewish converts and had been circumcised. Notably among these gathered were "visitors from Rome."

In this verse, Paul affirms that these Jewish believers were true children of Abraham, following the same faith he had before his circumcision.

4:13 ***So it was not by obeying Moses' Teachings that Abraham or his descendants received the promise that he would inherit the world. Rather, it was through God's approval of his faith.***

While the Jews believed they had received God's favor as His chosen people through their obedience to the law, Paul explained how this inheritance actually is born of faith and not of race, reaffirming his previous arguments that not all heirs of God are Jewish nor are all Jews heirs of God. Abraham and his descendants received God's promise not through strict adherence to the law but by their faith. This is the only way to receive God's approval:

> [21]*Those who want to be controlled by Moses' laws should tell me something. Are you really listening to what Moses' Teachings say?* [22]*Scripture says that Abraham had two sons, one by a woman who was a slave and the other by a free woman.* [23]*Now, the son of the slave woman was conceived in a natural way, but the son of the free woman was conceived through a promise made to Abraham...* [31]*Brothers and sisters, we are not children of a slave woman but of the free woman. (Galatians 4:21–23, 31)*

> [6]*Abraham serves as an example. He believed God, and that faith was regarded by God to be his approval of Abraham.* [7]*You must understand that people who have faith are Abraham's descendants.* [8]*Scripture saw ahead of time that God would give his approval to non-Jewish people who have faith. So Scripture announced the Good News to Abraham ahead of time when it said, "Through you all the people of the world will be blessed."* [9]*So people who believe are blessed together with Abraham, the man of faith.* (Galatians 3:6–9)

This affirms the biblical truth that there is only one way of salvation, and that way is through faith. The law was never intended as a means of gaining God's approval.

4:14 *If those who obey Moses' Teachings are the heirs, then faith is useless and the promise is worthless.*

If the Jews could truly obey the law and thereby inherit God's promise, faith would be of no use and the promise would be invalid. "*If we have to gain the inheritance by following those laws, then it no longer comes to us because of the promise. However, God freely gave the inheritance to Abraham through a promise*" (Galatians 3:18).

Calvary would not have been necessary if our obedience to the law could have in any way given us right standing before God. It is, however, abundantly clear in all Scripture that no one can meet His standard of perfection. Only by faith in God's promise will salvation be realized. In fact, "it is ominously bold presumption, when God is calling all to behold His Lamb, to be found asking God to behold your goodness, your works."[6]

4:15 *The laws in Moses' Teachings bring about anger. But where laws don't exist, they can't be broken.*

The primary consequence of the law is to reveal God's holy anger. "*God's anger is revealed from heaven against every ungodly and immoral thing people do as they try to suppress the truth by their immoral liv-*

ing" (Romans 1:18). This is the holy God's wrath as He observed humankind's sin and rebellion. This may sound harsh to human ears, but God's passion against sin also expresses His divine love for His creation:

> Like the Gospel, the Law is a gift of the love of God. The Law is still regarded in this way by the Jews. Again, as wrath is provoked by despising the goodness and longsuffering of God in the Gospel, so it is by despising the Law. This is not the purpose of the Law. Only from the standpoint of the transgressor does it look like this. If God is angry because of transgression of the Law, this is the reaction of spurned love, which sought to benefit man through the Law.[7]

The natural law condemns all humanity, but God's written revelation in the Bible condemns us even more. Consider the mockery of so many through the ages who have done everything possible to destroy or suppress the Scriptures. Still, it is these very Scriptures that God has used to bring the good news into the world to call out a people for Himself from all nations. "*Whoever believes in the Son has eternal life, but whoever rejects the Son will not see life. Instead, he will see God's constant anger" (John 3:36)*. God's righteous anger remains on all who reject His truth, but He gives eternal life to all who believe in His Son, the Lord Jesus Christ.

4:16–17a ***16Therefore, the promise is based on faith so that it can be a gift. Consequently, the promise is guaranteed for every descendant, not only for those who are descendants by obeying Moses' Teachings but also for those who are descendants by believing as Abraham did. He is the father of all of us, 17as Scripture says: "I have made you a father of many things."***

This understanding of faith does away with any possibility that we can do anything to save ourselves. Good works are not the grounds for salvation, but rather, they are the result of God's working in individual lives. "*God has made us what we are. He has created us in Christ*

Jesus to live lives filled with good works that he has prepared for us to do" (Ephesians 2:10).

Notes/Applications

We cannot fully comprehend God's kindness to us. Our human instinct is to earn God's favor by our good works, but because of His demand for perfection, we are always "weighed on a scale and found to be too light" *(Daniel 5:27)*.

We claim to be moral church members, generous givers, and hard workers, hoping these attributes will give them right standing before God. The message in Romans is clear: No one can merit God's approval; people can be saved only through believing God's promise of forgiveness through His Son Jesus.

> *The payment for sin is death, but the gift that God freely gives is everlasting life found in Christ Jesus our Lord. (Romans 6:23)*

> *Christ died for us while we were still sinners. This demonstrates God's love for us. (Romans 5:8)*

> *[9]If you declare that Jesus is Lord, and believe that God brought him back to life, you will be saved. [10]By believing you receive God's approval, and by declaring your faith you are saved. (Romans 10:9–10)*

We need to thank Almighty God for His grace and for loving us enough to save us. We express our love and thanks by walking in His ways. The popular hymn "Amazing Grace" expresses the wonder of His grace in saving undeserving sinners:

Amazing grace! How sweet the sound
That saved a wretch like me!
I once was lost, but now am found;
Was blind, but now I see.[8]

Romans 4:17b–25

4:17b–18 ***[17]Abraham believed when he stood in the presence of the God who gives life to dead people and calls into existence nations that don't even exist. [18]When there was nothing left to hope for, Abraham still hoped and believed. As a result, he became a father of many nations, as he had been told: "That is how many descendants you will have."***

Abraham and Sarah actually laughed when they heard the prophecy that they would have a child *(Genesis 17:17; 18:12)*. Their circumstances seemed hopeless, yet Abraham eventually believed the Lord's seemingly impossible promise because of the hope that came from God. God's promise assured Abraham even though it was beyond human comprehension *(Genesis 15:5–6)*.

4:19–21 ***[19]Abraham didn't weaken. Through faith he regarded the facts: His body was already as good as dead now that he was about a hundred years old, and Sarah was unable to have children. [20]He didn't doubt God's promise out of a lack of faith. Instead, giving honor to God for the promise, he became strong because of faith [21]and was absolutely confident that God would do what he promised.***

Abraham's body was already weakened by age, but he remained strong in his confidence in God. He continued to believe in God's promise even though he struggled within the frailty of his body. By his response, he honored God and was reassured that this promise would be fulfilled. His faith would not meet disappointment. God kept His promise, and from Abraham and Sarah was born the nation of Israel and ultimately the Messiah, the Son of God, by Whom all the redeemed are called to salvation.

4:22 ***That is why his faith was regarded as God's approval of him.***

Regardless of the implausibility of God's promises, Abraham always took God upon His word and obeyed with confidence. This unwavering faith was credited to him as righteousness in God's eyes and was ultimately fulfilled through the Messiah.

4:23–24 ***[23]But the words "his faith was regarded as God's approval of him" were written not only for him [24]but also for us. Our faith will be regarded as God's approval of us who believe in the one who brought Jesus, our Lord, back to life.***

The account of Abraham was not recorded in the Old Testament as just a historical event. It was written for instruction. "*Everything written long ago was written to teach us so that we would have confidence through the endurance and encouragement which the Scriptures give us*" (*Romans 15:4*). God has given us the entire Bible to reveal Himself to us and to teach us His ways; therefore, all of His teachings are relevant, applicable, and beneficial to every generation. "[16]*Every Scripture passage is inspired by God. All of them are useful for teaching, pointing out errors, correcting people, and training them for a life that has God's approval. [17]They equip God's servants so that they are completely prepared to do good things*" (*2 Timothy 3:16–17*).

We who believe have God's promise that we are His people and the assurance that He will faithfully work to perfect us according to His will:

> *[20]The God of peace brought the great shepherd of the sheep, our Lord Jesus, back to life through the blood of an eternal promise. [21]May this God of peace prepare you to do every good thing he wants. May he work in us through Jesus Christ to do what is pleasing to him. Glory belongs to Jesus Christ forever. Amen. (Hebrews 13:20–21)*

4:25 ***Jesus, our Lord, was handed over to death because of our failures and was brought back to life so that we could receive God's approval.***

The Lord Jesus went to the cross for the sins of the world and was raised again for the justification of all who believe. In 1 Corinthians 15:17, Paul declared that if Christ had not risen from the dead faith would be worthless and we would still be in our sins. Jesus' birth would have been meaningless without the cross. His cross would have been meaningless without the empty tomb. If these facts are not true, then our faith is false, and we are doomed to face the penalty of our sin *(1 Corinthians 15:19)*. But such is not the case. In Christ, we have the fulfillment of God's promise to Abraham. "*God had Christ, who was sinless, take our sin so that we might receive God's approval through him*" *(2 Corinthians 5:21)*.

Notes/Applications

Paul explained that Jesus was "handed over to death because of our failures and was brought back to life so that we could receive God's approval" *(verse 25)*. God has provided one way of salvation and that way is by believing in the finished work of His beloved Son. For those of us who believe, He has written on our death sentence, *Paid in full with the precious blood of Jesus:*

> [18]*Realize that you weren't set free from the worthless life handed down to you from your ancestors by a payment of silver or gold which can be destroyed.* [19]*Rather, the payment that freed you was the precious blood of Christ, the lamb with no defects or imperfections.* [20]*He is the lamb who was known long ago before the world existed, but for your good he became publicly known in the last period of time.* [21]*Through him you believe in God who brought Christ back to life and gave him glory. So your faith and confidence are in God.* *(1 Peter 1:18–21)*
>
> *This is true because Christ suffered for our sins once. He was an innocent person, but he suffered for guilty people so that he could bring you to God. His body was put to death, but he was brought to life through his spirit.* *(1 Peter 3:18)*

In view of such an amazing expression of God's love, we are assured that since salvation is God's work and not our own, we can rest in His wonderful, sustaining grace.

ROMANS 5

Romans 5:1–8

5:1 ***Now that we have God's approval because of faith, we have peace with God because of what our Lord Jesus Christ has done.***

This is one of three transitions in Romans (along with chapters eight and twelve) in which Paul took time to apply what he had taught in the previous section. Chapters one through three outlined the extent of human depravity. Chapter four taught clearly that we are saved out of this sinful condition by God's grace alone, not by our good works. Here in chapter five, Paul addressed the benefits of salvation: Having received God's approval through faith, believers have peace with God through the death of His Son.

"We have peace with God" is one of the most profound statements in all of Scripture. Turmoil and confusion fill the world, yet Christ bestows peace on those He redeems. The redeemed have this assurance of peace because salvation is God's gift of grace. "*I'm leaving you peace. I'm giving you my peace. I don't give you the kind of peace that the world gives. So don't be troubled or cowardly*" (*John 14:27*).

It is a miracle that sinful humanity can experience peace with the perfect, sinless God. Spiritual birth is just that—a miracle from God by way of Calvary. When originally created, Adam and Eve were at one with God. When they sinned, the harmony they experienced with their Creator was destroyed. From that moment on, all people have suffered from the separation that this broken relationship produced. Through God's gift on Calvary, this relationship is restored.

We have this peace "because of what our Lord Jesus Christ has done"—specifically, Christ came to save people from their sins. "*Indeed, the Son of Man has come to seek and to save people who are lost*" (*Luke 19:10*). Only through His sacrifice, when His blood was poured out for the remission of sin, can people be set free from their guilt and the penalty of their wrongdoing. "[18]*Realize that you weren't set free from the worthless life handed down to you from your ancestors by a payment of silver or gold which can be destroyed.* [19]*Rather, the payment that freed you was the precious blood of Christ, the lamb with no defects or imperfections*" (*1 Peter 1:18–19*).

As much as we long for some sense of contentment, we fail to achieve any degree of peace through power, possessions, or position. This world cannot provide the answer to our fundamental need for restoration. Only God can provide this kind of peace. "[6]*Never worry about anything. But in every situation let God know what you need in prayers and requests while giving thanks.* [7]*Then God's peace, which goes beyond anything we can imagine, will guard your thoughts and emotions through Christ Jesus*" (*Philippians 4:6–7*). God has conquered sin and given peace to us through His Son. Everyone who accepts His gift of salvation is restored to the harmonious relationship that God intended and discovers the great joy and perfect peace of union with the Creator and Redeemer. "*God was also pleased to bring everything on earth and in heaven back to himself through Christ. He did this by making peace through Christ's blood sacrificed on the cross*" (*Colossians 1:20*). What a marvelous gift! When doubts and confusion intrude, when peace in the world seems like a hopeless dream, the Word says that the true and eternal peace treaty has already been signed, sealed, and delivered in the blood of Christ.

5:2 ***Through Christ we can approach God and stand in his favor. So we brag because of our confidence that we will receive glory from God.***

Believers now have access to God through the Lord Jesus Christ. This is the wonderful result of what Christ accomplished for those who believe in Him!

> [13]*But now through Christ Jesus you, who were once far away, have been brought near by the blood of Christ.* [14]*So he is our peace. In his body he has made Jewish and non-Jewish people one by breaking down the wall of hostility that kept them apart.* [15]*He brought an end to the commandments and demands found in Moses' Teachings so that he could take Jewish and non-Jewish people and create one new humanity in himself. So he made peace.* (Ephesians 2:13–15)

This is what Christians mean when they speak of God's grace. God invites people to come to Him in faith. He has created this new relationship by adopting us as His children. "[1]*Consider this: The Father has given us his love. He loves us so much that we are actually called God's dear children. And that's what we are . . .* [2]*Dear friends, now we are God's children*" (1 John 3:1–2). As God's children, the redeemed are escorted into the holy presence of the eternal God. We "stand in his favor" as we live in constant communion with Him.

The promise of the glory that believers receive from God generates the confidence that enables them to brag about their position in Him. What does this really mean? Our confidence is in Jesus Christ Who has redeemed us for all eternity. If our hope were based upon our futile efforts, we would certainly be lost forever. Because our hope is in the eternal Son of God, our lost condition is removed. This gives direction and purpose to our lives now and the glorious promise of eternal life.

5:3–4 ***[3]But that's not all. We also brag when we are suffering. We know that suffering creates endurance, [4]endurance creates character, and character creates confidence.***

Verse three continues Paul's thoughts on bragging, but for an unexpected reason: "when we are suffering." How can this be? By nature, this is impossible. But in confidence of the glory of God, suffering produces the kind of person that God intends for the believer to be. We can rejoice in suffering when we know that it is for our good. *"We know that all things work together for the good of those who love God—those whom he has called according to his plan" (Romans 8:28)*. What then is God's grand design in suffering? This text answers that "suffering creates endurance, endurance creates character, and character creates confidence." Our difficult experiences produce in us a greater maturity, thereby increasing our usefulness to God and to other people.

5:5 ***We're not ashamed to have this confidence, because God's love has been poured into our hearts by the Holy Spirit, who has been given to us.***

The confidence spoken of here is based on God's promises and integrity, not on our capacity to endure suffering. Scriptures affirm that our confidence rests not on ourselves but on the unchanging nature of God. *"We have this confidence as a sure and strong anchor for our lives" (Hebrews 6:19)*. Our faith is based on this certain confidence, secured by Christ's death and resurrection from the dead.

Paul went even further to assure us that this confidence is not only objectively affirmed in the Scriptures but experienced in our lives as the Holy Spirit witnesses to our spirits. *"That helper is the Spirit of Truth. The world cannot accept him, because it doesn't see or know him. You know him, because he lives with you and will be in you" (John 14:17)*. This explains the condition under which the believer lives from the time of regeneration. *"When the Spirit of Truth comes, he will guide you into the full truth. He won't speak on his own. He will speak what he hears and will tell you about things to come"* (John 16:13). The Spirit lives in believers' hearts, impressing on them the reliability, truth, and inerrancy of Scripture. The resulting confidence provides unquenchable reliance on God's faithfulness to accomplish all that He has promised.

5:6 ***Look at it this way: At the right time, while we were still helpless, Christ died for ungodly people.***

When we were literally helpless, Christ died for us. We had no chance of rescuing ourselves. He didn't wait for humanity to turn to Him and love Him. We were not only weak but ungodly. In verse ten of this chapter, Paul went further still: Christ's death came "while we were still his enemies." Barnhouse wrote of our dilemma:

> He did not attempt to reform us; but He planned to die for us to give us new life. He did not plan to alter or patch us; His purpose was to create us anew in Christ and to give us His own life through Him. Here, then is our sure and steadfast hope. Christ has died. He has died for the ungodly. He has died for the weak, the helpless, the powerless, the infirm, the sinner. He has died for those who were dead. Out of His death has come life for us. We have obeyed the call of the Spirit and have learned that we are the objects of His love; since He found no merit in us but knew what we were before He saved us, we are confident our being beloved is an unchangeable attitude from the Father because of the very nature of His being.[1]

"At the right time," that time ordained by God, He sent His Son to accomplish this redemption. Bethlehem and Calvary were on God's calendar before He created the world. "*Before the creation of the world, he chose us through Christ to be holy and perfect in his presence*" (*Ephesians 1:4*).

5:7–8 ***[7]Finding someone who would die for a godly person is rare. Maybe someone would have the courage to die for a good person. [8]Christ died for us while we were still sinners. This demonstrates God's love for us.***

Occasionally, we hear of someone dying for another: a parent for a child or a friend for a friend. Of course, those accepting responsibility for protecting others (such as military, police, and fire personnel) risk their lives every day. With this exception, rarely would anyone give his life for someone he did not already love or, at least, felt was worthy of the sacrifice.

The good news is that while we were sinners Christ died for us. Everyone has sinned, and no one really looks for God. Nevertheless, God's love was expressed to all mankind in a way that is inconceivable. He sent His Son as the only acceptable sacrifice for sin even while humanity still rebelled against Him. Seven centuries before Christ, Isaiah foretold this amazing provision: "We have all strayed like sheep. Each one of us has turned to go his own way, and the LORD has laid all our sins on him" *(Isaiah 53:6)*. What unimaginable love, beyond our comprehension: God's holy Son died in our place. "*God had Christ, who was sinless, take our sin so that we might receive God's approval through him*" *(2 Corinthians 5:21)*. "*Christ suffered for our sins once. He was an innocent person, but he suffered for guilty people so that he could bring you to God*" *(1 Peter 3:18)*.

Notes/Applications

One of our most precious possessions as Christians is God's peace, which is beyond our understanding *(Philippians 4:7)*. This is a reality, not an illusion. It is tested and proven through adversity, even suffering, which here is declared to be a blessing. Most believers who have walked with the Lord for a lifetime can testify that their greatest growth has occurred during times of severe testing. God has promised to continue His work of salvation in us until He takes us home. "*I'm convinced that God, who began this good work in you, will carry it through to completion on the day of Christ Jesus*" *(Philippians 1:6)*.

Time and again, the Scriptures affirm that suffering is the pathway to our maturity in Christ. Therefore, we should rejoice in tribulations because God is working in our lives, molding a character that reflects the new life of Christ in us by the power of the Holy Spirit.

> [6]*You are extremely happy about these things, even though you have to suffer different kinds of trouble for a little while now.* [7]*The purpose of these troubles is to test your faith as fire tests how genuine gold is. Your faith is more precious than gold, and by passing the test, it gives praise, glory, and honor to God. This will happen when Jesus Christ appears again. (1 Peter 1:6–7)*

Hebrews 12:2 also exhorts us to "focus on Jesus, the source and goal of our faith. He saw the joy ahead of him, so he endured death on the cross and ignored the disgrace it brought him." With our eyes on Him for time and eternity, we have strength to persevere through the hard times in this life, trusting our Lord and giving glory and honor to Him.

Romans 5:9–14

5:9 ***Since Christ's blood has now given us God's approval, we are even more certain that Christ will save us from God's anger.***

Our redemption through the blood of Christ has provided God's approval. This could not be earned by keeping the law or secured by the sacrifice of animals. However, the divine blood of the perfect Lamb of God has made us acceptable to the holy God. *"John saw Jesus coming toward him the next day and said, 'Look! This is the Lamb of God who takes away the sin of the world'" (John 1:29). "But now through Christ Jesus you, who were once far away, have been brought near by the blood of Christ" (Ephesians 2:13).* Now in Christ we are enabled to walk in His presence. *"But if we live in the light in the same way that God is in the light, we have a relationship with each other. And the blood of his Son Jesus cleanses us from every sin" (1 John 1:7).*

The assurance of our new standing with God through the blood of His Son gives us confidence that we will not face His holy anger. Jesus gave this promise: "I can guarantee this truth: Those who listen to what I say and believe in the one who sent me will have eternal life. They won't be judged because they have already passed from death to life" *(John 5:24).*

5:10 ***If the death of his Son restored our relationship with God while we were still his enemies, we are even more certain that, because of this restored relationship, the life of his Son will save us.***

As unrepentant sinners, we were enemies of God. The past tense used here demonstrates that what was true of our lives in the past is no longer the case in the present. Similarly, Paul wrote to the Ephesian believers: "[1]You were once dead because of your failures and sins. [2]You followed the ways of this present world and its spiritual ruler. This ruler continues to work in people who refuse to obey God" *(Ephesians 2:1–2).* Through His death, the Son of God has restored our relationship with the Father. In Christ, we have His forgiveness from our sins and the promise of eternal life *(2 Corinthians 5:18–21)*.

Christ's life provides even greater confidence for the believer. The life He lived carried the full weight of the law in absolute perfection, making Him the blameless sacrifice for all sin. After His resurrection, Christ's life became the confirmation of every promise in the Old Testament and every promise He had spoken, especially His promise that He would give eternal life to those who were His. His life in heaven provides continuing intercession on behalf of His children. We are restored to God through His death and kept by His intercession until that day when we see Him face to face.

5:11 ***In addition, our Lord Jesus Christ lets us continue to brag about God. After all, it is through Christ that we now have this restored relationship with God.***

As Paul already said in verses two and three, we have something to brag about. This can have a negative or positive connotation. The meaning here is that, in Christ, we truly have something positive to brag about, namely our God and the salvation He has provided to us through His Son. In Galatians 6:14, Paul clarified the narrow focus our "bragging" must have in order to be acceptable: "It's unthinkable that I could ever brag about anything except the cross of our Lord Jesus Christ." When we reflect on God's mercy given to us through Christ, we can rightly brag about Him, rejoicing with thanks in His person and work.

This rejoicing comes because of our restored relationship with God. This is exactly what Jesus Christ did at Calvary. He met all the just demands of the law and paid the penalty for our sins. Through faith we are forgiven and stand before God in Christ's righteousness. Our reconciliation to the eternal Creator of the universe should fill us with inexpressible joy. "[8]*Although you have never seen Christ, you love him. You don't see him now, but you believe in him. You are extremely happy with joy and praise that can hardly be expressed in words* [9]*as you obtain the salvation that is the goal of your faith*" *(1 Peter 1:8–9)*.

5:12 ***Sin came into the world through one person, and death came through sin. So death spread to everyone, because everyone sinned.***

God created Adam and Eve without sin but with the capability to obey or disobey His command. Unfortunately, they chose disobedience. The first human being to sin was Eve, and Adam quickly followed. They were both guilty, but God held Adam accountable because He had given Adam clear instruction even before Eve was created, as recorded in Genesis 2:16–17: "[16]You are free to eat from any tree in the garden. [17]But you must never eat from the tree of the knowledge of good and evil because when you eat from it, you will certainly die." However, they both disobeyed their Creator. "*The woman saw that the tree had fruit that was good to eat, nice to look at, and desirable for making someone wise. So she took some of the fruit and ate it. She also gave some to her husband, who was with her, and he ate it*" (*Genesis 3:6*).

In this way, sin entered the human race. Because God is righteous, He cannot and will not tolerate sin, and so the penalty for sin is death. Since every human being is a descendant of this couple, sin and its resulting death penalty are the condition and destiny of all humanity. This message of the Scripture is demonstrated in all of human experience. To deny this fact is to deny the Word of God.

> [8]*If we say, "We aren't sinful" we are deceiving ourselves, and the truth is not in us.* [9]*God is faithful and reliable. If we confess our sins, he forgives them and cleanses us from everything we've done wrong.* [10]*If we say, "We have never sinned," we turn God into a liar and his Word is not in us. (1 John 1:8–10)*

5:13 ***Sin was in the world before there were any laws. But no record of sin can be kept when there are no laws.***

As we studied in chapter two, God's moral law existed long before it was written down by Moses. Therefore, this verse confirms that God held mankind accountable for its sinfulness before the written law was provided. We need to look no further into God's Word for evidence of this than when Adam and Eve disobeyed God by eating from the tree of the knowledge of good and evil *(Genesis 3)* or in the example of Cain, the firstborn son of Adam, who murdered his brother *(Genesis 4)*. Though the written law was centuries away from being recorded, God still imposed consequences for their sinfulness *(Genesis 3:16–19; 4:10–12)*.

What, then, was the purpose of the written law if right and wrong have always been established in mortal hearts and if the Almighty has always kept a record of transgressions? In essence, this "record of sin" would be established to provide evidence by which mankind could fully understand its hopeless position in contrast to "the one who would come" and provide the only means of reconciliation between the Creator and His creation as explained in the following verses.

5:14 ***Yet, death ruled from the time of Adam to the time of Moses, even over those who did not sin in the same way Adam did when he disobeyed. Adam is an image of the one who would come.***

The widespread escalation of sin from Adam to Moses is documented in the books of Genesis and Exodus. Although people did not have direct commands from God as Adam and Eve did, they had their oral tradition to guide them, as well as the witness of their consciences. Just nine generations after Adam, it is recorded in Genesis 6:5, "The LORD saw how evil humans had become on the earth. All day long their deepest thoughts were nothing but evil." Through Noah, He chose to bring His judgment by a flood and His deliverance in the ship.

As Adam was formed in the image of his Creator *(Genesis 1:27)*, the description of Adam as "an image of the one who would come" depicts how, just as sin entered the world through one man, so, too, would the redemption of man enter the world through one man *(1 Corinthians 15:21–22)*. This One became flesh, entered His creation, and lived among sinful people *(John 1:1–3, 14)*. The first man was created from the earth without sin but sinned willfully and subjected the world to the consequences of sin. The "last Adam" *(1 Corinthians 15:45)* existed eternally in heaven but came into His creation without sin, lived a sinless life, and died for the redemption of the sinful human race thereby reversing the curse that God had imposed upon His insubordinate creation.

Notes/Applications

Under the curse of Adam's sin, we all deserve the just consequences of God's righteous anger. Left to our own futile attempts at righteousness, we have no escape, no reprieve, no pardon, and no stay of execution. We are orphans and slaves to sin.

However, because of Jesus Christ, our condition is no longer hopeless. God removes the penalty of sin from those who believe upon Him. Christ's death and resurrection have given us the gift of eternal life and eternal hope. As the nineteenth century pastor and evangelist Charles Hadden Spurgeon comments, we must "cast the anchor of [our] faith on this...":[2]

> Personally, I could never have overcome my own sinfulness. I tried and failed. My evil tendencies were too much for me until, in the belief that Christ died for me, I cast my guilty soul on Him. And then I received a conquering principle by which I overcame my sinful self. The doctrine of the cross can be used to slay sin like the old warriors used their huge two-handed swords and mowed down their foes at every stroke. There is nothing like faith in the sinner's Friend; it overcomes all evil. If Christ has died for me—ungodly as I am, without strength as I am—then I can no longer live in sin, but must arouse myself to love and serve Him who has redeemed me. I cannot trifle with the evil which slew my best Friend. I must be holy for His sake. How can I live in sin when He has died to save me from it?[3]

When we are redeemed, we are saved from God's wrath, and we are set free to live holy lives. We are transformed from being enemies of God to being more than His creation, even more than His friends. We are given new life as His children.

Romans 5:15–21

5:15 ***There is no comparison between God's gift and Adam's failure. If humanity died as the result of one person's failure, it is certainly true that God's kindness and the gift given through the kindness of one person, Jesus Christ, have been showered on humanity.***

God's gift of redemption is free; it cannot be earned. Adam's failure was deadly but not fatal to those who believe. The contrast is well-stated in Romans 8:3: "It is impossible to do what God's standards demand because of the weakness our human nature has. But God sent his Son to have a human nature as sinners have and to pay for sin. That way God condemned sin in our corrupt nature." In calling to Himself a new people, saved by His grace, He reversed the universal effects of Adam's sin *(1 Peter 2:9)*.

Sin is offensive to the holy God. By Adam's sin all people are born sinful, but God sent another man into the world, His only Son, to bring salvation to sinners. By this man, Jesus, God's kindness (grace) has been "showered on humanity." *"Jesus was made a little lower than the angels, but we see him crowned with glory and honor because he suffered death. Through God's kindness he died on behalf of everyone" (Hebrews 2:9)*.

5:16 ***There is also no comparison between God's gift and the one who sinned. The verdict which followed one person's failure condemned everyone. But, even after many failures, the gift brought God's approval.***

Having contrasted God's gift with Adam's failure, Paul proceeded to compare the one through whom sin entered creation with the One through Whom salvation entered creation. God's gift is the very Lamb of God Who takes away the sin of the world. Through these comparisons in verses sixteen and seventeen, Paul illustrated the supremacy of God's gift by emphasizing that there really is no comparison at all.

When Adam and Eve sinned, God pronounced a guilty verdict upon mankind, and the resulting sentence was death. But in pronouncing this sentence in the garden of Eden, he also promised a deliverer *(Genesis 3:15)*. Even at that terrible moment in history, and regardless of the depths of mankind's sinfulness that would follow, God provided a means of salvation that was more than sufficient to forgive the sins of the world.

5:17 ***It is certain that death ruled because of one person's failure. It's even more certain that those who receive God's overflowing kindness and the gift of his approval will rule in life because of one person, Jesus Christ.***

Adam's transgression brought death, which has ruled mankind ever since. While the actions of the first Adam were consequential, devastating, and destructive, the grace of the last Adam, Jesus Christ, is far greater and nullifies the consequences of the first. This gracious gift of righteousness imputed to all believers provides victory over sin and guilt. "*Our Lord was very kind to me. Through his kindness he brought me to faith and gave me the love that Christ Jesus shows people*" *(1 Timothy 1:14)*. As Christians, the Lord Jesus Christ governs our lives so that His grace may be experienced and lived out. Death has no power or victory. "*Thank God that he gives us the victory through our Lord Jesus Christ*" *(1 Corinthians 15:57)*.

5:18 ***Therefore, everyone was condemned through one failure, and everyone received God's life-giving approval through one verdict.***

Because of Adam's one sin, everyone has an appointment with death and judgment *(Hebrews 9:27–28)*. Although Jesus fulfilled the letter of the law in absolute perfection, He willingly accepted the death penalty in order to conquer sin and death forevermore. As such, God has pronounced a verdict of "not guilty" on those who are redeemed *(1 Timothy 2:5–6)*. We were on death row, but this verdict has set us free. Certainly, we still face physical death, but we will not subjected to eternal punishment in hell *(Revelation 20:6)*.

5:19 ***Clearly, through one person's disobedience humanity became sinful, and through one person's obedience humanity will receive God's approval.***

This verse summarizes the previous seven verses. God created Adam perfect and holy and placed him in a perfect setting. He gave Adam dominion over creation, and Adam enjoyed direct communion with God in the garden.

When Adam disobeyed God's one rule about not eating of the tree of the knowledge of good and evil, he broke his relationship with Almighty God. He, therefore, became a sinner, and the entire human race became stained by this transgression. Yet even before Adam sinned, God knew it would happen and had planned a way to provide salvation. God could not overlook sin or simply decide that He wouldn't be so hard on people. Sin has a penalty, death, which cannot be evaded. The penalty had to be paid, but God Himself paid it. The Messiah, the perfect Lamb of God, was provided before creation—"the lamb who was slaughtered before the creation of the world" *(Revelation 13:8)*.

In contrast, the obedience of our Lord Jesus Christ and His sacrificial death for sinners mended the break between God and humanity caused by Adam's disobedience. Jesus willingly gave His innocent life for our guilty lives *(John 10:17–18)*. This magnificent obedience of the Son makes all who believe in Him acceptable again before Almighty God. "*[5]Because of his love he had already decided to adopt us through Jesus Christ. He freely chose to do this [6]so that the kindness he had given us in his dear Son would be praised and given glory*" *(Ephesians 1:5–6)*.

5:20 ***Laws were added to increase the failure. But where sin increased, God's kindness increased even more.***

If people did not sin, there would be no need of laws. In his letter to the Galatians, Paul gave an extensive explanation of the purpose of Moses' laws in relation to the promise given to Abraham:

> [19]*What, then, is the purpose of the laws given to Moses? They were added to identify what wrongdoing is. Moses' laws did this until the descendant to whom the promise was given came. It was put into effect through angels, using a mediator.* [20]*A mediator is not used when there is only one person involved, and God has acted on his own.* [21]*Does this mean, then, that the laws given to Moses contradict God's promises? That's unthinkable! If those laws could give us life, then certainly we would receive God's approval because we obeyed them.* [22]*But Scripture states that the whole world is controlled by the power of sin. Therefore, a promise based on faith in Jesus Christ could be given to those who believe.*
>
> [23]*We were kept under control by Moses' laws until this faith came. We were under their control until this faith which was about to come would be revealed.*
>
> [24]*Before Christ came, Moses' laws served as our guardian. Christ came so that we could receive God's approval by faith.* [25]*But now that this faith has come, we are no longer under the control of a guardian.* (Galatians 3:19–25)

The law was never intended as a way of salvation but rather to expose our sin and guilt before God. The law condemns; it does not pardon. This passage teaches that the law was primarily a guardian for God's people until Christ came as a fulfillment of the promise.

The effect of the law through the centuries was to increase people's awareness of their sinfulness. Under the Pharisees and scribes, the people felt burdened by their sins—the laws were too difficult to keep perfectly. In fact, no one could do it. Jesus, and later the apostles, exposed the sinful hypocrisy of the Jewish leaders who demanded perfect obedience to every law because they saw it as the way of salvation. Jesus' condemnation and insistence upon belief in Him for salvation led those leaders to reject the good news and to kill the only One Who could save them.

The Psalms and the writings of the prophets in the Old Testament speak often of the mercy of God and His desire for willing obedience as opposed to empty ritual. *"Is the LORD as delighted with burnt offerings and sacrifices as he would be with your obedience? To follow instructions is better than to sacrifice. To obey is better than sacrificing the fat of rams" (1 Samuel 15:22)*. In fact, our Lord is full of mercy, and some of the most powerful statements in the Bible to that effect can be found in the Old Testament prophets *(Micah 7:18–20)*. As sin increased, God's kindness through our Lord Jesus Christ was given to us in ever-increasing proportions *(Titus 3:3–7)*.

5:21 ***As sin ruled by bringing death, God's kindness would rule by bringing us his approval. This results in our living forever because of Jesus Christ our Lord.***

There was no death until sin came. When Adam sinned, death resulted. The entire human race fell under the dominion of the sin nature, ushering in the inevitable separation from the Creator and the related death penalty.

Even as believers, we continue to battle with sin in our flesh. Sin's hold on us is tough and relentless, but God's grace breaks that stronghold. We have victory only through the beloved Son of the living God. By His grace, we have regained what Adam lost. In the first Adam, there is only death. In the second Adam, there is life abundant and eternal. This is not just a promise and prospect for the future, but a present possession.

> [11]*This is the testimony: God has given us eternal life, and this life is found in his Son.* [12]*The person who has the Son has this life. The person who doesn't have the Son of God doesn't have this life.* [13]*I've written this to those who believe in the Son of God so that they will know that they have eternal life. (1 John 5:11–13)*

Notes/Applications

Words cannot express our gratitude to God for this gift secured for us in the sacrifice of Jesus Christ, His Son, our Lord. Our overwhelming response to this portrait of God's grace should be hearts full of gratitude to our heavenly Father. No other religious system claims a Creator God Who loves His alienated people so much that He would send His Son to die for them. Psalm one hundred seven gives a beautiful account of God's faithfulness to His people. Opening with the words, "Give thanks to the LORD because he is good, because his mercy endures forever," the psalm writer repeats this wonderful refrain four more times *(Psalm 107:1, 8, 15, 21, 31)*.

The hymn, "The Mercy of God Is an Ocean Divine," also eloquently expresses God's deep, unfathomable mercy in sending His Son:

The mercy of God is an ocean divine,
A boundless and fathomless flood.
Launch out in the deep, cut away the shore line,
And be lost in the fullness of God.

But many, alas! only stand on the shore,
And gaze on the ocean so wide.
They never have ventured its depths to explore,
Or to launch on the fathomless tide.

And others just venture away from the land,
And linger so near to the shore
That the surf and the slime that beat over the strand
Dash o'er them in floods evermore.

Oh, let us launch out on this ocean so broad,
Where floods of salvation o'erflow.
Oh, let us be lost in the mercy of God,
Till the depths of His fullness we know.

Refrain:

Launch out, into the deep.
Oh let the shore line go.
Launch out, launch out in the ocean divine,
Out where the full tides flow.[4]

In view of the indescribable mercies of our great God, let us worship Him and obey what Jesus called the "greatest and most important" commandment: "Love the Lord your God with all your heart, with all your soul, and with all your mind" *(Matthew 22:37)*.

ROMANS 6

Romans 6:1–7

6:1 ***What should we say then? Should we continue to sin so that God's kindness will increase?***

Building on his argument in the previous chapter, Paul posed this question to refute any unbalanced response to his emphasis on God's kindness and grace. He had declared that God demonstrated His great love through the death of His Son while we were sinners and even His enemies. This was *in spite of* our sinfulness and *because of* it. Paul certainly did not want his readers to infer that their state of sinfulness could enhance God's kindness.

In fact, even to contemplate *any* way to increase God's outpouring of kindness would be foolishness, if not heresy. God's kindness is unmerited favor; it cannot be earned, and people's sinfulness can neither increase nor diminish it. Furthermore, God's kindness in no way gives people license to sin. Paul already made that clear when he reminded his readers that God's kindness functioned not to excuse His people, but to lead them to change *(Romans 2:4)*. In his letter, Jude also described such people:

> *Some people have slipped in among you unnoticed. Not long ago they were condemned in writing for the following reason: They are people to whom God means nothing. They use God's kindness as an excuse for sexual freedom and deny our only Master and Lord, Jesus Christ. (Jude 4)*

6:2 *That's unthinkable! As far as sin is concerned, we have died. So how can we still live under sin's influence?*

Paul's answer to his question in verse one was an emphatic no. We must not "continue to sin." His reasoning? When we receive God's kindness through Christ's death, we have died to sin. Paul explained this when he wrote to the church in Galatia describing his new life in Christ: "[19]I have been crucified with Christ. [20]I no longer live, but Christ lives in me. The life I now live I live by believing in God's Son, who loved me and took the punishment for my sins" *(Galatians 2:19–20)*. This same reasoning can be seen in Jesus' teachings. Jesus told His disciples that if they wanted to follow Him, they would have to take up their crosses daily; in other words, they would need to be willing to die to their old way of life *(Luke 9:23)*.

Still, our human experience demonstrates that believers are continually engaged in a spiritual battle to rid themselves of sin. Even Paul, though he emphasized that the genuine believer is no longer subject to sin, was very much aware that this was humanly impossible. Keep in mind that when Paul wrote of believers being dead to sin, he was not saying that we are immune to sin or can no longer sin; rather, he was affirming our position in Christ. In God's eyes, Christ's work in us is already an accomplished fact. We are righteous in God's eyes. "*You have died, and your life is hidden with Christ in God*" *(Colossians 3:3)*. In Christ, we should live every day with the profound awareness that we have been freed from the power of sin. "*Christ carried our sins in his body on the cross so that freed from our sins, we could live a life that has God's approval*" *(1 Peter 2:24)*.

6:3 ***Don't you know that all of us who were baptized into Christ Jesus were baptized into his death?***

Paul used the word *baptized* here in a figurative sense, not speaking of the physical activity but rather describing the way that the believer is joined to Christ in a redeemed union. The word is used more often in the New Testament to refer to our union and identification with Christ than to water baptism.[1] Therefore, the union of the redeemed with the death of Christ means this: While Christ died to pay the penalty for our sin, we are immersed into that death so that we have died, and remain dead, to sin.

6:4 ***When we were baptized into his death, we were placed into the tomb with him. As Christ was brought back from death to life by the glorious power of the Father, so we, too, should live a new kind of life.***

The redeemed join their Savior both in His death and in His burial. While the believer is not physically buried, Paul used this imagery to describe what happens to us when we are saved. We are taken through the process of dying to self and sin and rising to newness of life, sharing the joy of our resurrected Lord. Paul used this same imagery in his letter to the Colossians: "This happened when you were placed in the tomb with Christ through baptism. In baptism you were also brought back to life with Christ through faith in the power of God, who brought him back to life" *(Colossians 2:12)*.

This is the basis upon which believers live the rest of their earthly days. Contrary to yielding to the sin nature in which we were born or attempting to rise above it by observing the law, we live this new life because we have joined Jesus Christ in His death, burial, and resurrection. The redeemed life is predicated on the work of Christ alone, not on anything we have done or can do.

6:5 ***If we've become united with him in a death like his, certainly we will also be united with him when we come back to life as he did.***

Jesus Christ came to earth like us and died that we might be like Him. The wonderful promise of 1 John 3:2 is that "we will be like him because we will see him as he is." Here, Paul moved from the metaphorical imagery of Christ's death and resurrection to a declaration that this spiritual rebirth will result in a physical resurrection of the believer's body. Because Jesus conquered death by His resurrection, death no longer has dominion over us *(1 Corinthians 15:51–54)*.

6:6 ***We know that the person we used to be was crucified with him to put an end to sin in our bodies. Because of this we are no longer slaves to sin.***

In every authentic believer, the transformation from death to life is a momentous event. The believer basks in the joyous experience of release from the consequence of sin. Charles Wesley, the beloved hymn writer, so graphically described this transformation in verse four of his classic hymn "And Can It Be That I Should Gain?":

Long my imprisoned spirit lay,
Fast bound in sin and nature's night;
Thine eye diffused a quickening ray—
I woke, the dungeon flamed with light;
My chains fell off, my heart was free,
I rose, went forth, and followed Thee.[2]

Knowing the persistence of our sin nature, how could Paul say that Christ has "put an end to sin in our bodies" and that we are no longer slaves to sin? It is a matter of ownership. The cruel master of our sin nature dominates every facet of our earthly existence, tenaciously controlling us until that moment when we die. However, when we are crucified with Christ, the hold of that merciless master is broken and replaced with the mastery of the Holy Spirit. We are no longer slaves to sin but the happy bondservants of our redeeming Lord.

6:7 *The person who has died has been freed from sin.*

The redeemed person, now servant to his new Master, Jesus Christ, becomes immersed in the new life that has been bestowed upon him. The Word of God opens new vistas of the goodness, mercy, and kindness of this new Master. He is no longer oppressed by his sin but is set free to enjoy an abundant life under the continual, superior guidance of the Holy Spirit.

Can a dead person commit murder, worship an idol, or act with self-righteous pride? Of course not! Once the believer has died to his old nature, once the cruel master has been expelled from his life, and once the believer has been raised to the newness of the redeemed life, the power and allure of his former nature begins its slow fade into the background and the influence of his new Master begins to emerge. Under the faithful supervision of the Holy Spirit, the redeemed person is directed into a maturing process in his new life while being kept from a headlong rush back into his dead nature.

Notes/Applications

Because God is holy, neither sin nor sinner can abide in His presence. Sin is a condition that is diametrically opposed to His very nature. The very idea that a recipient of His grace should continue to sin in order to magnify the measure of His holiness and kindness is unimaginable. That is why Paul reacted so strongly to such an absurd notion. It presumes upon the goodness of God and lowers Him to a product of humanity's vain imagination, attempting to exploit His goodness in a way that justifies a sinful agenda. The scope of His every attribute is immeasurable and unfathomable to the human mind.

The very idea that we could ever do anything to magnify the graciousness of God further undermines our understanding of the salvation that God has provided by the sacrifice of His Son, the Savior, Jesus Christ. Such thinking is the epitome of foolishness and self-righteousness. How could man denigrate the goodness of God as it is so clearly demonstrated by this supreme sacrifice? God's righteousness demands satisfaction, and the offense of our sin has been thoroughly eradicated by the blood of His Son shed on the cross. That is the price God required, and His Son paid that price in full. Nothing else could ever better express the depths of His love for His creation.

We know that our love for Christ is trivial in comparison to His love for us. May His patient goodness lead us to surrender to Him, the sacrifice for our sin and the keeper of our eternal souls. He is Master, Savior, and Lord. May we simply bow in adoration and gratitude.

Romans 6:8–14

6:8 *If we have died with Christ, we believe that we will also live with him.*

Since we have been crucified with Christ, we have died to our old ways. We are alive in Jesus Christ. This is the daily process in which we yield our own wills to the will of our new Master.

This new life is stronger than the curse of sin and the penalty of death. This occurs only because it is derived from the perfect life that Christ lived, the sacrifice that He suffered, and the victory that He secured. When He said, "It is finished," He meant that the full penalty for sin had been paid. He conquered sin and abolished all its consequences: death, hell, and eternal damnation. "*The one who is in you is greater than the one who is in the world*" (*1 John 4:4*).

6:9 *We know that Christ, who was brought back to life, will never die again. Death no longer has any power over him.*

Paul expanded his argument about the believer's confidence in Christ. He wanted his readers to be profoundly aware of the person Who validated their new lives. Not only did Christ rise from the dead, but He will never die again. "*I was dead, but now I am alive forever*" (*Revelation 1:18*). He is forever alive; death is forever conquered. Paul wanted believers to capture the essence of the assurance that is theirs in the resurrection of Christ. What is true of Christ is true of us as well.

6:10 *When he died, he died once and for all to sin's power. But now he lives, and he lives for God.*

The testimony of Christ's apostles affirmed the appalling death that Jesus suffered on the cross, but much more was happening in the spiritual realm. The courts of heaven mourned as the Father turned away from His only Son and laid the sins of the world on His shoulders. At that moment, Jesus ended sin's dominion, effectively ending its reigning power. When He rose from the dead, He brought God's offer of eternal life into the realm of our existence, and He conferred that life on the redeemed. Thus, Jesus fulfilled the will of the Father by ending sin and by perpetuating life. He is now enthroned in heaven as the Lamb of God, Who is forever worthy of all praise and adoration.

***6:11** So consider yourselves dead to sin's power but living for God in the power Christ Jesus gives you.*

This magnificent sacrifice for humanity's sin should cause us to recognize that our selfish and self-righteous lifestyle is over. As Christians, we should recognize that this is the import of Paul's declaration. The word *consider,* *λογίζεσθε* (logizesthe), means "to keep records of commercial accounts, involving both debits and credits—to put into one's account, to charge one's account, to regard as an account."[3] This is an accounting term, conveying the idea of charging to one's account. Our sin was charged to Jesus' account, and the books have been balanced. From now on, we should act upon this new life that has been given to us. "[19]*You don't belong to yourselves.* [20]*You were bought for a price. So bring glory to God in the way you use your body"* *(1 Corinthians 6:19–20)*.

Living this new life, we discover that in Christ we are alive to God. Our lives, supervised and directed by the Holy Spirit, are the expression of our new life in Christ. Believers are then the bearers of the Son's image, living unto God just as Jesus did. "*Everything you say or do should be done in the name of the Lord Jesus, giving thanks to God the Father through him" (Colossians 3:17)*.

***6:12** Therefore, never let sin rule your physical body so that you obey its desires.*

Even those who have been buried and raised with Christ still sin. The essential distinction between believers and unbelievers is that believers are forgiven, have eternal life, and now live under the authority of the risen Christ. The mastery of their sin nature has been forever destroyed. Although this mastery has been wiped out, Paul cautioned us that the practical power of sin over our human faculties is still a very real threat. The battle between the redeemed nature and the old nature will continue to plague us all of our lives. Jesus alone is our strength through this struggle against sin *(Colossians 3:15–16)*.

6:13 ***Never offer any part of your body to sin's power. No part of your body should ever be used to do any ungodly thing. Instead, offer yourselves to God as people who have come back from death and are now alive. Offer all the parts of your body to God. Use them to do everything that God approves of.***

Paul exhorted believers to avoid their own selfish desires and Satan's cunning temptations. As believers in Christ, bought by His blood, every part of our bodies belongs to Him and, therefore, should be surrendered to Him. Any part of our bodies—our hands, our feet, our eyes—can lead us into evil. That first touch, first step, or first look might seem small, but it is the beginning of a very dangerous pathway. Similarly, when we resist temptation, avoiding even the smallest enticements, we gain confidence and strength. "[7]*So place yourselves under God's authority. Resist the devil, and he will run away from you.* [8]*Come close to God, and he will come close to you*" *(James 4:7–8)*.

So how can we do things "that God approves of"? How can we know? We have the Holy Spirit Who enables us to understand the truth of God's Word. His abiding presence helps us make decisions that are in harmony with God's sovereign will. However, as we say no to our sin-directed predispositions, we must say yes to the Lord and seek His direction. Our highest worship is submission to our indwelling Lord, daily offering our bodies as living sacrifices. The whole of our lives should be the expression of such a daily worship. "*Brothers and sisters, in view of all we have just shared about God's compassion, I encourage you to offer your bodies as living sacrifices, dedicated to God and pleasing to him. This kind of worship is appropriate for you" (Romans 12:1).*

Through the Lord Jesus Christ, His death, burial, and resurrection, the battle between the flesh and the spirit has already been won. However, we must commit every day to the disciplines of prayer, meditation on the Word, and obedience to God.

6:14 ***Certainly, sin shouldn't have power over you because you're not controlled by laws, but by God's favor.***

Sin should no longer have control over us because God has taken us out from under the rule of the law and its condemning consequences. *"For the law was given by Moses, but grace and truth came by Jesus Christ" (John 1:17, KJV).* This does not mean that there is no sin in a Christian's life, but that sin is no longer the predominant force, having no entitlement in controlling the believer's life.

Believers are no longer condemned by the law, and while we no longer seek to gain God's favor by keeping the law, we do seek to obey God's commandments as the expression of our love for Him. The believer's righteousness is the gift of God's grace, received by faith, which is also a gift bestowed by God.

Notes/Applications

The essential theme of this section is new control over the believer's life. Paul affirmed that a profound change takes place as the believer spiritually dies, is buried, and rises again, aligned with the historical events of Jesus' life. Paul established this thesis in the early verses of this chapter. As the believer grows in understanding of this eternal truth—that he is purchased by the blood of Jesus Christ—Paul asserted that this growth should be demonstrated in the believer's life by the conduct that flows out of his gratitude for such a wonderful gift.

The first question raised in the treatise of the historic Heidelberg Catechism says it well: "What is your only comfort in life and in death?" The answer is deeply profound and compelling:

> *That I am not my own, but belong—body and soul, in life and in death—to my faithful Savior Jesus Christ. He has fully paid for all my sins with his precious blood, and has set me free from the tyranny of the devil. He also watches over me in such a way that not a hair can fall from my head without the will of my Father in heaven: in fact, all things must work together for my salvation. Because I belong to him, Christ, by his Holy Spirit, assures me of eternal life and makes me wholeheartedly willing and ready from now on to live for him.*[4]

These words powerfully express the Scriptures, reminding us that we have been bought with the price of the blood of the eternal Son of God. There is no greater motivation and challenge to submit ourselves daily to the loving care of our sovereign God, living out our salvation in willing, joyful obedience.

Romans 6:15–23

6:15 ***Then what is the implication? Should we sin because we are not controlled by laws but by God's favor? That's unthinkable!***

Does this new freedom in Christ mean that believers can sin because they are no longer controlled by laws or subject to their penalty? Paul's answer is an emphatic no! Freedom from the condemnation of the law in no way permits behavior that expresses itself in lawlessness. The law exposes guilt; it cannot forgive. God's sacrifice on the cross offers forgiveness to everyone. However, it is obvious that no one can keep the law at all times. The believer, therefore, is at the same time both set free from the dominion of his sin nature and obedient to the will of the One Who has redeemed him.

The key word here is "controlled." When we are set free from the domination of the law, we are ruled instead by God's favor and do not want to displease Him. Paul explained this to Titus:

> [11]*After all, God's saving kindness has appeared for the benefit of all people.* [12]*It trains us to avoid ungodly lives filled with worldly desires so that we can live self-controlled, moral, and godly lives in this present world.* [13]*At the same time we can expect what we hope for—the appearance of the glory of our great God and Savior, Jesus Christ.* [14]*He gave himself for us to set us free from every sin and to cleanse us so that we can be his special people who are enthusiastic about doing good things. (Titus 2:11–14)*

6:16 ***Don't you know that if you offer to be someone's slave, you must obey that master? Either your master is sin, or your master is obedience. Letting sin be your master leads to death. Letting obedience be your master leads to God's approval.***

Everyone is a slave to someone or something. We are either controlled by sin and self or by Christ. If sin is our way of life, we are its slaves. "*Jesus answered them, 'I can guarantee this truth: Whoever lives a sinful life is a slave to sin*'" (John 8:34).

We cannot serve sin and God at the same time *(Matthew 6:24)*. Obedience to the desires of the flesh leads to bondage and spiritual death. Obedience to God and His Word leads to freedom and life. Obedience to self-will yields frustration. Obedience to God's ways yields happiness, contentment, and genuine freedom.

6:17 ***You were slaves to sin. But I thank God that you have become wholeheartedly obedient to the teachings which you were given.***

Paul happily commended the Roman Christians for their wholehearted obedience to the teachings that had been given to them. Everyone begins life as a slave to sin, but thanks be to God, we do not need to remain in that hopeless state. By God's work in us, we have been set free to obey His word as an expression of our devotion to Him and not as a futile attempt to attain righteousness. In fact, we are enabled by grace to obey that first great commandment to "love the Lord your God with all your heart, with all your soul, and with all your mind" *(Matthew 22:37)*. We sinners have been delivered from sinful bondage through the gracious work of Christ on our behalf *(Titus 3:3–7)*.

6:18 ***Freed from sin, you were made slaves who do what God approves of.***

In becoming God's bondservant to His righteousness, real freedom is gained. "O LORD, *I am indeed your servant . . . You have freed me from my chains*" (Psalm 116:16). "[31]*So Jesus said to those Jews who believed in him, 'If you live by what I say, you are truly my disciples.* [32]*You will know the truth, and the truth will set you free…* [36]*So if the Son sets you free, you will be absolutely free*" *(John 8:31–32, 36)*. Genuine freedom is given by the Son of God, resulting in genuine fellowship with God and with all His people.

6:19 ***I'm speaking in a human way because of the weakness of your corrupt nature. Clearly, you once offered all the parts of your body as slaves to sexual perversion and disobedience. This led you to live disobedient lives. Now, in the same way, offer all the parts of your body as slaves that do what God approves of. This leads you to live holy lives.***

Paul applied his slavery analogy to the idea of willfully yielding to sinfulness or to God's ways. Even within believers there is the ongoing battle between the desire to do good works and the ability to implement them:

> [21]*So I've discovered this truth: Evil is present with me even when I want to do what God's standards say is good.* [22]*I take pleasure in God's standards in my inner being.* [23]*However, I see a different standard at work throughout my body. It is at war with the standards my mind sets and tries to take me captive to sin's standards which still exist throughout my body.* [24]*What a miserable person I am! Who will rescue me from my dying body? (Romans 7:21–24)*

As we once used our bodies to fulfill our fleshly pleasure, Paul encouraged us to use our bodies to do what pleases God. We cannot do this in our own strength, however, and Paul found only one answer to his question: "I thank God that our Lord Jesus Christ rescues me!" *(Romans 7:25)*. Only the power of the Holy Spirit living in us is sufficient to enforce the authority of our new Master and overcome the ways of our old nature *(1 Peter 4:2–3)*. As we submit ourselves to Him, we will lead holy lives that are pleasing to the Lord.

6:20 ***When you were slaves to sin, you were free from doing what God approves of.***

Ironically, slavery to sin affords freedom from obeying God's will. This is the natural way of thinking. "*There is a way that seems right to a person, but eventually it ends in death*" *(Proverbs 14:12)*.

A person who is under the control of sin can do good works, but those good works do not merit God's approval because the only criteria required for gaining God's approval has not been satisfied—acceptance of His Son's sacrifice. In good works alone, there is only the illusion of freedom, as expressed by W. E. Henley (1849–1903) in the poem "Invictus," which was a deathbed affirmation of his atheism: "I am the master of my fate; I am the captain of my soul."[5] This "freedom" may bring enjoyment for a time, but the end is only terrible loss, destruction, and death.

6:21 *What did you gain by doing those things? You're ashamed of what you used to do because it ended in death.*

This is a good question to ask when we are tempted to enjoy the momentary pleasures of sin. As Christians we must always beware of the consequences of our actions. "[14]*Everyone is tempted by his own desires as they lure him away and trap him.* [15]*Then desire becomes pregnant and gives birth to sin. When sin grows up, it gives birth to death*" *(James 1:14–15)*. Most Christians regret the times they yielded to temptations that looked so attractive, and even some Christians have fallen into grievous sin that has hurt themselves and others deeply.

Sin always damages its victims, often severely *(Galatians 6:7–8)*. The fruit of sin for the believer is shame and for the unbeliever is death and hell.

6:22 *Now you have been freed from sin and have become God's slaves. This results in a holy life and, finally, in everlasting life.*

In gaining freedom from sin, we become God's willing slaves. In most of his letters, Paul identified himself as a slave of Jesus Christ, a title he treasured. When we submit to the Lord as our Master, we find true liberty in Him. We are free at last to become what God intended us to be.

Jesus gave His disciples a profound example of His humility when He washed their feet just before going to the cross to give His life for them. Then, He modeled what was expected of them:

> *[12]After Jesus had washed their feet and put on his outer clothes, he took his place at the table again. Then he asked his disciples, "Do you understand what I've done for you? [13]You call me teacher and Lord, and you're right because that's what I am. [14]So if I, your Lord and teacher, have washed your feet, you must wash each other's feet. [15]I've given you an example that you should follow. [16]I can guarantee this truth: Slaves are not superior to their owners, and messengers are not superior to the people who send them. [17]If you understand all of this, you are blessed whenever you follow my example." (John 13:12–17)*

As genuinely redeemed servants of Jesus Christ, our lives are fruitful only when we serve as our Lord served us—in humility and faithfulness. This fruit is one of the main evidences of our faith, and the Holy Spirit produces it in us for the benefit of those around us *(Galatians 5:22–23)*.

6:23 ***The payment for sin is death, but the gift that God freely gives is everlasting life found in Christ Jesus our Lord.***

What an apt climax to chapter six! Paul unequivocally concluded with this clear description of the ultimate destinations of these two pathways—death or life. This conclusion was precisely the same as that found in Moses' law. "*Today I offer you life and prosperity or death and destruction*" *(Deuteronomy 30:15)*.

The Greek word for *payment* conveys an end result from some activity, viewed as something which one receives in return—"wages, result."[6] Wages are earned by a worker as payment for services. As sinners, we have earned God's death penalty. In our sinful nature, we relentlessly pursued our self-righteous cravings, and we, therefore, stand convicted, deserving God's judgment of death.

Thanks be to God, this is not the end of the story. God graciously provided salvation through the work of Jesus Christ on our behalf. "*[4]But God is rich in mercy because of his great love for us. [5]We were dead because of our failures, but he made us alive together with Christ*"

(Ephesians 2:4–5). This salvation gives us the certain promise of eternal life with our Redeemer in heaven.

What a wonderful assurance that although we deserved eternal death our Lord Jesus Christ has provided eternal life by His finished work. *"This is the testimony: God has given us eternal life, and this life is found in his Son" (1 John 5:11)*.

Notes/Applications

This chapter closes with Paul's forcefully-stated description of the authority of Christ to save and keep His people securely within the boundaries of His power. The completion of Jesus' finished work on the cross, His resurrection, and His heavenly intercession combine effectively to protect and keep His children until that day when He comes again to judge all people according to their works *(2 Timothy 1:12)*.

Once redeemed, our thoughts and actions are brought into conformity with God's decrees by the new life that has been given to us. Even though our practical experience tells us that we are far from a finished work or a holy people, this passage brings us into the realm of His peace and comfort, realizing that Jesus Christ alone is able to confer upon us His own righteousness, securing our position for all eternity. Christ alone dethroned the old master that cruelly held us in the bonds of our sinful nature. The transformation that has taken place by the work of Christ provides confidence as the Holy Spirit witnesses to our spirits and enables us to live obedient lives in His service.

Further, Paul completely dismantled the false conclusion of some who might say that they can sin as they choose because God's grace is sufficient. While it is true that God's grace is greater than all our sin, that is still no reason to test God's goodness. While believers are no longer ruled by the law, God's favor invokes us to worship Him through grateful obedience to all of His decrees.

God's gift of His Son as the sacrifice for our sin satisfied God's holy and righteous requirements. That sacrifice, that goodness, should so overpower us that we are horrified to think of offending the One Who so willingly died in our place.

ROMANS 7

Romans 7:1–6

***7:1** Don't you realize, brothers and sisters, that laws have power over people only as long as they are alive? (I'm speaking to people who are familiar with Moses' Teachings.)*

Having outlined how we have gained freedom from sin's power through Christ's fulfillment of the law *(Romans 6)*, Paul now provided a provoking transition to help his Jewish audience and all believers better understand the implications of their new life in Christ. This transition is concisely explained as follows:

> Romans seven is one of the most misunderstood chapters in the Bible because most people read it with the attitude, "It can't mean what it says!" The theme is that the believer is no longer under the law of God because he has been joined to Christ in His resurrection. Like an inexperienced swimmer, the average Christian stands in terror of such deep water as complete abandonment to the grace of God. He fears to be borne along on the will of God in his daily life—to cast himself

> completely on the direction of the Holy Spirit. But, once he gets over the panic of such self-abandonment, he finds that the grace of God sustains, carries, cradles, and calms him—and he lives eternity in time. This is the purpose of Romans seven: to help the willing believer to cast himself into the depths of grace.[1]

God's moral law has been integrated into each person's conscience. According to Paul's doctrine outlined in chapter six, the believer is dead to the law by virtue of Christ's sacrificial death on the cross. While the law endures forever as God's mandate for creation and for moral living, the believer is exempt from the judging aspect of the law; nevertheless, he remains subject to the moral statutes of the law as it relates to the way in which Christ lives in him.

7:2–3 ***[2]For example, a married woman is bound by law to her husband as long as he is alive. But if her husband dies, that marriage law is no longer in effect for her. [3]So if she marries another man while her husband is still alive, she will be called an adulterer. But if her husband dies, she is free from this law, so she is not committing adultery if she marries another man.***

Paul illustrated the function of the law in terms of the institution of marriage. The bond of marriage is not to be broken for any reason while both partners are alive. When one partner dies, however, that union no longer exists, and the other is free to remarry.

When people decide to disobey the law and bow to their personal desires, the principle of the marriage institution is shattered, and God's law is violated. God's law does not tolerate such disobedience and identifies such a person as an adulterer—one who is unfaithful to the spouse but, more importantly, unfaithful to God Who established the institution of marriage.

***7:4** In the same way, brothers and sisters, you have died to the laws in Moses' Teachings through Christ's body. You belong to someone else, the one who was brought back to life. As a result, we can do what God wants.*

Here, Paul took the illustration outlined in verses one through three and applied it in a practical way to the believer's life. He basically stated that every believer's death to the consequences of sin is accompanied by new ownership—the ownership of Christ. It is through Christ's ownership that believers can obey God. This is the full expression of the truth Paul had built on throughout chapter six. The One Who now owns the believer is the same One Who was resurrected by God's power.

***7:5** While we were living under the influence of our corrupt nature, sinful passions were at work throughout our bodies. Stirred up by Moses' laws, our sinful passions did things that result in death.*

In contrast to the God-pleasing lifestyle that he explained above, Paul described life under the influence of humanity's corrupt nature. As a result of the innate sinful nature, sinful passions are at work in us. People who are under the mastery of that corruption may have the false illusion that they are living the "good life" because they can do anything they please. Just like children who test the limits of their parent's discipline, people will want to do what is prohibited. That's how Moses' law stimulated greater disobedience, fostering self-righteous rebellion that ultimately resulted in death—not just physical death but spiritual death that received God's rightful judgment.

***7:6** But now we have died to those laws that bound us. God has broken their effect on us so that we are serving in a new spiritual way, not in an old way dictated by written words.*

The corrupt nature no longer dominates the believer's life. Instead, believers have died to those laws that kept them in bondage. God has broken the law's grip on us and has set us free to serve Him under the influence of the Spirit. The comparison between the old and the new is also described in Paul's second letter to the Corinthians:

> [7]*That old system of law etched in stone led to death, yet it began with such glory that the people of Israel could not bear to look at Moses' face. For his face shone with the glory of God, even though the brightness was already fading away.* [8]*Shouldn't we expect far greater glory when the Holy Spirit is giving life?* [9]*If the old covenant, which brings condemnation, was glorious, how much more glorious is the new covenant, which makes us right with God!* [10]*In fact, that first glory was not glorious at all compared with the overwhelming glory of the new covenant.* [11]*So if the old covenant, which has been set aside, was full of glory, then the new covenant, which remains forever, has far greater glory. (2 Corinthians 3:7–11,* NLT*)*

Notes/Applications

How many Christians would love to know that they do those things that God really wants them to do? Many Christians go through their whole lives struggling with terrible uncertainty of God's approval. They wander in a dark valley between "good days" and "bad days," sometimes seeming to do those things that are pleasing to God and then plunging into dark despair as they are overwhelmed by circumstances or their own failure to live up to God's standard.

Paul wanted believers to understand that being dead to sin means we are now under new ownership *(Romans 7:4)*. When we are joined with Christ in the finished work of redemption—His death, burial, and resurrection—we die to our old nature and are raised to a new life in Christ. From that moment on, we live in a viable relationship with the One Who has redeemed us. Since Christ was resurrected from the dead and lives forever, that relationship never dies. Since Christ also bestows the gift of eternal life on believers, neither partner in our relationship dies. Thus, Christ's ownership never ends and the relationship is never severed. For the rest of our lives, Jesus walks hand in hand with us, continuing His saving and keeping work, securing our salvation, and placing His stamp of protection on us until that day when we meet face to face in Christ's kingdom.

Romans 7:7–14

7:7 ***What should we say, then? Are Moses' laws sinful? That's unthinkable! In fact, I wouldn't have recognized sin if those laws hadn't shown it to me. For example, I wouldn't have known that some desires are sinful if Moses' Teachings hadn't said, "Never have wrong desires."***

Following Paul's logic in the previous verses, it would be very easy to conclude that the law is sinful. "That's unthinkable," Paul declared. In fact, the law is a reflection of the standard that God has set before His people. The law given through Moses is the perfect Word of God and expresses His character, perfection, righteousness, and holiness. His Son, Jesus Christ, perfectly obeyed the law and declared that He came not to set aside "Moses' Teachings or the Prophets" but to make them come true *(Matthew 5:17–18)*.

The law was given to expose our innate sinful nature. Like a mirror, it reflects who we really are. James' epistle challenges us to hear God's Word and obey it *(James 1:22–24)*. The perfect law of God makes clear that our inclinations are directed toward those things that are self-fulfilling. Outside of the law, it would be perfectly natural to assume that our self-directed human behavior was completely acceptable. However, the law exposes the true nature of those inclinations, revealing their destructive results. Our Creator gave the law so that we could understand how far from His will we have strayed. God meant the law for our good to show us how we should live securely in the world He created. It also shows the extent of our rebellion and our inability to live by it.

7:8 ***But sin took the opportunity provided by this commandment and made me have all kinds of wrong desires. Clearly, without laws sin is dead.***

The law does not cause us to sin but exposes our sinfulness. Then, unlike what we would claim for ourselves, this exposure magnifies the full extent of our evil desires. "*The human mind is the most deceit-*

ful of all things. It is incurable. No one can understand how deceitful it is" (Jeremiah 17:9). In our desperate attempt to "touch up" this picture, we resort to comparing ourselves to others, saying, "I'm as good as that person" or "At least I'm not as bad as that other person." However, that method of figuring our self-worth is terribly flawed. When we measure ourselves by God's perfect standard, we discover that we are hopeless, falling far short of what our Creator expects of us.

The phrase "without laws sin is dead" further accentuates the point that without the law there would be no standard by which our sinfulness would be made evident. It is not that sin would be non-existent. Rather, the very purpose of the law is to reveal our sin nature and to make clear our need for a Savior.

7:9–10 ***[9]At one time I was alive without any laws. But when this commandment came, sin became alive [10]and I died. I found that the commandment which was intended to bring me life actually brought me death.***

Citing his own experience, Paul asserted that at one time he considered himself very much alive in a spiritual sense "without any laws." This seems odd in light of the fact that he was a Pharisee living with fervent devotion to the law. However, we must understand that Paul was speaking of his ignorance to the true purpose of the law and the impact of Christ's fulfillment of the law. When he fully grasped the horrible truth of his position before Christ, he understood that he was actually dead—a desperately wicked sinner unable to fulfill all aspects of the law *(James 2:10)*. Paul knew the law as well as anyone but, like most, perceived them as guidelines for righteous living. In looking back on that same lifestyle as a new creature in Christ, he was awakened to the startling truth of the law—that adherence was impossible and the only means of attaining righteousness was through Christ's sacrifice.

7:11 ***Sin, taking the opportunity provided by this commandment, deceived me and then killed me.***

What is this sin that deceived and killed Paul? He knew the law better than most Jews of his day. He was educated by one of the most respected rabbis, Gamaliel. Not only did he know the law, but in his religious devotion, he followed every aspect of the law. Like the Pharisees who harassed Jesus throughout His earthly ministry, Paul was driven by his religious convictions and persecuted the "heretical" Christians. Like those Pharisees, he could not tolerate the idea that Jesus died to save sinners. Believing himself to be the fountain of wisdom and religious zeal, he never realized that he was blind to the truth *(John 9:41)*. Like those Pharisees, Paul served the law rather than the Lawgiver with blind fidelity. From his religious perspective, the law had become his god. Paul's own self-righteousness was the sin that deceived him and, if not for Christ's intervention, would have sealed his eternal destination.

7:12 ***So Moses' Teachings are holy, and the commandment is holy, right, and good.***

God's law, given through Moses, was perfect. Even though Paul emphasized what appears to be the negative aspect of the law, he asserted that the law is not bad but good. The law in itself is the very expression of God's will for all mankind. It is the very Word of God, expressing His holiness and perfection *(Psalm 19:7)*. Our failure to observe its precepts results in punishment and death. The law cannot save us, but it reveals our imperfection and need for salvation.

The law does not create sin in people; it simply exposes the sin that has always existed. Believers must acknowledge the goodness of the law and the truth of their sinful condition. Otherwise, we spend the sum of our earthly energy dodging the law and shifting the blame for our sins onto others. Paul's legalism had been unable to save him.

***7:13** Now, did something good cause my death? That's unthinkable! Rather, my death was caused by sin so that sin would be recognized for what it is. Through a commandment sin became more sinful than ever.*

Is the law, therefore, the cause of death? Paul responded with a resounding no. The cause of death is our sin. God clearly ordered Adam: "[16]You are free to eat from any tree in the garden. [17]But you must never eat from the tree of the knowledge of good and evil because when you eat from it, you will certainly die" *(Genesis 2:16–17)*. However, in the events that followed, Adam and Eve listened to the serpent and disobeyed God's clear command. Consequently, their death, and ours, was caused by disobedience to God's clear instruction.

***7:14** I know that God's standards are spiritual, but I have a corrupt nature, sold as a slave to sin.*

The law, both Old and New Testaments, constitute God's standards given to humanity both to convict of sin and to show the pathway to freedom from the burden of that sin and its consequences. Therefore, the entire expression of the law is God-breathed and therefore spiritual *(2 Timothy 3:16)*.

Our human nature is corrupt and enslaved by sin as pictured in the first three chapters of Romans. The holy and perfect law of God removes the scales from our eyes and reveals the horrible reality of our sin nature. Only when we see the spiritual character of the law do we realize how wretched we really are.

Notes/Applications

Contrary to what many people believe, the law is perfect, holy, and good—God's standard by which everyone is measured. No one is able to adequately satisfy the requirements of this standard; instead, all fall hopelessly short of its criteria and stand condemned before God's throne. However, some assert that they are really "good" people and, therefore, falsely believe that God accepts them on their own merit. Nevertheless, Jesus raised that standard to such a degree that even "good" people have to confess their hopelessness *(Matthew 5:17–20)*.

Paul did a masterful job of helping us understand the goodness of the law and the desperate condition of our sinful existence. We might even ask, "If the criteria are so impossible to achieve, who can be saved?" The answer, revealed in the rest of the chapter, is as simple as it is profound. Jesus Christ alone, God's Son, was the only person who kept the law perfectly. The sinless Lamb of God became our sacrifice by fulfilling the law's demands and suffering the penalty that we deserved because of our sins. Thus, Jesus dealt the death blow to sin's dominion by His atoning death on the cross and His resurrection from the tomb. Thanks be to God for providing salvation and freedom from the bondage of sin. *"God loved the world this way: He gave his only Son so that everyone who believes in him will not die but will have eternal life" (John 3:16)*.

Romans 7:15–25

7:15–17 ***[15]I don't realize what I'm doing. I don't do what I want to do. Instead, I do what I hate. [16]I don't do what I want to do, but I agree that God's standards are good. [17]So I am no longer the one who is doing the things I hate, but sin that lives in me is doing them.***

Paul vividly described the spiritual struggle that every believer faces. He was clearly redeemed, a son of the living God, but he still possessed the old nature inherited from Adam *(Psalm 51:5)*. Even though believers are no longer slaves to sin *(Romans 6:2)*, the sin nature has not been removed from them *(Romans 7:21)*. Even though the eternal punishment for sin has been defeated by Christ's sacrifice *(Romans 3:24)*, believers still live under the sway of sin's influence. Believers are not immune from sinful selfish cravings.

This very struggle proves that the law is good and holy; the real problem lies within us. As children of God, we need the help of the Holy Spirit to live the Christian life. We desire to obey God's ways but cannot do so without the Spirit's abiding, continual help. That is why we do those things that we should not do and do not do those things that we should do. It is a spiritual battle that will rage within us until the day we die.

7:18 ***I know that nothing good lives in me; that is, nothing good lives in my corrupt nature. Although I have the desire to do what is right, I don't do it.***

As believers, our inclination is to do what Christ wants, but we discover that we are virtually incapable of fulfilling this goal. Our corrupt nature is still very much alive and offers no help in our heartfelt wish to do those things that please God. As long as our old nature exists, we will struggle in our Christian lives. Very often, the harder we try, the more we find ourselves frustrated with our inadequacy. *"What your corrupt nature wants is contrary to what your spiritual nature wants, and what your spiritual nature wants is contrary to what your corrupt nature wants. They are opposed to each other. As a result, you don't always do what you intend to do"* (Galatians 5:17).

7:19–20 ***[19]I don't do the good I want to do. Instead, I do the evil that I don't want to do. [20]Now, when I do what I don't want to do, I am no longer the one who is doing it. Sin that lives in me is doing it.***

The dominance of the self provides the best evidence that all are sinners. When a person becomes a believer and the Holy Spirit enters his life, the battle between the old self and the Spirit begins. This struggle comes from the reaction of the old nature to the Spirit taking up residence in his life. God and His law are not the cause of this battle; it is the "sin that lives in me."

This is not a battle of conscience in choosing to do right or do wrong, for even unbelievers are subject to their conscience. Even the good an unbeliever does is but "as filthy rags" apart from receiving the righteousness of Christ *(Isaiah 64:6)*. Rather, this is a spiritual battle that exists only in the lives of believers who, having received freedom in Christ, are empowered by the Holy Spirit to engage in the battle to do those things that are pleasing to the Lord.

7:21 ***So I've discovered this truth: Evil is present with me even when I want to do what God's standards say is good.***

This truth is a comfort, knowing that this struggle is common to all Christians and a very real evidence of their faith. More than that, believers are comforted by their knowledge that God is with them in the midst of this struggle. Even when one's own will continues its conflict with God's will, the presence of evil can never take away God's abiding presence.

7:22 ***I take pleasure in God's standards in my inner being.***

In his spirit, Paul loved God's law. The Spirit of God within him had created a genuine desire to obey God's will and ways. The same can be said for everyone who has been redeemed by the work of the Holy Spirit. As Christians, we love God, and our deepest desire is to please Him *(Psalm 119:97–104)*.

7:23 ***However, I see a different standard at work throughout my body. It is at war with the standards my mind sets and tries to take me captive to sin's standards which still exist throughout my body.***

From the perspective of his redeemed life, Paul looked back at his sinful nature and recognized that the rules of his old nature were still in effect. The standard of the sinful nature was at war with his redeemed nature, which should have been dominating his thinking self. He was profoundly aware that his old nature wanted to seduce him and take him captive again. Every Christian can testify to the truth of this experience. This battle is very real for mature as well as young Christians. There are times of respite and triumph, and then the battle rages again. The war never ends in this life.

7:24 ***What a miserable person I am! Who will rescue me from my dying body?***

Paul recognized an important principle: The closer he walked with God in the Spirit, the more he realized how dreadfully close his sin nature really was. Several truths become clearly evident from summarizing Paul's personal testimony. First, the old nature and the new nature were simultaneously present within him. Second, the war that ensued took place within him—the redeemed mind versus the old sinful nature. Finally, Paul understood that though the Lord's will would be evident in so many situations he would often resort to doing what the sin nature wanted. Paul was not being unnecessarily "theatrical" in this statement; rather, this appeared to be an unsolvable puzzle, a constant and bitter struggle that provided no rest but a constant tension that knew no bounds.[2]

7:25 I thank God that our Lord Jesus Christ rescues me! So I am obedient to God's standards with my mind, but I am obedient to sin's standards with my corrupt nature.

Because of Jesus Christ, the answer to this otherwise unsolvable dilemma is clear and simple: Jesus Christ our Lord! In Him, through His completed work, by the indwelling Holy Spirit, with the bands of our sinful bondage shattered, it is possible to please God. Paul continued to develop this wonderful resolution in the following chapter.

Nevertheless, despite the security that this truth offers, the struggle persists. Paul asserted that with his mind he served God's standards and yet simultaneously obeyed the dictates of sin in his corrupt nature. In truth, the battle is waged within the confines of our daily experience where we simultaneously serve both natures. These two opposing forces seek to control the entire person. As this discourse unfolds, it becomes clearly evident that we are our own worst enemy.

Notes/Applications

Romans seven directly tackles the most difficult dilemma that Christians face: If we are redeemed, why do we fail to live up to God's expectations? Why do we fail to live up to the standards that we expect of ourselves? Why are the pathways of our lives strewn with so many potholes that jar our anticipation of a smooth journey?

Paul's answer to this quandary was remarkable both in its insight and in its honesty. Paul bared his soul, confessing that the struggle, if not for Christ's intervention, would virtually destroy him. He was completely transparent as he proceeded through the process of self-analysis, admitting the weaknesses he could see in his corrupt nature. In the end, his conclusion was startling: "I've discovered this truth: Evil is present with me even when I want to do what God's standards say is good" *(Romans 7:21)*. The truth is that there is no solution to this disturbing predicament. Instead, believers operate under this divinely induced stress from the moment of their new birth until the day they die. "*So I am obedient to God's standards with my mind, but I am obedient to sin's standards with my corrupt nature*" *(Romans 7:25)*.

Paul concluded that believers should accept the reality of the struggle, serving Christ under the direction of their redeemed nature and subjecting the old nature to the discipline of the new. Like Paul, we cry at one and the same time, "What a miserable person I am!" and "I thank God that our Lord Jesus Christ rescues me!"

ROMANS 8

Romans 8:1–8

***8:1** So those who are believers in Christ Jesus can no longer be condemned.*

Based on Paul's discourse in the previous chapter, the believer's escape from the penalty of God's judgment is exchanged for a life lived in Jesus Christ. God's righteous judgment has forever been satisfied by the sacrificial death of His Son.

> [17]*God sent his Son into the world, not to condemn the world, but to save the world.* [18]*Those who believe in him won't be condemned. But those who don't believe are already condemned because they don't believe in God's only Son.* [19]*This is why people are condemned: The light came into the world. Yet, people loved the dark rather than the light because their actions were evil. (John 3:17–19)*

This great truth assures believers and sets them free—free from the domination of the sin nature and free to serve Christ. We do not need to wait for eternity to receive the verdict of "not guilty." It is a present reality. Although believers are still sinful and continue to struggle with the sin nature, the penalty for sin has been paid by the Savior. "*I can guarantee this truth: Those who listen to what I say and believe in the one who sent me will have eternal life. They won't be judged because they have already passed from death to life*" (John 5:24). While we still have faults and failures, these have been paid for by Christ and are no longer charged against us or to our eternal account.

The powerful phrase "in Christ Jesus" is the foundation on which we live every day of our lives. The Spirit lives in us, influencing our decisions and directing our paths. "*On that day you will know that I am in my Father and that you are in me and that I am in you*" (John 14:20). This is an awesome assurance guaranteed by none other than the One Who was raised from the dead and lives forevermore. "*God has said, 'I will never abandon you or leave you'*" (Hebrews 13:5).

8:2 ***The standards of the Spirit, who gives life through Christ Jesus, have set you free from the standards of sin and death.***

Through Christ, the standards of the Holy Spirit have set believers free from the standards of the law, which only lead to sin and death. The more believers abide in Christ, the more freedom is gained from the dominance of the old sin nature. "*It is the Spirit who gives eternal life. Human effort accomplishes nothing. And the very words I have spoken to you are spirit and life*" (John 6:63, NLT).

8:3 ***It is impossible to do what God's standards demand because of the weakness our human nature has. But God sent his Son to have a human nature as sinners have and to pay for sin. That way God condemned sin in our corrupt nature.***

Since Adam and Eve sinned in the garden, no one has been able to obey the law. Therefore, it is impossible to earn God's favor. It is also impossible for the law to save anyone, or else salvation would have been by the law instead of through the costly sacrifice of God's dear Son. "[19]*What, then, is the purpose of the laws given to Moses? They were added to identify what wrongdoing is . . .* [21]*If those laws could give us life, then certainly we would receive God's approval because we obeyed them" (Galatians 3:19, 21).*

Humanity cannot obey those laws, however. Our sin nature makes it impossible for us to obey God's law completely. We might be able to be "pretty good," but that is not good enough. "*If someone obeys all of God's laws except one, that person is guilty of breaking all of them" (James 2:10).* Clearly, humanity was without hope.

But God had another plan. He sent His Son. As both fully God and fully man, Jesus lived a sinless life, fulfilling the requirements of the law, and He then offered His life as a sacrifice for our sin. He did this willingly out of love for and obedience to His Father.

8:4 ***Therefore, we, who do not live by our corrupt nature but by our spiritual nature, are able to meet God's standards.***

Having clearly established the basis for the salvation of believers through the sacrifice of the perfect Lamb of God, Paul declared that we who are in Christ are now able to satisfy God's just demands and meet His perfect standards. This is accomplished not by God's lowering of His standards, but by His providing a qualified substitute to die for our sins. By the undeserved grace of God, our sins have been laid on Christ and His righteousness has been placed on us. "*God had Christ, who was sinless, take our sin so that we might receive God's approval through him" (2 Corinthians 5:21).*

Our salvation is an instant transaction when we trust in Christ as our Savior and receive His righteousness. On the other hand, our sanctification (learning to live in obedience to His will) is a lifelong process. The process of sanctification is that ongoing work in which the Spirit applies the righteousness of Christ to the life of believers, gradually conforming them into the image of God's Son.

8:5–6 ***[5]Those who live by the corrupt nature have the corrupt nature's attitude. But those who live by the spiritual nature have the spiritual nature's attitude. [6]The corrupt nature's attitude leads to death. But the spiritual nature's attitude leads to life and peace.***

In verse four, Paul affirmed that believers who live by the Spirit and not by their corrupt nature are able to please God. In these verses, he reaffirms the truth that living under the corrupt nature and the Spirit have enduring consequences upon the life each governs. A life that persists under the corrupt nature would operate under a corrupt attitude and end in death and condemnation while a life governed by the Spirit would adopt the Spirit's influence and would harvest life eternal. Paul found it necessary to reiterate this fundamental truth to underscore the disparity between the appropriate spiritual authority over the life of the redeemed and the corrupt attitude seen in a believer's daily walk.

Even though believers know that they should live under the control of the Holy Spirit, very often they remain caught up in themselves. Their eyes focus upon earthly matters rather than God's heavenly call. They set out on the journey of living redeemed lives, but they continue to walk in the temporal rather than pursue the eternal. This mentality and lifestyle contradict their new life in Christ and defeat the purpose for which God redeemed them. Further, it cripples the joy that He intended them to experience while living on earth as His children and as His servants.

If people are living for their selfish pleasure with no apparent inclination to please the Lord, it is evident that they have not submitted to the direction of the Holy Spirit. It is not that those who live by the spiritual nature are able to live perfect lives; it is that they are sensitive to the Holy Spirit. Those believers who encounter inner conflict when obeying selfish desires know that their behavior is wrong. It becomes obvious that the Spirit dwells within them, convicting them of sin and leading them to repentance.

8:7–8 ***[7]This is so because the corrupt nature has a hostile attitude toward God. It refuses to place itself under the authority of God's standards because it can't. [8]Those who are under the control of the corrupt nature can't please God.***

In a simple statement of fact, Paul declared that the corrupt nature is the enemy of God. Continuing to live under the dictates of that nature is not only a blatant defiance of Christ's redeeming work, but also a refusal or a failure to submit to the Holy Spirit's direction. People who consistently live under their former nature cannot please God in any way because they fail to abandon their selfish cravings.

Notes/Applications

In these first verses of chapter eight, Paul asserted that when we surrender control to Christ, the Spirit delivers us from an otherwise wretched existence and gives us a new way to live—a way that pleases the Father. Under new management in Christ, it is not only *possible* that we can live up to God's standards—it is a *promise*!

How does the Holy Spirit accomplish this work in us? The Holy Spirit resides inside of us as our command center. He stakes God's claim upon our hearts and minds. Although we still daily fight the desires of the old nature, we are no longer under the corrupt nature's control. In Christ, we have the ability to withstand sin and temptation. When we, however, do grieve the Spirit by disobeying, we are met with conviction and the consequences of our rebellion, not the least of which is a broken fellowship with our heavenly Father.

In order to abide in the Spirit, we need daily fellowship with Christ and with one another *(1 John 1:7)*. We need a daily "bath" in His Holy Word *(2 Timothy 2:15 and Psalm 119:1)*.

Just as an athlete seeking victory will train rigorously every day, so we who desire victory in Christ must train faithfully in order to fulfill God's purpose in our lives. "*Training the body helps a little, but godly living helps in every way. Godly living has the promise of life now and in the world to come*" *(1 Timothy 4:8)*.

Romans 8:9–14

8:9 ***But if God's Spirit lives in you, you are under the control of your spiritual nature, not your corrupt nature. Whoever doesn't have the Spirit of Christ doesn't belong to him.***

The Spirit takes up residence in people's hearts at the moment of redemption; He "lives in" them. Under the influence of this new master, the lives of the redeemed take a radically different direction. Believers can never undo the control of God's Spirit. Any deviation from this profound transformation indicates the prevalence of a spiritual infancy that continues to enable the old nature to undermine the new man.

There is a sense here in which Paul was drawing a line in the sand. It is true that the believer still struggles with the sin nature that resides within him, but the Holy Spirit that has now taken up residence in his life is to be the controlling influence of that person's decisions, actions, and behavior. When this is not the case, the evidence suggests a return to the demands of the corrupt nature and contradicts the redeemed status that has been given to believers. To this, Paul states plainly, "Whoever doesn't have the Spirit of Christ doesn't belong to him." Such people may appear religious and even be church members, but they are not genuinely redeemed children of God. Only those who trust Christ and submit to the direction of His Spirit demonstrate that they are His children.

8:10 ***However, if Christ lives in you, your bodies are dead because of sin, but your spirits are alive because you have God's approval.***

There is no doubt our existence is temporal. No one gets out of this life except through the portal of death. Paul's assertion was that just as surely as believers' bodies will die, redeemed people are also alive because the work of Christ has received God's approval. Their righteousness is sealed by Christ's resurrection from the dead. Since Christ lives in all believers through the Holy Spirit, it is unnatural for us to seek to serve the corrupt nature. We ought, instead, to desire to remain dead to sin.

8:11 ***Does the Spirit of the one who brought Jesus back to life live in you? Then the one who brought Christ back to life will also make your mortal bodies alive by his Spirit who lives in you.***

Without any more elaboration on doctrine, Paul squarely confronted his readers with an uncompromising question. It was a question that reached deeply into the authenticity of Paul's testimony about his position in the Spirit. He asked his readers if their lives had been transformed by the work of the Spirit. If the answer was yes, then something remarkable was in store. The Spirit had raised Christ from the dead; therefore, He would also raise their mortal bodies from the dead as well. In both cases, the Spirit is the same Spirit, performing the same function both for Christ and for those who have lived and died under the protective covering of His grace and power.

8:12 ***So, brothers and sisters, we have no obligation to live the way our corrupt nature wants us to live.***

In view of God's mighty presence and His work in believers, nothing is owed to the continuing cravings of the flesh. As willing servants of Almighty God, the burden of serving the old nature is gone. The deceptiveness of the flesh is still evident, but the much greater power of Christ within should be the motivating force in their lives. The temptations to disobey come from within our own corrupt nature and from the enticements of the outside world, assaulting us on every side. Nevertheless, we are no longer under any compulsion to submit to such seduction because "the one who is in you is greater than the one who is in the world" *(1 John 4:4)*.

8:13 ***If you live by your corrupt nature, you are going to die. But if you use your spiritual nature to put to death the evil activities of the body, you will live.***

Believers are reminded that there are two consequential forces constantly at work in their lives: the corrupt nature resulting in sin and death and the Spirit of God imputing holiness and life. Paul's statement could not be made more clearly: "If you live by your corrupt nature, you are going to die." Yet, it can hardly be supposed that Paul was speaking here of physical death since this is the fate of all, both believers and unbelievers, as a result of sin *(Romans 6:23)*. Rather, it is apparent that Paul was continuing to build his case that redeemed people cannot persist in allowing the flesh to control their lives in such a way that is contrary to their new nature. As Douglas Moo explains, "Neither the 'indicative'—what God has done for us in Christ—nor the 'imperative'—what we are commanded to do—can be eliminated. Nor can they be severed from one another; they are inextricably connected."[1] So, then, it seems clear that Paul was speaking of the evidence in a person's life which reveals that he is truly redeemed or that he has not, in fact, experienced salvation in Christ.

DIG DEEPER: ***Christians Dying Because of Sin***

There are times when God will remove His child from the earth because that believer's witness has been tainted by sin. While the Scriptures never speak of a person achieving sinless perfection in this life, there are, nonetheless, situations in which the Lord will not allow a person to continue to live because of blatant transgression *(1 Corinthians 11:27–30; Acts 5:1–4;* and *1 Corinthians 5:1–5)*. The first two examples indicate that a believer may physically die as punishment for disobeying God. The third example shows the removal of a man from the body of believers because of an unacceptable indiscretion. The examples also affirm that these people belonged to Christ and therefore were redeemed. Let us beware of the severe consequences of sinful rebellion against Almighty God, even after we have received the gift of God's forgiveness and salvation.

All believers are responsible for working out their salvation *(Philippians 2:12)*, but they are able to do so only through the power of the Holy Spirit working within them. Only His intervention can overcome the temptations and enticements of the old nature. As He carefully forms His character into our lives, He replaces the inclinations of the sin nature with attributes that please God. Apart from this ability to reject "the evil activities of the body," the evidence again suggests that the Spirit of God is not present *(Romans 8:9)*.

8:14 ***Certainly, all who are guided by God's Spirit are God's children.***

The certainty of our inheritance as God's children is that the Holy Spirit lives in us. As children of Almighty God, we have the awesome privilege of addressing him as Father *(Galatians 4:6)*. Imagine being the child of a king, a president, or other world leader, sitting on his knee, and calling him "Daddy." How much greater our privilege to have this father-child relationship with the Creator of the universe *(1 John 3:1–3)*!

Notes/Applications

The focus of this passage is on the life-and-death struggle we all experience. In Adam, we were all under the curse of death and without hope. In Christ, hope was restored through His perfect life, atoning death, and triumphal resurrection *(1 Peter 1:3)*.

The transforming truth of the gospel motivates us to live for Christ every day. We cannot do this by our own determination to be faithful. Jesus taught the disciples important truths during the Last Supper, and these became vital to them after His ascension when the Holy Spirit came to live in them. The Lord taught them that He is the vine and that believers are the branches, but He did so with sober warning: "Without Me you can do nothing" *(John 15:5, NKJV)*. As with these men who became mighty apostles to proclaim this message, God wants to enable us to spread His word in our own day and time. This is our mandate:

> [12]*[God's saving kindness] trains us to avoid ungodly lives filled with worldly desires so that we can live self-controlled, moral, and godly lives in this present world.* [13]*At the same time we can expect what we hope for—the appearance of the glory of our great God and Savior, Jesus Christ.* [14]*He gave himself for us to set us free from every sin and to cleanse us so that we can be his special people who are enthusiastic about doing good things.* [15]*Tell these things to the believers. Encourage and correct them, using your full authority. Don't let anyone ignore you. (Titus 2:12–15)*

As believers, we must live in subjection to the One Who is our master. Jesus Christ dwells in us, vanquishing our corrupt nature so that the power of the Holy Spirit has full access to our redeemed nature *(Galatians 5:24–25)*. By God's grace, we must put to death the deeds of our flesh, which will produce holy lives in our mortal bodies that glorify Almighty God and honor our Lord and Savior.

Romans 8:15–21

***8:15** You haven't received the spirit of slaves that leads you into fear again. Instead, you have received the spirit of God's adopted children by which we call out, "Abba! Father!"*

Our corrupt nature held us under the bondage of sin. Under that bondage, we lived in the fear of God's punishment, but now that we are God's adopted children, Paul argued that we have been set free from that fearful bondage. In this new relationship, we dare to call God our "Father."

The Holy Spirit is not the spirit of bondage but the Spirit of freedom from slavery to sin *(1 Corinthians 2:12)*. God, our heavenly Father, has given us assurance to approach Him freely, addressing Him as we would address a devoted and loving parent.

As His children, we have been adopted by the God of the universe. Paul used the word *adopted* to describe what God has done in making us His children.[2] In Greek culture, such adoption was a public ceremony when a son came of age and was entering manhood. Therefore, this passage is not referring to salvation but to growing up under the care of the heavenly Father:

> *[1]Let me explain further. As long as an heir is a child, he is no better off than a slave, even though he owns everything. [2]He is placed under the control of guardians and trustees until the time set by his father. [3]It was the same way with us. When we were children, we were slaves to the principles of this world. [4]But when the right time came, God sent his Son into the world. A woman gave birth to him, and he came under the control of God's laws. [5]God sent him to pay for the freedom of those who were controlled by these laws so that we would be adopted as children. [6]Because you are God's children, God has sent the Spirit of his Son into us to call out, "Abba! Father!" [7]So you are no longer slaves but God has made you children. Since you are God's children, God has also made you heirs. (Galatians 4:1–7)*

8:16 The Spirit himself testifies with our spirit that we are God's children.

The Spirit that has brought us into the joys of Christ's redeeming work is that same Spirit Who nurtures us in a maturing relationship with the Father. From the moment of our redemption, the Spirit confirms our adoption as God's children. We are nurtured and strengthened by the influences of God's Holy Word as we read and learn what God expects of those He has redeemed. This relationship never changes as we mature in the faith; in fact, the more we mature, the more we realize our need for His guidance and control.

Expressing the importance of the Scriptures as the Spirit consistently instills the confidence of our adoption, Barnhouse explains:

> It must be understood that no spiritual experience is valid in itself. Every experience can be counterfeited, and therefore, no experience is valid that is not solidly based in correct theology. It is disastrous to build one's theology upon some experience; it is always necessary to explain our experience by the Word of God. In the course of past centuries of church history abundant evidence has been accumulated to show that it is possible to mistake the voice of Satan for the voice of God, and that it is even more possible to mistake the voice of self for the voice of God. That is why we must always be willing to turn to the Word of God, why we must repudiate any voice that speaks contrary to the Word of God, and avoid any experience that is an end in itself. We want no "inner light" experience, "divine voice" experience, we want no ecstatic mysticism that feels rather than thinks. The certain fact of our reception as sons of God must be based objectively on the written Word of God, and then subjectively on the fact of the Holy Spirit's joint witness with our spirit.[3]

The testimony of the Holy Spirit with our human spirit must be verified by the Word of God. When the Word enters our thinking and motivates our responses to the Lord, we have the sure witness of the Holy Spirit that we are children of the Most High God.

8:17 ***If we are his children, we are also God's heirs. If we share in Christ's suffering in order to share his glory, we are heirs together with him.***

As sons and daughters of the sovereign God, we are His heirs. An heir is someone who receives an inheritance by virtue of the will and testament of the benefactor. As adopted children of God by our faith in Christ, we receive eternal life and all its benefits. "*If you belong to Christ, then you are Abraham's descendants and heirs, as God promised*" *(Galatians 3:29)*.

Our inheritance is eternal, so we can never lose it. It is received only by the death of the one who made the will, Jesus Christ. As those who have died to self and been made alive in Christ *(1 Corinthians 15:22)*, we will likewise "share his glory" in the greatest blessing of all, eternal life with Him.

8:18 ***I consider our present sufferings insignificant compared to the glory that will soon be revealed to us.***

In the light of the glory that will be given to us in the life to come, our momentary suffering is trivial. Christians are sustained in their daily struggles by looking ahead, confident in the promise that Jesus gave them: "My Father wants all those who see the Son and believe in him to have eternal life. He wants me to bring them back to life on the last day" *(John 6:40)*. It is in this manner that Christians share in Christ's sufferings *(Hebrews 12:2–3)*. Understanding the privilege that we have to suffer as our Lord did gives us a better perspective on who we are as God's adopted children.

8:19 ***All creation is eagerly waiting for God to reveal who his children are.***

The earth longs to be delivered from the curse of sin pronounced in the garden of Eden. John Calvin states: "I understand the passage to have this meaning—that there is no element and no part of the world which, being touched, as it were, with a sense of its present misery, does not intensely hope for a resurrection."[4]

However, there is a sense in which the emphasis of the verse is not so much on those who encompass "his children" but on what will be revealed about them. Within the context of the previous verses, believers can look past their present suffering to that day when they will be revealed before all creation for what they truly are—God's precious children and heirs of His glorious inheritance.[5]

8:20–21 ***[20]Creation was subjected to frustration but not by its own choice. The one who subjected it to frustration did so in the hope [21]that it would also be set free from slavery to decay in order to share the glorious freedom that the children of God will have.***

Paul arrived at the conclusion of his argument regarding suffering. He explained that suffering became the natural world order as the result of God's sovereign judgment on the entire universe because of sin. Ever since sin entered the world, all creation has suffered. The result was futility, for all creatures of the earth are suppressed under God's curse even though they were not responsible for humanity's sin. When God pronounced judgment on Adam for his sin, He said, "[17]The ground is cursed because of you. Through hard work you will eat food that comes from it every day of your life. [18]The ground will grow thorns and thistles for you, and you will eat wild plants" *(Genesis 3:17–18)*.

God is in control of all His creation, and He cares for His creatures even in their present limited capacity. Jesus illustrated the concept of God's providential care in His Sermon on the Mount:

> *[26]Look at the birds. They don't plant, harvest, or gather the harvest into barns. Yet, your heavenly Father feeds them. Aren't you worth more than they? . . . [28]And why worry about clothes? Notice how*

> *the flowers grow in the field. They never work or spin yarn for clothes. [29]But I say that not even Solomon in all his majesty was dressed like one of these flowers.* (Matthew 6:26, 28–29)

The rest of the world yearns for that same hope that is already given to the children of God. Unfortunately, they fail to attain this same hope because they search for it on their own terms, rejecting the mandates of the eternal God as revealed in the provision of His Son, Jesus Christ. The hope for the restoration of the creation is related to what Peter calls "a living hope through the resurrection of Jesus Christ from the dead" *(1 Peter 1:3,* NKJV*)*. His resurrection represented a new beginning, which might well be called a "reverse of the curse."

When Christ returns to establish the new heavens and the new earth, all people who are found in Christ will regain the true freedom to fellowship with their Creator as they were originally created to do *(Revelation 22:3–5)*.

Notes/Applications

All creation seeks relief from pain and suffering, the bitter realities of sin's curse. Whether people believe in Christ or not, there is little doubt about the cursed condition of their life experience. Nevertheless, Christians should not be surprised by this harsh reality since they have lived through the deep waters of their own sin and were then released from its curse by the gift of Christ's salvation. More than that, Christians stand as witnesses to this salvation and should expect the hostilities imposed upon them by an unfriendly world that rejects their Savior. Not only should Christians expect and accept such suffering for the hope that they have in Christ, but they should also recognize it as the earthly reality of their redeemed lives.

There is more to it than that, however. God uses suffering as the refining and maturing process by which His children grow in their dependence upon Him. More importantly, God uses the example of

His children to show the sinful world His faithfulness. Unbelievers carefully observe believers, waiting for them to falter or fail, but God is completely dependable in the way that He sustains and directs their lives. In this way, God reveals who His children really are through suffering.

May believers learn to rejoice in suffering that they experience because of their faith in Christ, knowing that "when they pass the test, they will receive the crown of life that God has promised to those who love him" *(James 1:12)*.

Romans 8:22–27

8:22 ***We know that all creation has been groaning with the pains of childbirth up to the present time.***

Paul previously stated that although creation yearns to be free it will not happen. Instead of experiencing redemption, the world is destined to suffer under the penalty of God's judgment. When God's predetermined time has arrived, this curse will be removed. However, it will be a long painful process, much like a woman struggling through the pain of childbirth.

8:23 ***However, not only creation groans. We, who have the Spirit as the first of God's gifts, also groan inwardly. We groan as we eagerly wait for our adoption, the freeing of our bodies from sin.***

Not only does all of creation groan, expressing deep longing to be freed from its bondage to the curse, but Christians also long for that day of deliverance. The Spirit living within makes us yearn for the day when our bodies will be free from sin and we will be like Jesus. Because we have experienced the regenerating work of the Spirit in our lives, we have a glimpse of what that glory will be. Therefore, while we endure the suffering that is prevalent throughout all nature, we also groan as we eagerly wait to be freed from our mortal bodies and clothed in glorified, immortal bodies. Suffering is a constant companion throughout our lives, even though we are redeemed. The completion of our redemption comes when Christ returns to take us home and transforms our mortal bodies into heavenly bodies *(1 Corinthians 15:40–44)*.

8:24–25 ***[24]We were saved with this hope in mind. If we hope for something we already see, it's not really hope. Who hopes for what can be seen? [25]But if we hope for what we don't see, we eagerly wait for it with perseverance.***

Believers eagerly look forward to that day when they will be set free, and they wait for the day of His redemption not with despair but with hope. When we are redeemed by the work of the Spirit, the Lord plants the seed of this hope deep within our hearts. At that time, we are given a new perspective on everything that we have experienced. We now understand the condition of our new life in Christ; we understand the way that the world suffers because of sin, and we eagerly look forward to that day when our hope will be realized. This hope is not some mere desire for something better than our current circumstances but a confident expectation of all that our inheritance in Christ entails.

8:26 ***At the same time the Spirit also helps us in our weakness, because we don't know how to pray for what we need. But the Spirit intercedes along with our groans that cannot be expressed in words.***

When hope falters, when believers are overwhelmed by inabilities and circumstances, there is always the reliability of God in the person of the Holy Spirit to intercede on their behalf. This same indwelling Spirit Who guides, directs, teaches, instructs, and explains God's truth recognizes the frailty of our human struggles. He recognizes that even redeemed believers only dimly perceive the salvation that has been imparted to them and the glory that awaits them.

The Amplified Bible offers an expanded description of Paul's argument:

> *So too the [Holy] Spirit comes to our aid and bears us up in our weakness; for we do not know what prayer to offer nor how to offer it worthily as we ought, but the Spirit Himself goes to meet our supplication and pleads in our behalf with unspeakable yearnings and groanings too deep for utterance. (Romans 8:26,* AMP*)*

***8:27** The one who searches our hearts knows what the Spirit has in mind. The Spirit intercedes for God's people the way God wants him to.*

God knows us better than we know ourselves. No matter how hard we try to live lives that reflect the new person we have become, challenging circumstances often arise and shake our resolve. When confronted with these obstacles, we often pray with passion to be released from such adversity. However, that prayer, although passionate and heartfelt, may not reflect God's will. In spite of our condition, the Spirit intercedes faithfully in absolute harmony with the Father.

Notes/Applications

"I consider our present sufferings insignificant compared to the glory that will soon be revealed to us" (Romans 8:18).

As believers, the knowledge that the Holy Spirit lives within us and intercedes for us provides unassailable confidence, although not in ourselves but in the One Who intercedes on our behalf. The reality of the Spirit's faithfulness sustains us through life's trials and temptations.

We are assured and comforted by the Holy Spirit within us as we eagerly wait for the completion of our redemption when we will be welcomed home to live with Christ eternally. This is truly our Christian hope, which is far different from the world's concept of hope. Hebrews 6:19 describes this hope as "an anchor of the soul, both sure and steadfast" (NKJV).

Romans 8:28–32

8:28 ***We know that all things work together for the good of those who love God—those whom he has called according to his plan.***

No matter what believers face, whether doubt or adversity, God is faithfully at work, making everything conform to His grand plan. God is sovereign and without equal; He is unchanging and unchangeable; and He has a divine plan for His entire creation as well as for each of us. There are no accidents in God's wise providence. Events occur only with His definitive purpose so that His people become what He wants them to be.

In the Old Testament, Joseph understood this truth in confronting his brothers about their evil intent against him. "[19]*Joseph said to them, 'Don't be afraid! I can't take God's place.* [20]*Even though you planned evil against me, God planned good to come out of it. This was to keep many people alive, as he is doing now'"* (Genesis 50:19–20).

8:29 ***This is true because he already knew his people and had already appointed them to have the same form as the image of his Son. Therefore, his Son is the firstborn among many children.***

In verse seventeen, Paul asserted that believers are God's heirs. As he developed his theme, he moved through this fundamental premise to the point where he assured that everything that happens to believers, whether good or bad in their eyes, really fulfills the purpose that God intends. Paul affirmed that this was true because God's plan has always existed. From eternity, God knew His people and "appointed them to have the same form as the image of his Son."

It should be understood that Paul is speaking here of spiritual traits, not physical ones. The "image of his Son" is righteousness; so, too, we are made righteous through Him. However, this righteousness is not only a reference to the glory that will one day be ours in heaven but also to the blessings that are ours in our earthly lives through the new nature we have been given.[6] Our inheritance is sure because Christ has gone before us as the "firstborn among many children." This is a reference to His resurrection, which secures our hope in our own resurrections one day. *"But now Christ has come back from the dead. He is the very first person of those who have died to come back to life" (1 Corinthians 15:20).*

8:30 ***He also called those whom he had already appointed. He approved of those whom he had called, and he gave glory to those whom he had approved of.***

Those whom God has already appointed have been called and preordained to be His adopted children *(Ephesians 1:11)*. All of God's redeemed people are called by Him according to His purpose *(2 Timothy 1:9)*. This gracious call by God affirms our certain transformation into the image of His Son, both in His suffering and in His glory. Those He has called have been approved, declared righteous because of Christ's atoning sacrifice.

Finally, those who have received God's approval are given His glory to the praise and honor of His beloved Son. Through the finished work of His Son, God has planned that the redeemed will also receive the same glory that His Son was given.

8:31 ***What can we say about all of this? If God is for us, who can be against us?***

Once Paul explained the purpose and calling of God, he embarked on a series of questions that can best be summed up by one overriding challenge: "If God is for us, who can be against us?" The conclusion of the theological discourse is self-evident, resulting in such a confidence that Christians can face anything and everything that life throws at us. If God is on our side, why should anything else matter? Such genuine confidence does not result in an arrogant attitude toward others, nor is it an unassuming naiveté. Christians still suffer, and the pain is real. They still face adversity, and the circumstances still appear to be insurmountable. They are often insulted because of their Christian testimony *(Acts 5:41)*.

When God tells us to do something, however, we have nothing to fear. He has all wisdom and power and will accomplish His purpose. When we belong to God, we offer our weakness, and He offers His strength *(2 Corinthians 12:10)*. We are nothing; God is everything *(2 Corinthians 13:4)*. God asserts that nothing will succeed in destroying what He has already determined to happen.

***8:32** God didn't spare his own Son but handed him over to death for all of us. So he will also give us everything along with him.*

The heart of the good news is that God loved us so much that He gave His only Son to die in our place. He did not spare the Lord Jesus Christ, the eternal Son of God and the perfect Son of Man, but handed Him over to His enemies *(Isaiah 53:10)*.

The wonderful truth is that not only did God hand over His Son, Jesus, as a "gift that words cannot describe" *(2 Corinthians 9:15)*, but along with Him, believers receive other innumerable blessings. They receive the gifts of the Spirit and the fruit of the Spirit; they receive the intercession of the Holy Spirit on their behalf; they receive the confidence that God imparts, affirming that each of them has been an integral part of God's plan from the beginning of time; and they receive the gift of eternal life.

Notes/Applications

Knowing that as Christians all circumstances in our lives are ordered by a loving and almighty God, why can we not relax and trust Him in everything that happens? We should realize that God, our Father, has planned what family we would be born into, where we would live on the face of the earth, the time frame in history that we would occupy, the mate we would marry, the children that we would or would not have, the persecution we would endure in His name, and ultimately where, when, and how we would die. All is preordained by a loving, compassionate, and merciful God.

As we experience difficult times, sorely tested by the trials we endure, we should realize that these are no surprise to God. He works through all of these circumstances to conform us to the image of His Son. In fact, the apostolic admonition is to rejoice in all things, even in our sufferings *(James 1:2–4)*.

When this life is over and we enter into our eternal rest with Him, we will have accomplished every purpose that He determined and finished the task for which we were created. Nothing that happens to us can ever gain victory over us because we know the truth of God's sovereign care for us from birth to death and on into eternity with Him. God Himself has determined our final resting place in Christ our Savior.

Romans 8:33–39

8:33 ***Who will accuse those whom God has chosen? God has approved of them.***

Paul continued to raise questions that would further define God's work, providing an unassailable stronghold against those deceptions that might cause believers to falter in their faith. This particular question addressed Christians facing hostile accusations. These accusations come from three main sources—Satan, other people, and their own doubts.

Satan, the great accuser of believers, has been overcome by the blood of the spotless Lamb of God, the Lord Jesus Christ *(Revelation 12:10–11)*. People also may hurl insults and accusations, scoffing at those who have a relationship with Christ. These have no lasting impact on His followers since they belong to the One Who has died in their place. There is a sense in which these accusations against Christians only serve to reveal that the accusers are rebelling against the Lord. Nevertheless, no accusation will have an actual impact on believers because God has already approved of them.

8:34 ***Who will condemn them? Christ has died, and more importantly, he was brought back to life. Christ has the highest position in heaven. Christ also intercedes for us.***

Paul built on the believer's position in Christ. He reaffirmed one's security in God by showing how God executed His plan through the death, resurrection, and continuing intercession of His Son.

God alone has the authority and power to condemn. Since He has acquitted believers through His Son, they are not condemned. "[17]*God sent his Son into the world, not to condemn the world, but to save the world.* [18]*Those who believe in him won't be condemned. But those who don't believe are already condemned because they don't believe in God's only Son" (John 3:17–18)*. As important as His death was, Jesus' resurrection was even more vital, for it sealed His work of redemption, completely conquered death, and secured our eternal life.

God's Son is interceding for us in heaven. He is at the Father's right hand, "the highest position in heaven," pleading our case. "[24]*But Jesus lives forever, so he serves as a priest forever.* [25]*That is why he is always able to save those who come to God through him. He can do this because he always lives and intercedes for them*" (Hebrews 7:24–25).

8:35 ***What will separate us from the love Christ has for us? Can trouble, distress, persecution, hunger, nakedness, danger, or violent death separate us from his love?***

Paul was not blind to the harsh realities of the difficulties that Christians face. There were real, life-threatening issues that intruded on these Christians' lives. But was that the overriding issue? The primary concern was that they knew that Christ's love surpassed any physical adversity that could infringe upon their lives.

God's everlasting love sustains us no matter how great the pressure we endure for our faith. As already asserted, persecution is to be expected in the lives of believers. As they express the reality of their faith, a hostile and rebellious world will assault their identity with Christ. This assault may escalate beyond verbal offense. As evidenced throughout history, Christians may face physical threats on their lives, in some cases even resulting in violent death. Paul assured believers that no matter what should happen, the most extreme cases of their earthly experience are powerless in the light of God's unquenchable love. The abiding affirmation of this passage is that He preserves believers in their suffering and finally delivers them into His loving presence forever.

8:36 ***As Scripture says: "We are being killed all day long because of you. We are thought of as sheep to be slaughtered."***

Paul, by quoting the Scriptures, reminded his readers of the dangers they face. "*Indeed, we are being killed all day long because of you. We are thought of as sheep to be slaughtered*" (Psalm 44:22). Hebrews eleven provides eloquent testimony to the generations of men and women who suffered and died for their faith:

> [33]*Through faith they conquered kingdoms, did what God approved, and received what God had promised. They shut the mouths of lions,* [34]*put out raging fires, and escaped death. They found strength when they were weak. They were powerful in battle and defeated other armies.* [35]*Women received their loved ones back from the dead. Other believers were brutally tortured but refused to be released so that they might gain eternal life.* [36]*Some were made fun of and whipped, and some were chained and put in prison.* [37]*Some were stoned to death, sawed in half, and killed with swords. Some wore the skins of sheep and goats. Some were poor, abused, and mistreated.* [38]*The world didn't deserve these good people. Some wandered around in deserts and mountains and lived in caves and holes in the ground. (Hebrews 11:33–38)*

Paul was unapologetically forthright both in the expression of God's faithfulness to His redeemed people and in the harsh realities of a world to which they no longer truly belonged. Therefore, Christians should not be surprised by the adversity and suffering that they witness or personally experience, just as they should never forget the One Who has called them, saved them, and sustained them. Christians must recognize that adversity and intense suffering are an integral part of the human experience and an even more profound reality of believers' lives.

8:37 The one who loves us gives us an overwhelming victory in all these difficulties.

In all these things—trouble, distress, persecution, hunger, nakedness, danger, and even death—we are victors through Christ Who loves us. He is the great conqueror, having triumphed over death. This is not just a close win but an "overwhelming victory" that is bestowed on the believer through the intercession of Christ. This victory is a great contrast to the suffering God's people have endured. This overwhelming victory comes only through the faithfulness of our living Lord. He is the only One able to keep us from falling *(Jude 24–25)*.

8:38–39 ***[38]I am convinced that nothing can ever separate us from God's love which Christ Jesus our Lord shows us. We can't be separated by death or life, by angels or rulers, by anything in the present or anything in the future, by forces [39]or powers in the world above or in the world below, or by anything else in creation.***

Paul began this climactic statement with the assuring words "I am convinced." Paul was fully confident that nothing on earth or in heaven could keep us from God's love. To make his point, Paul enumerated several such forces.

All believers, whether in life or death, are in the hands of their sovereign Lord. Physical death cannot separate believers from God; rather, it delivers them into His presence. Life cannot separate us from Christ's love because He is living in us. This affirmation has been the whole thrust of Paul's discourse throughout this chapter. Paul generalized those adversities that are powerless to change the believers' position in Christ—trouble, distress, persecution, hunger, nakedness, danger, or even violent death.

If nothing in our lives or deaths can separate us, the natural inclination might be to wonder what things beyond this physical word might prevail against us. However, Paul negated such possibilities by refuting the abilities of even "angels" or "powers in the world above or in the world below" to separate us from the love that has saved us. All of creation, whether of this world or of a different realm, is subject to the sovereign will of Almighty God *(Psalm 139:7–8)*.

Notes/Applications

Chapter eight begins with the declaration that "believers in Christ Jesus can no longer be condemned" and climaxes with the statement that "nothing can ever separate us from God's love which Christ Jesus our Lord shows us." What a marvelous expression of God's unfathomable love! He is on our side, as shown by the sacrifice of

His dear Son and the continual intercession of the Spirit before the Father's throne. He has saved us, and He faithfully keeps us in the safety and security of His will, calling us His sons and daughters and making us heirs together with Christ.

This is the gracious work of our God. There is nothing that we can contribute to our salvation or even to our own position in Christ. Every moment of our lives should be a moment of thanksgiving for God's amazing love, the eternal life He has so freely given us, and the faithful intercession of His Holy Spirit.

ROMANS 9

Romans 9:1–5

***9:1** As a Christian, I'm telling you the truth. I'm not lying. The Holy Spirit, along with my own thoughts, supports me in this.*

Having reached the summit of God's wonderful grace in Jesus Christ, Paul made a seemingly abrupt change in focus. He opened with an emphatic declaration, "I'm telling you the truth. I'm not lying." He was speaking the very Word of God. In this case, Paul revealed something that affected him profoundly, coming from deep within his heart. This deeply held conviction was confirmed by the witness of the Holy Spirit living within him. As in other cases, Paul affirmed his apostolic authority under the control of the Holy Spirit. "*God is my witness that what I'm writing is not a lie*" *(Galatians 1:20)*.

***9:2–3** [2]I have deep sorrow and endless heartache. [3]I wish I could be condemned and cut off from Christ for the sake of others who, like me, are Jewish by birth.*

Paul was deeply grieved about something that was extremely important to him. This grief was so profound that he actually felt as though he carried a heavy burden. Like the Old Testament prophets, he grieved over his people, the Jews, who did not seek after their God.

> *My people have done two things wrong. They have abandoned me, the fountain of life-giving water. They have also dug their own cisterns, broken cisterns that can't hold water. (Jeremiah 2:13)*

> *Streams of tears run down from my eyes over the ruin of my dear people. (Lamentations 3:48)*

Paul unveiled one of the greatest expressions of love in all of history. In his genuine love for his people and filled with the testimony of the Holy Spirit, Paul desired their salvation. Although he was called to minister to the Gentiles, he was always a Jew first. He was weighed down with sorrow that most Jews rejected their promised Messiah—the One sent to save them. Paul's love was so intense that he was willing to be condemned for eternity so that they could be saved. What amazing love, the very love of Christ!

9:4 They are Israelites, God's adopted children. They have the Lord's glory, the pledges, Moses' Teachings, the true worship, and the promises.

The Israelites are God's chosen people through Abraham, Isaac, and Jacob. Jacob, renamed Israel, had twelve sons who became the twelve tribes comprising the nation of Israel. God adopted them as His children and conferred on them His glory, His law, His way of true worship, and His promises. God told them through Moses:

> *[4]You have seen for yourselves what I did to Egypt and how I carried you on eagles' wings and brought you to my mountain. [5]If you will carefully obey me and are faithful to the terms of my promise, then out of all the nations you will be my own special possession, even though the whole world is mine. (Exodus 19:4–5)*

> *You are a holy people, who belong to the LORD your God. He chose you to be his own special possession out of all the nations on earth. (Deuteronomy 7:6)*

Through Israel, the glory of God came to earth. While fleeing the Egyptian army, the Lord protected their escape by His personal intervention. "*While Aaron was speaking to the whole community of Israelites, they looked toward the desert. Suddenly, they saw the glory of the LORD in the column of smoke" (Exodus 16:10)*. The Lord's presence traveled with them through their wilderness journey. When Solomon built the temple, the Lord again graced Israel with His presence. "[10]*When the priests left the holy place, a cloud filled the LORD's temple.* [11]*The priests couldn't serve because of the cloud. The LORD's glory filled his temple" (1 Kings 8:10–11)*.

The pledges, or covenants, were given for Israel to live distinctively as examples to the rest of the world. "*Then he took the Book of the LORD's Promise and read it while the people listened. They said, 'We will obey and do everything the LORD has said'" (Exodus 24:7)*. The law, also referred to as Moses' teachings, was first for Israel but also for the benefit of all people.

The "true worship" given to the Israelites refers to worship that is acceptable to God. This worship, which He established through Israel, is the very foundation of Christian worship. Sacrifice in the Old Testament required the shedding of blood for the sins of the people, looking forward to the promised Lamb of God, Jesus Christ, Who was sacrificed on Calvary to redeem His own. In Romans 12:1, we are exhorted to present our bodies "as living sacrifices," having been saved through the blood of Christ. This, Paul declares, is the believer's deepest expression of worship.

Finally, there are numerous promises given to Israel throughout the Old Testament. The promises given us through Abraham, Moses, and the prophets are perfectly fulfilled in Christ. "*Don't ever think that I came to set aside Moses' Teachings or the Prophets. I didn't come to set them aside but to make them come true" (Matthew 5:17)*.

9:5 The Messiah is descended from their ancestors according to his human nature. The Messiah is God over everything, forever blessed. Amen.

More than all of the distinctions outlined in verse four, the Jews were the people through whom God's Messiah was brought into the world. The other aspects were conceptual in nature, but the Messiah became the most tangible evidence of God's blessing on Israel. Messiah was the historical fulfillment of all that was expressed in the Old Testament Scriptures.

The ancestry of Jesus Christ, God's Messiah, was recorded in Matthew chapter one, beginning with Abraham, Isaac, and Jacob, and continuing through the kingly line of David. Luke 3:23–38 records the ancestors of Jesus the Messiah through Mary his mother. This also includes Abraham, Isaac, Jacob, and David. Abraham was the father of the nation Israel through whom God would provide salvation for all the peoples of the world. *"Through you every family on earth will be blessed" (Genesis 12:3).*

Despite all of these God-given resources and the historical fulfillment in the appearance of God's Messiah, the Jewish people continued in obstinate rejection of all that God had promised them. Born in the richness of this Jewish heritage, Paul was brokenhearted over his nation's apathy.

Notes/Applications

Having expressed how he reached the summit of God's grace in the previous chapter, Paul looked into the valley below and saw his fellow Israelites living in the futility of seeking God's approval through the law. He was genuinely grieved that his people, with their rich heritage in the Lord's covenant with Abraham, had rejected the good news of salvation through Jesus their Messiah. God's promises did not fail, but His people lost their way through their unbelief. *"He went to his own people, and his own people didn't accept him" (John 1:11).*

After expressing the security that he had experienced in Christ, and after his passionate discourse in chapter eight ending with his affirmation that "nothing can ever separate us from God's love which Christ Jesus our Lord shows us," Paul found it terribly difficult to understand why his own people could not see the truth of Christ's love. His grief was so intense that he articulated his wish that he could be condemned so that they could be saved. What kind of love would motivate Paul to such extreme measures? It is only by the love of Christ flourishing in his heart through the indwelling Spirit that he could dare to speak such unspeakable desires.

Such love makes us wonder about the level of our own love for humanity. Would we dare to make such an appeal to God if those around us did not believe in Christ—our family members, our coworkers, church members, and others who cross our path? Unfortunately, many of us are fearful even to let others know that we belong to Christ, let alone make such a passionate appeal for their salvation.

Let us appeal to God in the name of Jesus Christ to give us the spirit of boldness and joy in the salvation that has been so graciously bestowed on us. Let us ask Him to make us fearless witnesses to all those we meet.

Romans 9:6–12

9:6–7 ***[6]Now it is not as though God's word has failed. Clearly, not everyone descended from Israel is part of Israel [7]or a descendant of Abraham. However, as Scripture says, "Through Isaac your descendants will carry on your name."***

The Word of God has not failed, for every word is true. "*God is not like people. He tells no lies. He is not like humans. He doesn't change his mind. When he says something, he does it. When he makes a promise, he keeps it*" (*Numbers 23:19*). All that God has spoken will be accomplished. "*My word, which comes from my mouth, is like the rain and snow. It will not come back to me without results. It will accomplish whatever I want and achieve whatever I send it to do*" (*Isaiah 55:11*).

Paul asserted that the people of Israel are descendants only of Isaac, the child of God's promise to Abraham. Abraham had other sons, for he was also the father of Ishmael through Hagar. After Sarah died, Abraham then married Keturah, and she gave birth to six sons (*Genesis 25:1–2*). There are eight biological lines that could claim Abraham as their paternal ancestor: Ishmael, Isaac, and the six sons of Keturah. While all eight sons could claim Abraham as their father through their bloodlines, only Isaac met both criteria as a biological son and the son of promise. Paul made the clear distinction that Israel was the descendant of Isaac, not any of Abraham's other children.

9:8 ***This means that children born by natural descent from Abraham are not necessarily God's children. Instead, children born by the promise are considered Abraham's descendants.***

Paul again clarified his point that the promise made to Abraham was only to his descendants through Isaac, not Ishmael (and then through Jacob, who received the blessing of Isaac, and not Esau, Jacob's brother). However, the greater point that Paul made was that a bloodline to Abraham is not what matters most. While the biological bloodline determines validity of one's human ancestry, the most important matter lies in the lineage of God's promise.

The phrase "children born by the promise" refers to those children who are descendants of Isaac. God promised through Moses and the prophets to send His Messiah to redeem Israel. Jesus came to earth as the fulfillment of that promise, the promise God made to Abraham that affects all nations of the earth. Earlier, Paul had affirmed that this promise has been given to all those who live as inheritors of Abraham's lineage in faith:

> *Therefore, the promise is based on faith so that it can be a gift. Consequently, the promise is guaranteed for every descendant, not only for those who are descendants by obeying Moses' Teachings but also for those who are descendants by believing as Abraham did. He is the father of all of us. (Romans 4:16)*

9:9 ***For example, this is what the promise said, "I will come back at the right time, and Sarah will have a son."***

Abraham and Sarah had left their native Ur and headed for the Promised Land when he was seventy-five years old and she was sixty-five. They were childless, but God had promised them innumerable descendants. Twenty-four years later, the Lord and two angels visited Abraham with special news. "*The LORD said, 'I promise I'll come back to you next year at this time, and your wife Sarah will have a son*'" *(Genesis 18:10)*. Sarah, who happened to be listening, laughed to herself, thinking, "Now that I've become old, will I enjoy myself again? What's more, my husband is old!" *(Genesis 18:12)*. When the Lord asked why Sarah laughed, she denied it, but He replied: "Is anything too hard for the LORD? I will come back to you next year at this time, and Sarah will have a son" *(Genesis 18:14)*.

The Lord kept his promise, and Sarah gave birth to Isaac when she was ninety and Abraham was one hundred. God is the God of the impossible. They believed His promise and by His miraculous working received their son of promise. Thus, God provided this son of promise, Isaac, through Sarah in order to send His Son of promise, Jesus, born two thousand years later, to Mary.

9:10 ***The same thing happened to Rebekah. Rebekah became pregnant by our ancestor Isaac.***

God's promise continued with Isaac and Rebekah, who also went childless for many years. Like his father before him, Isaac worried that time was passing and they were getting too old to have children. If Abraham's line was to continue through Isaac, then Rebekah would also have to provide a male heir. Finally, "Isaac prayed to the LORD for his wife because she was childless. The LORD answered his prayer, and his wife Rebekah became pregnant" (*Genesis 25:21*). God answered Isaac's prayer not only by enabling Rebekah to become pregnant but by giving her twins, Esau and Jacob.

9:11–12 ***[11]Before the children had been born or had done anything good or bad, Rebekah was told that the older child would serve the younger one. This was said to Rebekah so that God's plan would remain a matter of his choice, [12]a choice based on God's call and not on anything people do.***

God chose the younger son over the older before they were born and before their earthly character was formed. He planned this even before they were conceived, not after He observed their deeds in life. In Isaac's culture, the oldest son always received the birthright from the father. However, in this case, God reversed the order, demonstrating that the line of Abraham's promise would develop the way that God alone had planned.

This truth about God's calling was revealed to Rebekah "so that God's plan would remain a matter of his choice." This could not be clearer or more emphatically stated, and it reminds us of the importance of believing God and accepting His divine will for our lives. Most important is the recognition that God chose Jacob to be in the line through whom His Son would be born (*Genesis 25:22–27*).

Notes/Applications

The Word of God has not failed, for every word is true. Paul wanted his readers to know that God has never and will never change. To prove his point, Paul provided the examples of the Israelite patriarchs. In those early years of God's redemptive history, God did things in an extraordinary way simply to affirm that nothing could stop the execution of His plan: not Sarah and Rebekah's barren wombs, Abraham's old age, or the standard traditions of existing cultures.

Nobody would argue that it was impossible for a couple in their nineties to conceive and bear a child through the rigors of pregnancy. Even if the woman could bear the child, why wouldn't both the child and the woman die in childbirth? Yet, that is exactly the way God chose to miraculously fulfill His promise in the lives of Abraham and Sarah and in the lives of Isaac and Rebekah.

God also broke cultural tradition by establishing the precedence of the younger son over the older. True, Jacob was less than honest when he disguised himself as the older, hairy Esau and virtually stole their father's blessing from Esau *(Genesis 27)*. Still, that is precisely how God worked through the lives of this dysfunctional family. Why? Because God wanted to show that His way was the only way that would accomplish His purposes.

We cannot help but rationalize our circumstances and attempt to put God into a box that we can understand and hopefully control. However, God will never be understood by His creation, nor will He ever be manipulated by unbelievers or even by believers. His will and sovereign plan are the only factors that count throughout the course of history. Knowing this, believers should realize that they bring nothing into the relationship that God has not already given to them. This induces a large dose of humility and a greater dose of thanksgiving.

Romans 9:13–21

9:13 *The Scriptures say, "I loved Jacob, but I hated Esau."*

Paul was quoting from what is now the Old Testament, in this case, from the prophet Malachi:

> [1]*This is a divine revelation. The* LORD *spoke his word to Israel through Malachi.*
> *"*[2]*I loved you," says the* LORD.
> *"But you ask, 'How did you love us?'*
> *"Wasn't Esau Jacob's brother?" declares the* LORD. *"I loved Jacob,* [3]*but Esau I hated. I turned his mountains into a wasteland and left his inheritance to the jackals in the desert'"* (Malachi 1:1–3).

Malachi spoke these words long after Jacob and Esau lived, interpreting clearly God's sovereign choice. Jacob was loved as the chosen son through whom God's holy Son would come to earth. No matter how Esau or any of his descendants might try, the Messiah would never come from his lineage.

The idea of God hating Esau (or *anyone*, for that matter) is one that is perplexing, even troubling, for believers to reconcile with their understanding of God's love for all people *(John 3:16)*. Some have attempted to explain the statement by suggesting that this was just a manner of expressing that God loved Esau *less* than He loved Jacob. However, this seems to fall short of satisfying the problem. Since Paul did not provide further explanation of the meaning, it is perhaps best to define *hate* in contrast to God's expression of *love* within the context of this passage. Professor and respected theologian Douglas Moo explains it this way:

> If God's love of Jacob consists in his choosing Jacob to be the "seed" who would inherit the blessings promised to Abraham, then God's hatred of Esau is best understood to refer to God's decision not to bestow this privilege on Esau. It might best

be translated "reject." "Love" and "hate" are not here, then, emotions that God feels but actions that he carries out.[1]

9:14 *What can we say—that God is unfair? That's unthinkable!*

Many people intensely dislike this view of God. They argue that God is unfair in the way that He treats people. Paul was very much aware of this reaction, and so he began to answer the objection.

By His very nature, God is perfectly righteous as taught in all of Scripture. "[3]*I will proclaim the name of the* LORD. *Give our God the greatness he deserves!* [4]*He is a rock. What he does is perfect. All his ways are fair. He is a faithful God, who does no wrong. He is honorable and reliable" (Deuteronomy 32:3–4).*

Almighty God created everything. Everything happens according to His will and plan. He will not commit evil and, therefore, is not chargeable with injustice in His choices. We cannot understand God's ways unless they are revealed to us *(Isaiah 55:8–9).* We can always rest assured, however, that God's ways are always right, holy, and fair *(Psalm 145:17).*

DIG DEEPER: ***Is God Fair?***

One of the most disturbing perceptions of God is the idea that He is really unfair. Many people think that God has treated them unfairly, that somehow their lives have been shortchanged by some unseen, capricious deity who directs their fate with casual disdain. This conclusion can only be held by those people who have little or no understanding for who God is. Job tried to honor God by obeying His law, but that was not enough. Cruel adversity made chaos out of what once had been great prosperity. Job, too, had to discover the majesty of the Lord and accept the reality of his own false perception about God's fairness *(Job 34:10–19).*

9:15 *For example, God said to Moses, "I will be kind to anyone I want to. I will be merciful to anyone I want to."*

God clearly revealed His sovereign will to Moses because Moses had an intimate relationship with Him *(Exodus 33:17–19)*. This is God's sovereignty. He is all-powerful, all-wise, and all-present, and yet He is merciful and gracious to His people *(Micah 7:18 and 2 Timothy 1:9)*.

God is in ultimate control of the lives of all people. That does not relieve us of our responsibility but rather affirms His sovereignty. "*God has made us what we are. He has created us in Christ Jesus to live lives filled with good works that he has prepared for us to do*" *(Ephesians 2:10)*.

9:16 *Therefore, God's choice does not depend on a person's desire or effort, but on God's mercy.*

God has chosen us in Christ according to His own mercy and not according to anything a person can do. It is only through His drawing people to Him that they can even respond in faith *(John 6:44)*. Jesus made this clear to His disciples just before the cross: "You didn't choose me, but I chose you" *(John 15:16)*.

9:17 *For example, Scripture says to Pharaoh, "I put you here for this reason: to demonstrate my power through you and to spread my name throughout the earth."*

God Himself spoke to Pharaoh through His servant Moses. Several times in the Exodus account, the words "the LORD said to Moses" are followed by Moses taking that word to Pharaoh, saying, "This is what the LORD God of the Hebrews says." Here Paul quoted Exodus 9:16, God's words to Pharaoh: "I have spared you for this reason. I want to show you my power and make my name famous throughout the earth." God's sovereign will and almighty power were shown to the land of Egypt through the stubbornness of the most powerful ruler of that time that all the earth might know the true God.

Kings and rulers are in God's control. "*The king's heart is like streams of water. Both are under the LORD's control. He turns them in any direction he chooses*" *(Proverbs 21:1)*. The prophet Isaiah said of

Cyrus, the great Persian ruler, "He is my shepherd. He will do everything I want him to do" *(Isaiah 44:28)*. In Isaiah 45:1, the Lord called Cyrus "his anointed one" whom He would use to rebuild Jerusalem after the Babylonian destruction. Isaiah spoke these words about 150 years before Cyrus ruled. *"I am the LORD, and there is no other. There is no other God besides me. I will strengthen you, although you don't know me, so that from the east to the west people will know that there is no God except me" (Isaiah 45:5–6)*.

9:18 *Therefore, if God wants to be kind to anyone, he will be. If he wants to make someone stubborn, he will.*

God's kindness or mercy is upon all whom He chooses. *"But from everlasting to everlasting, the LORD's mercy is on those who fear him" (Psalm 103:17)*. No one is worthy of His mercy, but some are shown mercy according to His plan.

Just as His mercy is given according to His purpose, so He makes stubborn (hardens) whom He will. This is evident with Pharaoh (*"I have made him and his officials stubborn," Exodus 10:1*) but also with Pharaoh's people (*"I am making the Egyptians so stubborn that they will follow the Israelites," Exodus 14:17*). This is shown again when Joshua defeated the Canaanite rulers in Joshua 11:20: "The LORD made their enemies stubborn enough to continue fighting against Israel so that he could claim them all for destruction without mercy, as he had commanded Moses."

9:19 *You may ask me, "Why does God still find fault with anyone? Who can resist whatever God wants to do?"*

The concept of God's sovereignty is beyond human comprehension *(2 Chronicles 20:6)*. Even though God is in complete control, people are still accountable. *"[13]When someone is tempted, he shouldn't say that God is tempting him. God can't be tempted by evil, and God doesn't tempt anyone. [14]Everyone is tempted by his own desires as they lure him away and trap him" (James 1:13–14)*.

God executes His sovereign will in the affairs of humanity. It was His will to crucify His beloved Son, but woe to those who were used in the process. Jesus said of Judas: "The Son of Man is going to die as the Scriptures say he will. But how horrible it will be for that person who betrays the Son of Man! It would have been better for that person if he had never been born" *(Mark 14:21)*. The apostle Peter, preaching at Pentecost, said, "By using men who don't acknowledge Moses' Teachings, you crucified Jesus, who was given over to death by a plan that God had determined in advance" *(Acts 2:23)*.

9:20 ***Who do you think you are to talk back to God like that? Can an object that was made say to its maker, "Why did you make me like this?"***

It is as if Paul read our minds. We are almost screaming in frustration, "That isn't fair!" In our own ignorance, we try to assume some status equal to God that would permit us to question why He chooses to do what He does. This is, of course, impossible. More so, we should respond to God's sovereignty with confidence and peace, not frustration or resignation.

The questions posed here by Paul are rhetorical, and their answers are self-evident. The creation is neither qualified to question the Creator, nor is the Creator obligated to provide us any reasons for His decisions. Demanding answers for His actions is pointless. *"How horrible it will be for the one who quarrels with his maker. He is pottery among other earthenware pots. Does the clay ask the one who shapes it, 'What are you making?' Does your work say to you, 'There are no handles'?" (Isaiah 45:9)*.

9:21 ***A potter has the right to do whatever he wants with his clay. He can make something for a special occasion or something for everyday use from the same lump of clay.***

Paul drove home the point of his message in these verses by using a familiar metaphor in which he compred God to a potter and His creation to a lump of clay *(Job 10:9; Isaiah 29:16 and 64:8)*. This simple illustration exemplifies both the control of the potter to do whatever he pleases with the clay as well as the utter inability of the clay to make anything meaningful of itself. The deeper implication is that the lump of clay represents all of humanity, from which God, in His divine providence, sees fit to take some portion of that clay and fashion it into something honorable or, in the spiritual sense, something acceptable to God and fit for heaven. In that vessels created for special purposes and vessels fitted for common use are formed from the same lump of clay, it should not be argued that His reasons for doing so are found in any answer other than His inestimable mercy *(Romans 9:16)*.

Notes/Applications

As we reflect on the unfathomable truth of these verses, may this be our prayer to the Master Potter:

My Maker and my King,
To Thee my all I owe;
Thy sovereign bounty is the spring
Whence all my blessings flow;
Thy sovereign bounty is the spring
Whence all my blessings flow.

The creature of Thy hand,
On Thee alone I live;
My God, Thy benefits demand
More praise than I can give.
My God, Thy benefits demand
More praise than I can give.

Lord, what can I impart
When all is Thine before?
Thy love demands a thankful heart;
The gift, alas! how poor.

Thy love demands a thankful heart;
The gift, alas! how poor.

O! let Thy grace inspire
My soul with strength divine;
Let every word and each desire
And all my days be Thine.
Let every word and each desire
And all my days be Thine.[2]

Romans 9:22–28

9:22 ***If God wants to demonstrate his anger and reveal his power, he can do it. But can't he be extremely patient with people who are objects of his anger because they are headed for destruction?***

Almighty God is not limited and can show His infinite power and wrath at any time. He is very patient with those who are bound for destruction, giving them time to repent of their rebellion. His dealing with Pharaoh is a perfect illustration of this. If He had cut Pharaoh down after the first plague, it would have seemed unfair not to not given Pharaoh a chance, and the Israelites and Egyptians would not have seen His full glory and power. Pharaoh was given many opportunities to repent, but he willfully chose to rebel. Nevertheless, through the suffering endured at Pharaoh's hand, God displayed His power throughout the world. Forty years later, when the Israelites entered the Promised Land under Joshua, the Canaanites had heard of the Israelites' God and what He had done to Pharaoh. Rahab, who lived in Jericho, told the spies:

> [10]*We've heard how the LORD dried up the water of the Red Sea in front of you when you left Egypt. We've also heard what you did to Sihon and Og, the two kings of the Amorites, who ruled east of the Jordan River. We've heard how you destroyed them for the LORD.* [11]*When we heard about it, we lost heart. There was no courage left in any of us because of you. The LORD your God is the God of heaven and earth. (Joshua 2:10–11)*

Our God is long-suffering toward sinful humankind *(Psalm 103:8)*, yet even in the midst of His patience, "The Lord isn't slow to do what he promised, as some people think. Rather, he is patient for your sake. He doesn't want to destroy anyone but wants all people to have an opportunity to turn to him and change the way they think and act" *(2 Peter 3:9)*.

9:23–24 ***[23]Can't God also reveal the riches of his glory to people who are objects of his mercy and who he had already prepared for glory? [24]This is what God did for us whom he called—whether we are Jews or not.***

God shows His glory not only in His wrath but also in His mercy, both to Jews and Gentiles. Believers should be very thankful that they are beneficiaries of God's wonderful salvation. In bestowing the gift of salvation on those who should seemingly be the recipients of His wrath, He shows how rich and wonderful His mercy really is. Not only do we experience the glorious mercy of God, but we also receive a share in His glory. He calls those whom He has already prepared to receive the riches of His mercy. "*[4]Before the creation of the world, he chose us through Christ to be holy and perfect in his presence. [5]Because of his love he had already decided to adopt us through Jesus Christ. He freely chose to do this*" *(Ephesians 1:4–5).*

9:25–26 ***[25]As God says in Hosea: "Those who are not my people I will call my people. Those who are not loved I will call my loved ones. [26]Wherever they were told, 'You are not my people,' they will be called children of the living God."***

There will come a day when all true Israel, composed of believing people from all nations, will call upon the name of the Lord. The phrase "my people" is used simply to represent the entire congregation of the redeemed, both Jews and Gentiles, who are the beneficiaries of God's matchless mercy and kindness. It includes those who are the legitimate descendents of Israel who have been redeemed and those who have been grafted into God's chosen people, the cultivated tree described in Romans 11:17 and 24. In that day, His people will be His beloved and live in His eternal home.

Paul quoted the prophet Hosea, who proclaimed this word from the Lord:

> *I will plant my people in the land.*
> *Those who are not loved I will call my loved ones.*

Those who are not my people, I will call my people.
Then they will say, "You are our God!" (Hosea 2:23)

Paul was affirming that God is now in the process of fulfilling His purpose as He draws people from all the nations of the earth into the citizenship of His kingdom. When everything is fulfilled completely, all nations will be drawn to the throne of God to celebrate the salvation that He has given them. This was foretold by the apostle John in a beautiful picture that unfolds in Revelation chapter seven, showing "[9]a large crowd from every nation, tribe, people, and language . . . [10]crying out in a loud voice: 'Salvation belongs to our God, who sits on the throne, and to the lamb!'" *(Revelation 7:9–10)*.

***9:27–28** [27]Isaiah also says about Israel: "Although the descendants of Israel are as numerous as the grains of sand on the seashore, only a few will be saved. [28]The Lord will carry out his sentence on the land, completely and decisively."*

In fulfilling His promise to Abraham, the people of Israel became so numerous that they could not be counted. Quoting the prophet Isaiah, Paul said that although there would be countless descendants, only a few would be saved *(Isaiah 10:21–23)*.

Jesus declared, "Many are invited, but few of those are chosen to stay" *(Matthew 22:14)*. This was true of Israel, and it is true in the church today. Many call themselves Christians but want to go their own way. "[13]*Enter through the narrow gate because the gate and road that lead to destruction are wide. Many enter through the wide gate.* [14]*But the narrow gate and the road that lead to life are full of trouble. Only a few people find the narrow gate*" *(Matthew 7:13–14)*.

God's judgment on the earth will be quick and decisive. In His perfect time He will accomplish His plan *(Psalm 9:8 and 1 Thessalonians 5:3)*. The Amplified New Testament translates the full impact of God's swift judgment: "For the Lord will execute His sentence upon the earth [He will conclude and close His account with men completely and without delay], rigorously cutting it short in His justice" *(Romans 9:28,* AMP*)*.

Notes/Applications

The apostle Paul contended that God's approval of us is based upon faith, yet that even this faith is a gift dispensed from the hand of God. Almighty God in His benevolence, wisdom, and perfection has seen fit to rescue us from dishonor, from the road to destruction.

And so, the rock that trips has become our sure foundation. The rock that offends has become our confidence. The rock that confounds has become our peace.

We who trust Him have glimpsed the truth of our disparity. We have emerged from the dark waters of death and have been made forever clean, never ashamed, and we realize that it is He Who has accomplished this for us:

Hail, sovereign love that first began,
The scheme to rescue fallen man;
Hail matchless free eternal grace,
That gave my soul a hiding place.

Against the God who rules the sky,
I fought with hand uplifted high,
Despised the mention of His grace,
Too proud to seek a hiding place.

Enwrapped in thick Egyptian night,
And fond of darkness more than light,
Madly I ran the sinful race,
Secure without a hiding place.

But thus th' eternal counsel ran,
"Almighty Love, arrest that man!"
I felt the arrows of distress,
And found I had no hiding place.

Indignant justice stood in view,
To Sinai's fiery mount I flew,
But Justice cried with frowning face,
"This mountain is no hiding place!"

Ere long a heavenly voice I heard,
And Mercy's angel form appeared.
Who led me on with gentle pace,
To Jesus Christ, my hiding place.

On Him Almighty vengeance fell,
That must have sunk a world to hell;
He bore it for a chosen race,
And thus became their hiding place.

Should storms of sevenfold vengeance roll,
And shake this earth from pole to pole;
No flaming bolt could daunt my face,
For Jesus is my hiding place.

A few more rolling suns at most,
Shall land me safe on Heaven's coast.
There I shall sing the song of grace,
To Jesus Christ, my hiding place![3]

Romans 9:29–33

9:29 ***This is what Isaiah predicted: "If the Lord of Armies hadn't left us some descendants, we would have been like Sodom and Gomorrah."***

This quote from Isaiah 1:9 reminds us that no one would be spared from judgment without the mercy of God. Through the prophets, God warned the ancients often of their sins and His coming judgment. They deserved to be destroyed like Sodom and Gomorrah. If not for God's sovereign plan to extend His mercy rather than His judgment, Israel's disobedience would have caused the nation's total destruction. "[21]*The reason I can still find hope is that I keep this one thing in mind:* [22]*the* LORD*'s mercy. We were not completely wiped out. His compassion is never limited.* [23]*It is new every morning. His faithfulness is great" (Lamentations 3:21–23).*

Our God is often portrayed as the "Lord of Hosts" or "Lord of Armies" with unlimited power. Sodom and Gomorrah were completely destroyed because they defied the "Lord of Armies." No one escaped except for Lot and his family—brought out by God's grace alone. "[24]*Then the* LORD *made burning sulfur and fire rain out of heaven on Sodom and Gomorrah.* [25]*He destroyed those cities, the whole plain, all who lived in the cities, and whatever grew on the ground" (Genesis 19:24–25).*

In His mercy, God did not treat Israel as He treated Sodom and Gomorrah. By His own counsel, He retained a believing "remnant" in Israel so that they continued as a people. Without His grace, they would have been obliterated.

9:30–31 [30]***So what can we say? We can say that non-Jewish people who were not trying to gain God's approval won his approval, an approval based on faith.*** [31]***The people of Israel tried to gain God's approval by obeying Moses' Teachings, but they did not reach their goal.***

Throughout his life as a prophet, Isaiah brought God's word of hope for those who would repent and believe, and God's warning of judgment for continued rebellion and unbelief. He foretold God's gracious response to the Gentiles who believed even though they had not been seeking Him.

> [1]*I was ready to answer those who didn't ask. I was found by those who weren't looking for me. I said, "Here I am! Here I am!" to a nation that didn't worship me.* [2]*I stretched out my hands all day long to stubborn people. They chose to go the wrong direction. They followed their own plans. (Isaiah 65:1–2)*

The Gentiles were no more holy or unholy than Israel, but now they were receiving God's approval by faith and not by keeping the law. In contrast, the people of Israel were continuing to seek His approval by their own futile efforts and by trying to keep the law. The good news is that all who trust in Jesus Christ receive salvation as God's gift, whether Jew or Gentile. Nevertheless, neither Jew nor Gentile can receive this salvation by their own works, no matter how seemingly impressive they are.

This good news was preached to Abraham and promised to the world. "*Scripture saw ahead of time that God would give his approval to non-Jewish people who have faith. So Scripture announced the Good News to Abraham ahead of time when it said, 'Through you all the people of the world will be blessed*'" (Galatians 3:8). Believers throughout history have been justified by faith alone: "No one receives God's approval by obeying the law's standards since, 'The person who has God's approval will live because of faith'" *(Galatians 3:11)*.

9:32 *Why? They didn't rely on faith to gain God's approval, but they relied on their own efforts. They stumbled over the rock that trips people.*

In their zeal for the law, the Jews forgot the Lawgiver. They missed the true meaning of the opening phrase of the Ten Commandments: "I am the LORD your God, who brought you out of slavery in Egypt"

(Exodus 20:2). They missed the essence of the law: "Love the LORD your God with all your heart, with all your soul, and with all your strength" *(Deuteronomy 6:5; Deuteronomy 30:6;* and *Matthew 22:37)*. This was intended to be the basis for their obedience to the law, but they made the law their primary way of seeking God's approval.

The law, which Paul said in Galatians was meant to be a guardian to lead to Christ *(Galatians 3:24)*, became a rock that the people stumbled over *(1 Corinthians 1:23)*. Why does it offend? God has given a command to live by faith *(Habakkuk 2:4)*, but people, by nature, want to earn everything. It is just too simple to "have faith," to just "believe." People by nature are unwilling to trust God and follow His arrangement for salvation. Therefore, the Jews, receivers of the law and God's chosen people, stumbled over this truth. "[13]*Remember that the LORD of Armies is holy. He is the one you should fear and the one you should be terrified of.* [14]*He will be a place of safety for you. But he will be a rock that makes people trip and a stumbling block for both kingdoms of Israel*" *(Isaiah 8:13–14)*.

9:33 ***As Scripture says, "I am placing a rock in Zion that people trip over, a large rock that people find offensive. Whoever believes in him will not be ashamed."***

Here Paul quoted from Isaiah 28:16: "This is what the Almighty LORD says: I am going to lay a rock in Zion, a rock that has been tested, a precious cornerstone, a solid foundation. Whoever believes in him will not worry." God gave to Zion His own Son, Who is the Messiah. He is the stone that the builders rejected. "*The stone that the builders rejected has become the cornerstone*" *(Psalm 118:22)*. This is an indisputable principle that explains how so many people respond to the good news of Jesus Christ.

The apostle Peter likewise affirmed this principle:

> [6]*That is why Scripture says, "I am laying a chosen and precious cornerstone in Zion, and the person who believes in him will never be ashamed."* [7]*This honor belongs to those who believe. But to those*

> *who don't believe: "The stone that the builders rejected has become the cornerstone, [8]a stone that people trip over, a large rock that people find offensive." The people tripped over the word because they refused to believe it. Therefore, this is how they ended up.* (1 Peter 2:6–8)

Once believers are established on the firm foundation of faith, Jesus Christ becomes their certain hope so that they embrace everything that they receive from the Lord. Therefore, they are the happy witnesses to God's salvation, and they are never again ashamed of Jesus Christ. "[2]*I trust you, O my God. Do not let me be put to shame. Do not let my enemies triumph over me. [3]No one who waits for you will ever be put to shame, but all who are unfaithful will be put to shame" (Psalm 25:2–3)*. Regardless of difficulties and trials, believers can never be shaken from the faith that God has instilled in them. "*For this reason I suffer as I do. However, I'm not ashamed. I know whom I trust. I'm convinced that he is able to protect what he had entrusted to me until that day" (2 Timothy 1:12)*.

Notes/Applications

Jesus Christ is the cornerstone that functions both as the foundation of faith for those who believe and as a stumbling block to those who do not believe. To some people, the Lord Jesus Christ is offensive. The very idea that a person would have to die in order to save people is offensive to their intellect. It is even more offensive to many people to be told that they need to be saved from anything. They believe that they don't need a Savior because they really do not think that they have done anything that bad. However, those who have been redeemed through the regenerating work of the Holy Spirit humbly rejoice that Jesus has saved them. Jesus becomes their most precious friend. He becomes the solid foundation for their lives. Jesus described it this way: "[24]Therefore, everyone who hears what I say and obeys it will be like a wise person who built a house on rock. [25]Rain poured, and floods came. Winds blew and beat against that house. But it did not collapse, because its foundation was on rock" *(Matthew 7:24–25)*.

Christ is the stumbling stone because people must, against the grain of their own sinful nature, acknowledge their total depravity and their desperate need for the Savior. This is a rock of offense for most people because they cannot accept that they can do nothing to save themselves and that salvation is attained solely by God's grace.

ROMANS 10

Romans 10:1–8

10:1 ***Brothers and sisters, my heart's desire and prayer to God on behalf of the Jewish people is that they would be saved.***

Paul loved his people, the Jews, and prayed earnestly that they would be saved. In chapter nine, he expressed the full depth of his love: "I wish I could be condemned and cut off from Christ for the sake of others who, like me, are Jewish by birth" *(Romans 9:3)*. Even though Paul was called by God to be the Apostle to the Gentiles, he never lost his deep love for his own people. He even opened this letter to the Romans with the point that the good news was for the Jews first *and also* for the Gentiles *(Romans 1:16)*.

10:2 ***I can assure you that they are deeply devoted to God, but they are misguided.***

Paul's own history served as a good example of a Jew who was deeply devoted to God but was desperately misguided in his understanding of the messianic hope. In Philippians chapter three, he indicated that he was a Pharisee, "a pure-blooded Hebrew." Note how he described his own intense devotion: "When it comes to being enthusiastic, I was a persecutor of the church. When it comes to winning God's approval by keeping Jewish laws, I was perfect" *(Philippians 3:6)*. Clearly, he gave his fellow Jews credit for their religious fervor.

Although the Jewish people were sincere, they were misguided. In observing the laws of Moses and the temple rituals, they had lost sight of the more important matters of the law—love, justice, mercy—and especially their longing for the Messiah. Again, Paul's own experience is helpful:

> [13]*You heard about the way I once lived when I followed the Jewish religion. You heard how I violently persecuted God's church and tried to destroy it.* [14]*You also heard how I was far ahead of other Jews in my age group in following the Jewish religion. I had become that fanatical for the traditions of my ancestors. (Galatians 1:13–14)*

Then he gave this simple testimony: "But God, who appointed me before I was born and who called me by his kindness, was pleased to show me his Son" *(Galatians 1:15–16)*.

10:3 They don't understand how to receive God's approval. So they try to set up their own way to get it, and they have not accepted God's way for receiving his approval.

There is only one way to receive God's approval—through His Son, Jesus Christ *(John 14:6)*. This is the clear teaching of the Gospels and the Epistles. "*God had Christ, who was sinless, take our sin so that we might receive God's approval through him*" *(2 Corinthians 5:21)*. God will not receive us on the basis of anything we have done or can do because we all are sinners and unable to meet His standard of perfect obedience.

Contrary to God's way for receiving His approval, the Jewish people of Paul's day typify religious people everywhere who strive through their good deeds to merit God's approval. They obey the moral law and certain religious rites that they hope God will accept.

No matter how much religious fervor they bring to these rituals, their knowledge of God is insufficient to establish a lasting relationship with Him. Unredeemed people will always establish what they believe to be their own, superior knowledge over the simplicity of the good news, for it has been stated: "Man's righteousness is that which man has evolved since he turned away in rebellion against God. Man did so in pursuit of the knowledge that the Devil had promised."[1]

10:4 *Christ is the fulfillment of Moses' Teachings so that everyone who has faith may receive God's approval.*

Jesus was the fulfillment of the Old Testament prophecies; He was sent by God to bring salvation and reconciliation. When Adam and Eve were created, they lived in perfect harmony with their Creator and were commanded to obey His directives. When they failed, sin came upon all humankind. Jesus Christ, the second Adam, kept the law perfectly and died to redeem His people from the curse of the law. In so doing, He fulfilled the just requirements of God, accepting the penalty for all sin. Thus, people who had no hope of keeping the law can be restored to a right relationship with their Creator through accepting Christ's sacrifice on their behalf. This is the good news that Paul preached in the synagogue at Antioch near Pisidia on his first missionary journey. "[38]*So, brothers, I'm telling you that through Jesus your sins can be forgiven. Sins kept you from receiving God's approval through Moses' Teachings.* [39]*However, everyone who believes in Jesus receives God's approval" (Acts 13:38–39).*

Christ was the consummation of God's plan as it had been expressed throughout Israel's history—through Moses' teachings and the writings of the prophets. All who trust in Him as their only way to salvation are placed in right standing before the eternal God. According to Isaiah 53:6, "the LORD has laid all our sins on him." Through the death and resurrection of Jesus Christ, our sins have been laid on Him and His righteousness has been given to us.

***10:5** Moses writes about receiving God's approval by following his laws. He says, "The person who obeys laws will live because of the laws he obeys."*

Perfect obedience to God's laws is the only way of "earning" His approval *(Leviticus 18:2, 4–5)*. The problem is that we are sinners by nature and fall far short of God's standard of perfection. Therefore, this standard is impossible to achieve; God sets the standard to illustrate our desperate need for His grace. *"Not one person can have God's approval by following Moses' Teachings. Moses' Teachings show what sin is" (Romans 3:20)*.

***10:6–7** [6]However, Scripture says about God's approval which is based on faith, "Don't ask yourself who will go up to heaven," (that is, to bring Christ down). [7]"Don't ask who will go down into the depths," (that is, to bring Christ back from the dead).*

This quotation is taken from Deuteronomy chapter thirty in which Moses focused upon the necessity of faith in true obedience to God's law. The context of the verses quoted is that God's words must be in our mouths and hearts so that we might correctly interpret and obey them.

> *[11]This command I'm giving you today isn't too hard for you or beyond your reach. [12]It's not in heaven. You don't have to ask, "Who will go to heaven to get this command for us so that we can hear it and obey it?" [13]This command isn't on the other side of the sea. You don't have to ask, "Who will cross the sea to get it for us so that we can hear it and obey it?" [14]No, these words are very near you. They're in your mouth and in your heart so that you will obey them. (Deuteronomy 30:11–14)*

It is helpful to note the contrast between verse five, which speaks of God's approval based on keeping the law, and verse six, which presents God's approval based on faith. This Deuteronomy reference focuses on the deep meaning of the law not just as a standard of righteousness but as a reflection of God. This is not uncommon in Deuteronomy. Whereas chapter five repeats the Ten Commandments as given in Exodus twenty, chapter six presents the overarching meaning of the law: "[4]Listen, Israel: The LORD is our God. The LORD is the only God. [5]Love the LORD your God with all your heart, with all your soul, and with all your strength" *(Deuteronomy 6:4–5)*.

No one can "bring Christ down" from heaven. The Father sent Him from heaven according to His own purpose and timing.

> *The Word became human and lived among us. We saw his glory. It was the glory that the Father shares with his only Son, a glory full of kindness and truth. (John 1:14)*

> *I haven't come from heaven to do what I want to do. I've come to do what the one who sent me wants me to do. (John 6:38)*

God sent His Son not only to live among us but to die for our sins. Then He brought Him back to life so that we can have eternal life through Him. By "[bringing] Christ back from the dead," God gave the Lord Jesus Christ complete jurisdiction over death and life *(1 Peter 3:18, 22)*.

***10:8** However, what else does it say? "This message is near you. It's in your mouth and in your heart." This is the message of faith that we spread.*

In essence, Paul was saying that God's approval-based faith is not really difficult. The argument that God's ways are impossible to achieve is shattered. Because God sent His Son from heaven and raised Him from the dead, people do not have to go looking all over the place for God's salvation. God has brought it to people in such a way that they can understand very well what God expects. In fact, the message is so near to them that God has placed it in people's hearts *(Jeremiah 31:31–34)*.

Notes/Applications

Paul powerfully expressed his deep, enduring love for his fellow Jews. He in no way compromised his message that Jesus Christ remained their only hope of salvation but rather showed empathy for their misguided zeal.

This does not nullify the importance of obeying God's law, even for Christians today. The early apostles took their stand for God, declaring "we must obey God rather than people" *(Acts 5:29)*. Obedience to God's law is never the grounds for our salvation, but it has temporal benefits of order and peace in our lives. Having been saved by God's grace, we are enabled to walk in obedience to His law. *"God has made us what we are. He has created us in Christ Jesus to live lives filled with good works that he has prepared for us to do" (Ephesians 2:10)*.

We may be guided by Paul's attitude and example as we relate to unbelieving relatives and friends. We must not forget that we once found ourselves in the very same position before God. While it is important that we demonstrate the sincerity of our beliefs, it is also crucially important that we clearly convey the substance of our beliefs—that righteousness is not attained by our devotion to living according to God's standards, but that living according to God's standards is the evidence of the righteousness we have attained through His grace. Our zeal for the Lord must be expressed in loving concern for them, but the message must never be misrepresented: "God's approval...is based on faith" *(Romans 6:6)*.

Romans 10:9–15

10:9 If you declare that Jesus is Lord, and believe that God brought him back to life, you will be saved.

This is the essence of the word of faith Paul proclaimed: to profess "Jesus is Lord" and believe that God has raised Him from the dead. This simple profession of faith affirms that we are children of God. When the Philippian jailer asked Paul what he needed to do to be saved, Paul replied, "Believe in the Lord Jesus, and you and your family will be saved" *(Acts 16:31)*.

Genuine believers will confess with their mouths what has miraculously taken place in their hearts. This good news is presented simply in 1 Corinthians 15:3–4: "[3]Christ died to take away our sins as the Scriptures predicted. [4]He was placed in a tomb. He was brought back to life on the third day as the Scriptures predicted." By confessing Jesus as Lord as the essential tenet of our salvation, we acknowledge His sovereignty in our lives. Our only hope for salvation is in Him. "*Through him you believe in God who brought Christ back to life and gave him glory. So your faith and confidence are in God*" *(1 Peter 1:21)*.

10:10 By believing you receive God's approval, and by declaring your faith you are saved.

God's approval is received by believing in the Lord Jesus, the Son of the living God. This is not merely an intellectual assent, but a heart response to the mighty work of God in us. "[28]*Then they asked him, 'What must we do to do the works God requires?'* [29]*Jesus answered, 'The work of God is this: to believe in the one he has sent'*" *(John 6:28–29, NIV)*.

When we profess with our mouths that Jesus is Lord, the Holy Spirit dwells within us. "*Does the Spirit of the one who brought Jesus back to life live in you? Then the one who brought Christ back to life will also make your mortal bodies alive by his Spirit who lives in you*" *(Romans*

8:11). This cannot be explained merely on an intellectual level. It is a work of God's grace, which transcends the law and confounds the human mind *(John 1:17)*. It is the work of God's Spirit in our hearts, which refers to our whole inner being. It enables us to fulfill the great commandment to "love the Lord your God with all your heart, with all your soul, with all your mind, and with all your strength" *(Mark 12:30)*.

10:11 ***Scripture says, "Whoever believes in him will not be ashamed."***

As he did in Romans 9:33, Paul again quoted from Isaiah: "This is what the Almighty LORD says: I am going to lay a rock in Zion, a rock that has been tested, a precious cornerstone, a solid foundation. Whoever believes in him will not worry" *(Isaiah 28:16)*. The firm foundation for our faith is the Lord Himself. In 1 Corinthians 3:11, Paul said, "No one can lay any other foundation than the one that is already laid, and that foundation is Jesus Christ." In 1 Peter 2:6, the apostle Peter uses this same verse from Isaiah as referring to Christ: "This is why Scripture says, 'I am laying a chosen and precious cornerstone in Zion, and the person who believes in him will never be ashamed.'" All who have been genuinely redeemed have nothing to be ashamed of before the Lord.

10:12 ***There is no difference between Jews and Greeks. They all have the same Lord, who gives his riches to everyone who calls on him.***

Once people are redeemed, they enter the protection of Christ's kingdom. As such, their primary citizenship is in that kingdom and their primary allegiance belongs to the King. Under His kind providence, national distinctions fade into the background, erasing normally held prejudices. To remind his readers of this new life, Paul restated what he had said before in chapters one and three:

> [22]*Everyone who believes has God's approval through faith in Jesus Christ. There is no difference between people.* [23]*Because all people have sinned, they have fallen short of God's glory.* [24]*They receive God's approval freely by an act of his kindness through the price Christ Jesus paid to set us free from sin. (Romans 3:22–24)*

10:13 ***So then, "Whoever calls on the name of the Lord will be saved."***

This promise is quoted from Joel 2:32. In his sermon at Pentecost, the apostle Peter quoted Joel 2:28–32, concluding with this same promise. Joel's prophecy spoke of that historic day when God would pour out His Spirit on everyone, and the risen Lord was proclaimed as the promised Messiah.

There is no higher name on earth to which we can appeal for deliverance from the consequences of our sin. This was the message that consumed the energy and passions of the apostles *(Acts 4:10–12)*.

10:14 ***But how can people call on him if they have not believed in him? How can they believe in him if they have not heard his message? How can they hear if no one tells the Good News?***

Unbelievers cannot appeal to God for their salvation if they do not believe in Him. They will have a hard time knowing what God expects of them if they never hear the message. As believers, it is our duty to proclaim the message of salvation to those who have not heard. This is the sacred commission that Jesus has laid on all who, drawn by the Father, come to Him. This was the sum and substance of His command in what is called the great commission. "*Wherever you go, make disciples of all nations: Baptize them in the name of the Father, and of the Son, and of the Holy Spirit. Teach them to do everything I have commanded you*" *(Matthew 28:19–20)*.

Commenting on Romans 10:14, R. C. Sproul says:

> The top priority enterprise for the Christian church is the preaching of the gospel of Jesus Christ, because people cannot believe or even hear about Jesus unless Jesus is preached . . . Not every Christian is responsible to go to the mission field, and not every Christian is called to be a preacher. But the body of Christ has the responsibility to send preachers and teachers and missionaries into the world.[2]

***10:15** How can people tell the Good News if no one sends them? As Scripture says, "How beautiful are the feet of the messengers who announce the Good News."*

Sends as used in this verse connotes a commission, as one who is sent with authority and with a specific purpose.[3] This projects the idea of being sent by God as in Acts 13:2: "While they were worshiping the Lord and fasting, the Holy Spirit said, 'Set Barnabas and Saul apart for me. I want them to do the work for which I called them'" *(Acts 13:2)*.

The individual is charged with heeding the message of the gospel. Believers are appointed to the witness and proclamation of the gospel. Here, Paul said that the church is commissioned to set apart designated messengers for specific tasks related to the proclamation of the gospel. However, these assigned tasks are not to be assumed under the guise of some organization, but under the direction of the Lord Who calls and equips His church for this sacred task. "[11]*He also gave apostles, prophets, missionaries, as well as pastors and teachers as gifts to his church.* [12]*Their purpose is to prepare God's people to serve and to build up the body of Christ" (Ephesians 4:11–12)*. While all believers are called to the work of the church, some leaders have been given a special commission to preach, teach, and equip God's people for ministry.

This verse concludes with a quotation from the prophet Isaiah: "How beautiful on the mountains are the feet of the messenger who announces the good news, 'All is well.' He brings the good news, announces salvation, and tells Zion that its God rules as king" *(Isaiah 52:7)*. This good news announces salvation—that God's Anointed One, His Messiah, has come in the person of His Son, the Lord Jesus Christ. Once He fulfilled the purpose for which His Father had sent Him into the world, He called and equipped His apostles to proclaim this good news to the whole world and then promised to return in power and glory to reign as king forever. Paul affirmed that both the message and the messenger are "beautiful."

Notes/Applications

The gospel message is very familiar to us as believers. However, a closer look at the context of Paul's presentation reveals an intentional progression in which the apostle presented a strategic case for faith in Christ.

First, in verse nine, Paul conveyed the vital aspect of lordship. Over the years, there has been the opinion that accepting Christ as Lord is a learned experience, a process that can only truly take place *after* one becomes a believer. The belief essentially classifies acceptance of Christ's lordship as part of the sanctification process. The argument is that after individuals are saved, they more fully appreciate what Christ has done and learn to make God first in their lives.

However, Paul clearly refuted such thinking throughout chapter eight of Romans, in which he taught that the Holy Spirit is the controlling influence over a believer's actions. While the sinful nature remains and the struggle persists, Paul clarified that understanding Christ's sacrifice for our sins and committing ourselves to full surrender to His will is an essential element in saving faith. We cannot accept the forgiveness Christ offers without turning our lives wholly over to Him. We cannot accept the remedy for our sinfulness through His sacrifice without sacrificing our own lives to His service.

Second, Paul also affirmed throughout this letter that we must understand that it is only through God's mercy that we have been saved and not the result of anything that we have done or can do to earn God's approval. To this point in his letter, Paul had declared time and again that there is no favor in God based in works. We are saved by "believing [we have] received God's approval." The action is explicitly in what God has done for us, not from what we have done for God.

Third, he stated that "whoever calls on the name of the Lord will be saved" *(verse 13)*. More than that, though, Paul preceded this statement by saying, "So, then." In so doing, he reaffirmed his prior message: It is only in accepting both the lordship and mercy of Christ that one can call upon the Lord to be saved. Without understanding the punishment that is deserved, one cannot understand God's mercy. Without understanding the enormity of the sacrifice that was made, one cannot understand that Christ must be made Lord over all. Only by understanding God's position as both righteous judge and merciful Savior can one be compelled to call out to Him for salvation.

Ironically, Scripture affirms that even a child can be saved and thus grasp the concept, even if in elementary understanding, of accepting Christ as both Lord and Savior, and yet Christ's lordship is many times the insurmountable stumbling block for many adults. *"But Jesus said, 'Let the little children come to Me, and do not forbid them; for of such is the kingdom of heaven'" (Matthew 19:14)*.

Being a child of God is no small thing to be taken lightly. Only with a complete appreciation for the remarkable redemption that is ours through God's grace are we properly motivated to "tell the Good News." Only when we are so motivated will we view spreading the gospel message not as a burden of the faith but as our greatest privilege and highest calling.

Romans 10:16–21

10:16 *But not everyone has believed the Good News. Isaiah asks, "Lord, who has believed our message?"*

Paul stated the obvious. Even the casual observer would have to admit that there are many people who do not believe this good news. This is affirmed throughout the entire biblical text. In Romans 3:11, Paul declared that "no one understands. No one searches for God." In John 6:44, Jesus said, "No one can come to Me unless the Father who sent Me draws him" (NKJV). In the early history of the Christian church, Luke commented, "Some of them were convinced by what he [Paul] said, but others continued to disbelieve" *(Acts 28:24)*. John's commentary on these words of Isaiah is especially piercing:

> [38]*In this way the words of the prophet Isaiah came true: "Lord, who has believed our message? To whom has the Lord's power been revealed?"* [39]*So the people couldn't believe because, as Isaiah also said,* [40]*"God blinded them and made them close-minded so that their eyes don't see and their minds don't understand. And they never turn to me for healing!" (John 12:38–40)*

10:17 *So faith comes from hearing the message, and the message that is heard is what Christ spoke.*

As we proclaim the good news, people hear, and some believe. We are not responsible for those who believe nor for those who do not; that is God's work alone, and it has nothing to do with the messenger's "effectiveness" *(1 Corinthians 1:18–24)*.

Those who are called by the Father receive Christ's words with gladness and, by His power, are transformed into the children of God. *"Here is another reason why we never stop thanking God: When you received God's word from us, you realized it wasn't the word of humans. Instead, you accepted it for what it really is—the word of God. This word is at work in you believers" (1 Thessalonians 2:13)*.

***10:18** But I ask, "Didn't they hear the message?" Certainly they did! "The voice of the messengers has gone out into the whole world and their words to the ends of the earth."*

God's revelation is seen and heard in all of His creation. People may reject what they see and hear, but that does not negate the truth *(Psalm 19:1–4)*.

People have no excuse as they stand before the holy God as their judge. Paul developed this theme in the first chapters of Romans, concluding that humankind is without excuse for neglecting God's natural revelation *(Romans 1:20 and Romans 2:15)*.

Here in chapter ten, Paul was speaking not of God's natural revelation in the evidence of His astounding creation but of the message concerning His redemptive salvation as the early church carried its good news throughout the known world. The voice of God's messengers has gone out through all the earth. "*The LORD will show his holy power to all the nations. All the ends of the earth will see the salvation of our God*" *(Isaiah 52:10)*.

***10:19** Again I ask, "Didn't Israel understand that message?" Moses was the first to say, "I will make you jealous of people who are not a nation. I will make you angry about a nation that doesn't understand."*

Paul asked a rhetorical question about the knowledge that God had given to Israel. From the time that God chose Abraham to father the Hebrew nation and through the terrible years of slavery in Egypt and their final rescue by Moses, God's appointed messenger, Israel had received the careful training and discipline that a father would use as he reared his children. Then, God gave the law to Moses and the Word of God began its long journey through the annals of Israel's history, establishing God's covenant relationship with His people. Yes, Israel surely did know God's Word. However, their history was marked by unfaithfulness, disobedience, and blatant rebellion. Therefore, in His righteous determination, God used heathen nations, Israel's enemies, to bring destruction on His chosen people *(Deuteronomy 32:15–21)*.

Long before their rebellion was obvious, Moses warned Israel of the penalty for their disobedience and the method by which God would destroy them. If they did not repent and turn from their disobedience and idolatry, He would make them jealous by blessing other nations with success and using those nations to punish them. This made His people angry because they were proud of their special favor with God, falsely assuming that they could do as they pleased while taking for granted His love, holiness, and righteous laws. They completely disregarded the mercy God had showered upon them.

10:20 ***Isaiah said very boldly, "I was found by those who weren't looking for me. I was revealed to those who weren't asking for me."***

Moses was not the only patriarch to prophesy of great judgment to come, so did the prophet Isaiah. He was called by God to warn Israel, but the people didn't want to hear his message:

> [1]*I was ready to answer those who didn't ask.*
> *I was found by those who weren't looking for me.*
> *I said, "Here I am! Here I am!"*
> *to a nation that didn't worship me.*
> [2]*I stretched out my hands all day long to a stubborn people.*
> *They chose to go the wrong direction.*
> *They followed their own plans.* (Isaiah 65:1–2)

Even though Israel had been chosen by God, their rejection of Him was well documented. Paul reminded his fellow Jews that they continued to reject the Word of God. He reminded them that they were still guilty of resisting God's repeated warnings. He sought to make them jealous by showing how their God was now reaching out to the Gentiles with the good news of deliverance through Jesus, their Messiah. The Gentiles were quick to understand and accept the message of Christ's salvation that Paul preached to them.

10:21 Then Isaiah said about Israel, "All day long I have stretched out my hands to disobedient and rebellious people."

This is the second verse of the above quotation from Isaiah sixty-five. This is a clear expression of the grace of God toward His rebellious people. This entire book could well be called "The Gospel According to Isaiah" for its frequent references to the Lord bringing salvation to His people. Chapter fifty-three is the well-known prophecy about the coming Messiah with the wonderful promise of redemption that He would bring.

Other prophets also warned Israel of coming judgment as a nation, but the people would not listen:

> *I have sent all my servants the prophets to you again and again. They said, "Turn from your evil ways, do what is right, and don't follow other gods in order to serve them. Then you will live in the land that I gave you and your ancestors." However, you refused to listen to me or obey me. (Jeremiah 35:15)*

Facing His crucifixion, Jesus condemned the Jewish leaders for their unbelief *(Matthew 23:29–32)*. After Jesus was crucified, resurrected, and returned to His Father in heaven, the leaders of the early church gave the same witness. In his sermon at Pentecost, the apostle Peter challenged his hearers: "All the people of Israel should know beyond a doubt that God made Jesus, whom you crucified, both Lord and Christ" *(Acts 2:36)*. As he gave his defense before the Jewish council just before his execution, Stephen accused them of continued treachery:

> [51]*How stubborn can you be? How can you be so heartless and disobedient? You're just like your ancestors. They always opposed the Holy Spirit, and so do you!* [52]*Was there ever a prophet your ancestors didn't persecute? They killed those who predicted that a man with God's approval would come. You have now become the people who betrayed and murdered that man. (Acts 7:51–52)*

If only Israel and all humankind would listen and obey the voice of God!

Notes/Applications

This chapter ends on a discouraging note, indicting Israel for chronic unbelief. Although the good news had been proclaimed again and again, the people stubbornly resisted the truth. In the midst of this widespread unbelief, some received the message by faith and received God's favor. The irony of Israel's history is characterized by their repeated rejection of God's messengers and their relentless persecution of the prophets whom God sent to warn them of His judgment. In Paul's day, the current religious leaders perpetuated this history.

In that day and in ours, God continues to reach out to His people, offering forgiveness and salvation. Jesus expressed His deep compassion for His rebellious people. "*Jerusalem, Jerusalem, you kill the prophets and stone to death those sent to you! How often I wanted to gather your children together the way a hen gathers her chicks under her wings! But you were not willing!*" *(Matthew 23:37)*. If He is so gracious to reach out to His people in spite of their sins, we should likewise continue to reach out to those around us.

The constant challenge to Christians today is to humble ourselves before God, pray, and repent from our own sins so that our people will be spared. "*If my people, who are called by my name, will humble themselves, pray, search for me, and turn from their evil ways, then I will hear their prayer from heaven, forgive their sins, and heal their country*" *(2 Chronicles 7:14)*. How often we evade these challenging words and keep blaming others for God's judgment! His righteous wrath remains on all unbelievers, but He seeks repentance among all people in order to bring healing to their nations. May Israel's bad example motivate us to face our sins squarely and bring us to true repentance through His grace and forgiveness.

ROMANS 11

Romans 11:1–8

11:1 ***So I ask, "Has God rejected his people Israel?" That's unthinkable! Consider this. I'm an Israelite myself, a descendant of Abraham from the tribe of Benjamin.***

In view of their rejection of Christ, is God now finished with the Israelites? Absolutely not. Israel has always been a part of God's eternal plan of redemption, which was completely fulfilled in the Lord Jesus Christ, God's Messiah. God cannot forsake His own word spoken in earlier times: "For the sake of his great name, the LORD will not abandon his people, because the LORD wants to make you his people" *(1 Samuel 12:22)*. Even though the Hebrew people were decimated by the Roman emperor Titus when he destroyed Jerusalem in AD 70, Israel emerged again as a nation, returning to political independence in 1948. Presently, as in the past, there is a remnant of Jewish Christians around the world. God will never forsake Israel because He promised Abraham an everlasting people, and God always keeps His promises.

God's chosen people have been very disobedient throughout their history, and yet there has always been a remnant of genuine believers. Israel's continued presence as a nation depends only on God's promise, grace, and faithfulness.

Paul said that he was living proof that God's mercy was endless and Israel had not been cast away. Paul was the perfect example of a righteous Jew:

> [5]*I was circumcised on the eighth day. I'm a descendant of Israel. I'm from the tribe of Benjamin. I'm a pure-blooded Hebrew. When it comes to living up to standards, I was a Pharisee.* [6]*When it comes to being enthusiastic, I was a persecutor of the church. When it comes to winning God's approval by keeping Jewish laws, I was perfect. (Philippians 3:5–6)*

11:2–4 [2]***God has not rejected his people whom he knew long ago. Don't you know what Elijah says in the Scripture passage when he complains to God about Israel? He says,*** [3]***"Lord, they've killed your prophets and torn down your altars. I'm the only one left, and they're trying to take my life."*** [4]***But what was God's reply? God said, "I've kept 7,000 people for myself who have not knelt to worship Baal."***

Elijah, one of God's mightiest prophets during the time of King Ahab and Queen Jezebel, complained bitterly that he was the only prophet left in his time. This shows the depths of Israel's rebellion against God. Through God's power, Elijah had just claimed a great historic victory over the 450 prophets of Baal at Mount Carmel. Nevertheless, he felt very much alone afterward when Jezebel pronounced his death sentence. "[1]*Ahab told Jezebel everything Elijah had done, including how he had executed all the prophets [of Baal].* [2]*Then Jezebel sent a messenger to Elijah. She said, 'May the gods strike me dead if by this time tomorrow I don't take your life the way you took the lives of Baal's prophets'" (1 Kings 19:1–2)*. Elijah responded by praying, "LORD of Armies, I have eagerly served you. The Israelites have abandoned your promises, torn down your altars, and executed your prophets. I'm the only one left, and they're trying to take my life" *(1 Kings 19:10)*.

Jezebel's threat was real, and Elijah felt abandoned by God. He had seen God's mighty hand destroying the prophets of Baal, but now he was confronted by the wicked queen.

As Elijah fled from Jezebel's wrath, God told him to "go out and stand in front of the LORD on the mountain" *(1 Kings 19:11)*. After Elijah again cried out that he was the only prophet and his life was threatened, the Lord told him to return and anoint Jehu as king of Israel and Elisha as prophet to take his place, then assured him with these words: "I still have 7,000 people in Israel whose knees have not knelt to worship Baal and whose mouths have not kissed him" *(1 Kings 19:18)*.

Upon hearing Paul's explanation of how people were saved solely by God's grace and not by virtue of their Jewish heritage, there would certainly have been many questions racing through the minds of these Jewish believers in Rome.

In verse one, Paul posed what was likely the most prevalent concern—has God abandoned or rejected the Jews? Paul replied with an emphatic, *No!* Then as if to illustrate the point, he reminded his Jewish audience of the familiar example of Elijah in order to assure them that no matter how dire the situation might appear God always preserves a remnant of faithful followers. Though Israel had corporately rejected its messiah, God did not sweepingly reject His people but still preserved a remnant according to His grace, thereby keeping His plan and His promise intact.

DIG DEEPER: ***Israel's Rebellion and God's Endless Compassion***

In his great intercessory prayer, Nehemiah spoke profoundly of the depths of Israel's rebellion and the heights of God's mercy. Find out more by reading Nehemiah 9:26–31.

11:5 ***So, as there were then, there are now a few left that God has chosen by his kindness.***

Paul affirmed that there were some believers in Israel, chosen by the grace of God. Although a small number in relation to all the Jews, it was similar to God's chosen remnant throughout Jewish history. The main difference was that with the revelation of Jesus as the promised messiah, these Jews had become Christians. Since then, the number of believing Jews has always been small in comparison with the total Jewish population, just as the number of believing Gentiles is small in comparison to the great numbers of the Gentile nations.

11:6 ***If they were chosen by God's kindness, they weren't chosen because of anything they did. Otherwise, God's kindness wouldn't be kindness.***

God's kindness, demonstrated by His unmerited favor, is the result of His own volition and not because of anything we do. In fact, if a person could do anything to merit His favor, it would no longer be grace. All that God does in our salvation is by His grace, just as it was in the days of Moses and the Israelites *(Deuteronomy 9:4–5 and Joshua 24:13)*. Clearly, the Israelites received the land because of God's purpose, kindness, and grace and not because of their worth or works.

All believers have been called by God's grace according to His own purpose. "*God saved us and called us to be holy, not because of what we had done, but because of his own plan and kindness. Before the world began, God planned that Christ Jesus would show us God's kindness*" *(2 Timothy 1:9)*. The death of our Lord Jesus Christ would be useless if anyone could obtain righteousness by keeping the law. "*I don't reject God's kindness. If we receive God's approval by obeying laws, then Christ's death was pointless*" *(Galatians 2:21)*.

11:7–8 ***[7]So what does all this mean? It means that Israel has never achieved what it has been striving for. However, those whom God has chosen have achieved it. The minds of the rest of Israel were closed, [8]as Scripture says, "To this day God has given them a spirit of deep sleep. Their eyes don't see, and their ears don't hear!"***

Paul asked and answered the question of what this means. What Israel has not achieved by its own efforts, God's chosen ones have achieved through His kindness and grace. The Louw-Nida Greek Lexicon explains it this way: "What the people of Israel sought, this they did not experience, but the chosen ones did experience it."[1] The Jews sought God's approval by their own efforts. This was impossible because of sin, which was so evident in their rebellious history. The prophets constantly exposed the sinful hearts of the people and called them to repent and return to the Lord. As the people of Israel continued to reject God's call, God closed their minds and hardened their hearts.

The idea that the Lord closed His people's minds is hard for us to accept. We might not understand it, but we must trust the reliability and infallibility of God's Word. The fact of Israel's rebellion is abundantly clear, and the Jews have continued to reject their Messiah.

To add weight to his argument, Paul quoted the prophet Isaiah: "The LORD has poured out on you a spirit of deep sleep. He will shut your eyes. (Your eyes are the prophets.) He will cover your heads. (Your heads are the seers)" *(Isaiah 29:10)*. Much earlier in Israel's history, Moses called Israel to hear the word of the Lord:

> *[2]You've seen with your own eyes everything that the LORD did in Egypt to Pharaoh, to all his officials, and to his whole country. [3]You also saw those terrible plagues, those miraculous signs, and those spectacular, amazing things. [4]But to this day the LORD hasn't given you a mind that understands, eyes that see, or ears that hear. (Deuteronomy 29:2–4)*

Just as the blind cannot see and the deaf cannot hear, we cannot see or hear the things of God without His miraculous work of grace.

This shows the sovereign authority of Almighty God. From Moses' day to the present, God has shut the eyes and ears of His people. He "has given them a spirit of deep sleep" so that they have no real sense of their sinfulness or need of salvation. The phrase "deep sleep" is derived from a Greek word which conveys a sense of lethargy, "which renders their souls torpid, so insensible that they are not affected at all by the offer made them of salvation through the Messiah."[2] The Lord repeated this judgment through Jeremiah, one of Israel's greatest prophets: "[21]'Hear this, you stupid and senseless people! You have eyes, but you cannot see. You have ears, but you cannot hear. [22]Don't you fear me?' asks the LORD. 'Don't you tremble in my presence?'" *(Jeremiah 5:21–22)*. The apostles also affirmed the warnings of the prophets. *"These people have become close-minded and hard of hearing. They have shut their eyes so that their eyes never see. Their ears never hear. Their minds never understand. And they never turn to me for healing" (Acts 28:27)*.

Notes/Applications

God's ways and thoughts are so much higher than the most brilliant human mind can possibly comprehend, and yet, He chose to reveal Himself to us in spite of our limited capacity to understand His love, grace, and mercy. "[8]'My *thoughts are not your thoughts, and my ways are not your ways,' declares the* LORD. [9]*'Just as the heavens are higher than the earth, so my ways are higher than your ways, and my thoughts are higher than your thoughts'" (Isaiah 55:8–9)*. The only way we can know Him is by faith. Israel disobeyed the Lord's commands and suffered grievously under God's punishment. Instead of submitting wholly to God's covenant, they consistently questioned His wisdom and went their own way, interrupted only by brief periods of repentance and faith. However, even during times of Israel's greatest unbelief, God called a small remnant of faithful believers who walked in His ways.

This condition is not unlike that seen in many people in the church today who presume upon God's mercy and live as they please, even while being challenged by the preaching of the Scriptures.

Every Christian needs to be warned by the words of the prophets. All believers have a responsibility to hear and obey God. Like the apostles, we have been given eyes to see and ears to hear the good news. We also need to heed Jesus' exhortation to His disciples: "Let the person who has ears listen!" *(Matthew 11:15)*. God's chosen, both Jews and Gentiles, at all times must bow in humble adoration and thankfulness to the Lord. We tremble in His presence! As we understand the real truth that we are saved by His grace through faith, our hearts burst forth in praise and gratitude for His great salvation, and we long to live in humble obedience.

Romans 11:9–14

11:9–10 ***[9]And David says, "Let the table set for them become a trap and a net, a snare and a punishment for them. [10]Let their vision become clouded so that they cannot see. Let them carry back-breaking burdens forever."***

Paul continued his quotations from the storehouse of Old Testament Scriptures demonstrating that God's consistent judgment has followed Israel throughout its rebellious history. Here he quoted King David from Psalm 69:22–23: "[22]Let the table set for them become a trap and a snare for their friends. [23]Let their vision become clouded so that they cannot see. Let their thighs continually shake." Under the direction of the Holy Spirit, David also had observed the headstrong disobedience of God's people and realized that God would have to deal with their sin.

Paul thus drew on the resources of the Old Testament Scriptures to prove his point—the Jewish people repeatedly acted in rebellion against God rather than submitting to His precepts. Three hundred years before Isaiah, God pronounced His verdict on His own people, stating that their vision had become clouded so that they could not see.

***11:11** So I ask, "Has Israel stumbled so badly that it can't get up again?" That's unthinkable! By Israel's failure, salvation has come to people who are not Jewish to make the Jewish people jealous.*

By the use of this rhetorical question, Paul declared that Israel's fall was not permanent; a permanent fall would suggest that God had retracted His ancient promise to Abraham, Isaac, and Jacob. Nevertheless, Israel's rebellion and unfaithfulness did provide the occasion for non-Jewish people to find salvation. The Jews' rejection and persecution of the early Christian church led Paul and others to carry the gospel to those who were not Jews. In his ministry, Paul often experienced the anger and jealousy of the Jews as he proclaimed the good news of salvation through Jesus Christ. After teaching in the synagogue in Antioch, he confronted the Jewish opposition:

> [45]*When the Jews saw the crowds, they became very jealous. They used insulting language to contradict whatever Paul said.* [46]*Paul and Barnabas told them boldly, "We had to speak the word of God to you first. Since you reject the word and consider yourselves unworthy of everlasting life, we are now going to turn to people of other nations."* (Acts 13:45–46)

On the Sabbath following Paul's sermon in Antioch, almost the whole city came together to hear the Word of God. Paul's message concluded with the assurance that salvation for the Gentiles was in God's sovereign plan from the beginning:

> *"*[47]*The Lord gave us the following order: 'I have made you a light for the nations so that you would save people all over the world.'"* [48]*The people who were not Jews were pleased with what they heard and praised the Lord's word. Everyone who had been prepared for everlasting life believed.* (Acts 13:47–48)

In this way, God's promise to Abraham that He would call out a special people and that through Abraham "every nation on earth will be blessed" *(Genesis 12:3)* was fulfilled.

11:12 *The fall of the Jewish people made the world spiritually rich. Their failure made people who are not Jewish spiritually rich. So the inclusion of Jewish people will make the world even richer.*

As God brings salvation and blessings, He also uses falls and failures to fulfill His sovereign plan. This is a mystery that is difficult to understand, but God is in control and uses all for His greater glory. He continues to build His church from every nation of the earth. "*God wanted his people throughout the world to know the glorious riches of this mystery—which is Christ living in you, giving you the hope of glory*" *(Colossians 1:27)*. If Israel's failures bring riches to the rest of the world, how much greater will the world be blessed when the

Jewish people join the host of the redeemed. Isaiah chapters eleven and twelve describe that coming day. At some appointed time in the future, the Jewish people will also be included in the gathering of God's people out of all nations.

R. C. Sproul, renowned Bible scholar, addressed the wide variation of interpretation among Bible-believing Christians about the future of Israel:

> One of the great controversies among Christians is how we are to understand biblical prophecies of the future, with specific reference to the Jewish people. Does God have in his plan another chapter to be written for Israel as a nation, as a people? Is what is going on today in Palestine significant to biblical prophecy? Or is it just part of the normal passage of secular history? Some take the position that there is no more to be done of any special character with the Jewish people, other than the conversions of individuals from Judaism to Christianity. Others are convinced that the Christian church has become the new Israel, the spiritual Israel, and all biblical prophecies in the Old Testament and the New that refer to the future of Israel, find their fulfillment totally and exclusively in the Christian church. Still others are of the opinion that God indeed does plan a new redemptive work, specifically targeted at the Jews, and with a view to their restoration in the kingdom of God. Personally, I have been persuaded that God does intend to write another chapter for the Jewish people. I do think that what is happening in Palestine today is significant, and I have been persuaded that there will be a restoration of the Jewish people to faith in Christ before the end of the age.[3]

Regardless of anyone's interpretation, it is clear that God has a plan for Israel that He is working out for His glory and for the fulfillment of His calling to Abraham and his descendants.

11:13 ***Now, I speak to you who are not Jewish. As long as I am an apostle sent to people who are not Jewish, I bring honor to my ministry.***

Having focused on God's plan for Israel, here Paul addressed the Gentiles to whom he was specifically called to bring the good news. He testified to this calling when he spoke before King Agrippa:

> [13]*Your Majesty, at noon, while I was traveling, I saw a light that was brighter than the sun. The light came from the sky and shined around me and those who were with me.* [14]*All of us fell to the ground, and I heard a voice asking me in Hebrew, "Saul! Saul! Why are you persecuting me? It's hard for a mortal like you to resist God."* [15]*I asked, "Who are you, sir?" The Lord answered, "I am Jesus, the one you're persecuting.* [16]*Stand up! I have appeared to you for a reason. I'm appointing you to be a servant and witness of what you have seen and of what I will show you.* [17]*I will rescue you from the Jewish people and from the non-Jewish people to whom I am sending you.* [18]*You will open their eyes and turn them from darkness to light and from Satan's control to God's."* (Acts 26:13–18)

Paul was certain of his calling and humbly accepted the privilege of being an apostle to the Gentiles. "*I am the least of all God's people. Yet, God showed me his kindness by allowing me to spread the Good News of the immeasurable wealth of Christ to people who are not Jewish*" *(Ephesians 3:8)*. After some controversy among the early believers, his calling was affirmed in the first church council in Jerusalem as recorded in Acts chapter fifteen.

11:14 ***Perhaps I can make my people jealous and save some of them.***

Paul still loved his fellow Jews intensely and hoped that as he preached to the Gentiles he would cause some Jews to be envious of the salvation that the Gentiles received. When they saw how God bestowed His Spirit on the Gentiles, Paul prayed that the Jews, too, would repent and receive God's salvation. Even though he loved everyone, both Jew and Gentile, Paul had a special place in his heart for his own people *(1 Corinthians 9:19–22)*.

Notes/Applications

Almighty God is sovereign in His decisions, but no one knows the determinations that He makes. Therefore, Christians must follow Paul's example in witnessing to everyone and trusting Him for the results. As we proclaim the good news, our message is simply to invite others to Jesus. When the Holy Spirit is drawing people to Himself, we can be certain of their positive response.

Jesus' parable of the farmer is informative for our task. He told about the farmer planting seeds. Some fell by the road and were quickly devoured by the birds. Some fell on rocky soil and withered quickly. Some were planted among thornbushes, which choked them, but some were planted on good ground and produced a good crop. After telling this story, Jesus taught the disciples that this was a picture of His harvest. As His "farmers," we are to plant the seed of the Word faithfully, and the Lord will bring forth His harvest *(Luke 8:4–15)*. When Jesus sent seventy disciples on their first "short-term mission," He said, "The harvest is large, but the workers are few. So ask the Lord who gives this harvest to send workers to harvest his crops" *(Luke 10:2)*.

Our calling, as theirs, is to be faithful in spreading the Word. God will be faithful in bringing a great harvest for His glory.

Romans 11:15–21

11:15 ***If Israel's rejection means that the world has been brought back to God, what does Israel's acceptance mean? It means that Israel has come back to life.***

Even as Israel was set aside so that the door to Gentiles could be opened, how much more wonderful it will be when God's plan to restore His covenant people becomes a historical reality. At that time, Israel will also be granted the gift of eternal life. Out of the dust of their desolation and rebellion, the Lord will bring His people back to life, restoring the breath of life in them and bringing glory to His name. Just as Ezekiel prophesied over bones, and God gave them life *(Ezekiel 37:1–14)*, so Israel's ending will be greater than its beginning. That is the way that God has determined to bring Israel back from the dead.

11:16 ***If the first handful of dough is holy, the whole batch of dough is holy. If the root is holy, the branches are holy.***

Paul introduced an example from the Levitical law. The Hebrew people were instructed to bring an offering to the Lord at each harvest. This offering was designed to remind the people that they were to give God the first portion of the whole harvest that God had already given to them. This was a reminder that all things come from the hand of the Lord *(Numbers 15:17–21)*.

In this way, the "first handful" is only an initial sampling of the whole. This first part taken from the whole is true of the whole; if the offering is holy, the entire harvest is holy. Thus, every blessing that the Hebrew people received from the Lord was a representation of their position in the covenant. They were God's people set apart for His purposes.

When God chose Abraham, Isaac, Jacob, and the subsequent twelve tribes of Israel, He made them holy (that is, set apart by God for His purposes). They were not holy in themselves but only because God chose them. He made the patriarchs holy when He chose them and set them apart as His own. The Jews are God's chosen people through whom all the people of the earth have received blessing. They are "the root" as a result of God's sovereign choice, ordained to bring forth the branches, which came through His Son, their Messiah.

11:17 *But some of the olive branches have been broken off, and you, a wild olive branch, have been grafted in their place. You get your nourishment from the roots of the olive tree.*

The branches, planted by God, have grown from the root of Abraham and the patriarchs but are now broken off. When the Lord delivered Israel from slavery, He brought His vine out of Egypt *(Psalm 80:8–19)*. In Psalm eighty, Israel is portrayed as a vine that grows to cover the whole Middle East, but at the Lord's hand, the vine is cut down, burned, and destroyed. However, there is a cry for the Lord to come and rescue the vine, restore its strength, and give it life again. This imagery was a representation of the future plan that God pursued as He carefully guided humanity's rescue from the slavery of sin.

Even though the branches were broken off, the root was never touched. Even though Israel rebelled, God never changed His plan to redeem them. As God was unfolding His plan for humanity's salvation, He needed to prune those branches that failed to produce fruit.

> [16]*The LORD called you a large olive tree that has beautiful fruit to look at. He will set fire to you with a mighty storm, and your branches will be broken.* [17]*The LORD of Armies planted you. He has pronounced disaster on you. This is because of the evil things that Israel and Judah have done. (Jeremiah 11:16–17)*

The wild olive branch is the non-Jew who is grafted into the tree, whose holy root is Abraham. Only believing Jews and believing Gentiles are part of the true Israel. The divine root from whom Abraham and the patriarchs sprang is the Lord Jesus Christ, the only source of life for all believers. "*At that time the root of Jesse will stand as a banner for the people to gather around. The nations will come to him. His resting place will be glorious*" *(Isaiah 11:10)*.

***11:18* So don't brag about being better than the other branches. If you brag, remember that you don't support the root, the root supports you.**

Gentile believers should never gloat over the misfortune of the Hebrew people. It is only by God's grace that anyone is saved—Jew or Gentile. Salvation in Christ grows out of the faith that was given to Abraham, the father of all who believe *(Romans 4:16)*. "*If you belong to Christ, then you are Abraham's descendants and heirs, as God promised*" *(Galatians 3:29)*.

The branch, no matter how productive it may be, cannot produce without the nourishment it receives from the root.

> *[4]Live in me, and I will live in you. A branch cannot produce any fruit by itself. It has to stay attached to the vine. In the same way, you cannot produce fruit unless you live in me. [5]I am the vine. You are the branches. Those who live in me while I live in them will produce a lot of fruit. But you can't produce anything without me. (John 15:4–5)*

He is our life, and without Him, we can do nothing worthwhile for His kingdom.

***11:19–20* [19]"Well," you say, "Branches were cut off so that I could be grafted onto the tree." [20]That's right! They were broken off because they didn't believe, but you remain on the tree because you do believe. Don't feel arrogant, but be afraid.**

Some may have falsely assumed that some branches were pruned from the tree so that Gentile believers could be grafted onto the tree. However, there was no basis for this conceited attitude. The natural branches (the Jews) were not broken off to make room for the wild branches (the Gentiles). The Jews were broken off the vine because of their unbelief. There is plenty of room for all the branches that God has determined to be a part of His family tree. The Jews are not less deserving and the Gentiles more deserving. God loved the world, Jews and Gentiles alike, and He is no respecter of persons.

God resists a proud heart and desires a grateful spirit. "*God opposes arrogant people, but he is kind to humble people*" *(James 4:6)*. "*Be humbled by God's power so that when the right time comes he will honor you*" *(1 Peter 5:6)*. We often need to be reminded of the frightful consequences of unbelief. All believers must be aware of falling into the same attitude of disobedience to the Word of God. This possibility should bring about a healthy distrust of personal conceit and instead promote living in the intense fear of a holy and almighty God.

***11:21** If God didn't spare the natural branches, he won't spare you, either.*

God has a plan for His chosen Israel, which He calls "the apple of his eye" *(Zechariah 2:8)*. If God chose to break off some natural (Jewish) branches, He was still by no means obligated to graft in unnatural (Gentile) branches that persisted in unbelief. The proper response to God's mercy in Christ, therefore, should be reverential fear, not arrogance.

Notes/Applications

Paul permitted believers to boast in only one thing: "the cross of our Lord Jesus Christ" *(Galatians 6:14)*. All other bragging is self-centered and self-destructive. This was one of Israel's great snares and should serve as a stern warning to Gentile believers. Proverbs 16:18 warns that "pride precedes a disaster, and an arrogant attitude precedes a fall."

Believers should always remember that salvation is not through their worth or works, but only through the worthy Lamb of God Whose blood was shed to take away their sins. When we see the majesty of our Savior and all that He has done for us, we are humbled *(Ephesians 3:14–17)*.

When we are truly humbled before Almighty God and firmly rooted in Christ's love, we will be equipped to please Him in our lives. Our prayer will be: "Let your kingdom come. Let your will be done on earth as it is done in heaven" *(Matthew 6:10)*. All glory be to the Lord Jesus Christ, the Root of David!

Romans 11:22–27

***11:22** Look at how kind and how severe God can be. He is severe to those who fell, but kind to you if you continue to hold on to his kindness. Otherwise, you, too, will be cut off from the tree.*

We enjoy speaking of God's kindness, but we must also recognize His severity. God knows everything, even the very motivations and intentions of our hearts. Accordingly, He showers His kindness on those who have received His forgiveness and pronounces His judgment on those who are disobedient.

These words from Paul are a similar warning to Gentile believers about the same promises of God, Whose character never changes. In His eternal nature, He demonstrates justice as equally as He demonstrates His love and mercy. In the apostasy of the "last days," all Christians are exhorted to be faithful and warned about the perils of unfaithfulness *(Jude 17–21)*.

As God's people, we need to repent from our pride and continue to live under the ongoing benefits of His matchless goodness and mercy. Believers should never take Him for granted but should remember their calling in Jesus Christ. *"Remember how far you have fallen. Return to me and change the way you think and act, and do what you did at first. I will come to you and take your lamp stand from its place if you don't change" (Revelation 2:5)*.

Paul further explained that Gentile believers must likewise remain steadfast in their pursuit of Christlike behavior. Those who do not cling to the new nature that they profess to have received will likewise "be cut off from the tree." This should not be misunderstood as meaning that true believers could lose the salvation they have in Christ; such is clearly contrary to Scripture *(John 6:37–40* and *John 8:12)*. Rather, Paul was again pointing to the fact that the evidence of faith is not in people's words but in consistent obedience that demonstrates that their lives are controlled by the Holy Spirit *(Romans 8:13)*.

11:23 ***If Jewish people do not continue in their unbelief, they will be grafted onto the tree again, because God is able to do that.***

This statement is conditional. Although the minds of many Jews have been blinded, God is able to restore their former position on the tree only through faith in Christ *(Zechariah 12:10)*. When their faith is restored and they understand the extent of their former disobedience, they will be grafted again into the tree of life.

Paul referred to this blindness as a veil that must be removed for anyone to see God's revelation:

> [14]*Their minds became closed. In fact, to this day the same veil is still there when they read the Old Testament. It isn't removed, because only Christ can remove it.* [15]*Yet, even today, when they read the books of Moses, a veil covers their minds.* [16]*But whenever a person turns to the Lord, the veil is taken away.* (2 Corinthians 3:14–16)

11:24 ***In spite of the fact that you have been cut from a wild olive tree, you have been grafted onto a cultivated one. So wouldn't it be easier for these natural branches to be grafted onto the olive tree they belong to?***

Paul wanted the Gentile believers to understand that they were rebellious when God called them into His family. They were branches of a *wild* olive tree. However, they were grafted into God's *cultivated* tree, which consists of the entire body of Christ; it is composed of all children of God, both Jew and Gentile, who are heirs in Christ through faith:

> [11]*Remember that once you were not Jewish physically. Those who called themselves "the circumcised" because of what they had done to their bodies called you "the uncircumcised."* [12]*Also, at that time you were without Christ. You were excluded from citizenship in Israel, and the pledges God made in his promise were foreign to you. You had no hope and were in the world without God.* [13]*But*

now through Christ Jesus you, who were once far away, have been brought near by the blood of Christ. (Ephesians 2:11–13)

11:25 ***Brothers and sisters, I want you to understand this mystery so that you won't become arrogant. The minds of some Israelites have become closed until all of God's non-Jewish people are included.***

The way God works often remains a mystery to His human creatures. However, Paul understood this mystery and unveiled it to those who believe, trusting that their understanding of how God was working among Jews and Gentiles would remove any remnant of arrogance. The minds of some Jews (not all Jews) will remain blinded until God has brought all non-Jewish people whom He has chosen into the fold of His family *(Ephesians 3:2–6)*.

It is clear that the Gentiles were included in God's plan of salvation from the beginning. Israel was blessed with God's revelation, His holy commandments, and His promises to Abraham, yet Israel rebelled against Him time and time again. In rejecting Jesus as their Messiah, they were cut off from the tree, and the message of Christ's salvation was preached to the Gentiles; those who believed were grafted in. The state of the Jewish people will remain in the condition of unbelief until God has accomplished everything among the Gentiles that He has determined.

11:26–27 ***[26]In this way Israel as a whole will be saved, as Scripture says, "The Savior will come from Zion. He will remove godlessness from Jacob. [27]My promise to them will be fulfilled when I take away their sins."***

Paul assured Jewish believers that the day was coming when Israel would return to the Lord, when they would return to the Messiah whom they rejected for so long. Paul quoted from Isaiah 59:20–21:

"[20]Then a Savior will come to Zion, to those in Jacob who turn from rebellion," declares the LORD. "[21]This is my promise to them," says the LORD. "My Spirit, who is on you, and my words that I put in

> *your mouth will not leave you. They will be with your children and your grandchildren permanently," says the* LORD.

It is not clear from Scripture how and when this will be fulfilled, but it seems evident that God will remove Israel's blind disobedience and pour out His love on them, and there will be a great return to Christ.

In view of other scriptural teaching, this would suggest that Israel as a people will be delivered from the severe judgment of God that came with their national rejection of the Messiah. This deliverance will result in a major awakening of the Jewish people.

Notes/Applications

The consummation of God's promise to redeem His people is portrayed in the magnificent scene in Revelation chapter five. The four living creatures and twenty-four leaders bowed before the Lord Jesus Christ, the Lamb of God, and sang a new song:

> [9]*You are worthy to take the scroll, and to open its seals; for You were slain, and have redeemed us to God by Your blood out of every tribe and tongue and people and nation,* [10]*and have made us kings and priests to our God; and we shall reign on the earth. (Revelation 5:9–10,* NKJV*)*

These verses accurately portray the sovereign grace of God. Our salvation, from beginning to end, is His design and His gift. We are assured from Scripture that He has everything in control and works everything for His glory and our good. The glorious picture of the Lamb of God, Who was slain to redeem us to God from every tribe and tongue and people and nation by His blood, should motivate us to pray "Come, Lord Jesus!" *(Revelation 22:20)*. Because our sins were laid on Him and His righteousness placed on us, we will stand before Him filled with wonder and humble gratitude. The last verse of Charles Wesley's great hymn "Love Divine, All Loves Excelling" expresses this vividly:

Finish, then, Thy new creation;
Pure and spotless let us be.
Let us see Thy great salvation
Perfectly restored in Thee;
Changed from glory into glory,
Till in heaven we take our place,
Till we cast our crowns before Thee,
Lost in wonder, love, and praise.[4]

Romans 11:28–36

11:28 The Good News made the Jewish people enemies because of you. But by God's choice they are loved because of their ancestors.

The good news proclaimed by the apostles was offensive to the Jews as a people, and they became God's enemies. Their complex system of legalism and morality had blinded them and created a barrier between them and their Creator. The gift of salvation that He offered to them was the complete opposite of the system of "law-abiding" works they had developed. Nevertheless, this was part of God's plan to bring salvation to the Gentiles.

Israel became God's enemy, forcing Paul and other Christians out of Jewish regions to proclaim the good news of salvation to the Gentiles. Although the good news was then preached to and accepted by non-Jews, God did not forget His covenant with Abraham and his descendants. "[8]*But you are my servant Israel, Jacob, whom I have chosen, the descendant of Abraham, my dear friend.* [9]*I have taken you from the ends of the earth and called you from its most distant places. I said to you, 'You are my servant. I've chosen you; I haven't rejected you'*" *(Isaiah 41:8–9)*.

11:29 God never changes his mind when he gives gifts or when he calls someone.

God's word is trustworthy. He does not break His promises or revoke His gifts. "*God is not like people. He tells no lies. He is not like humans. He doesn't change his mind. When he says something, he does it. When he makes a promise, he keeps it*" *(Numbers 23:19)*. God never changes. "*For I am the LORD, I do not change; therefore you are not consumed, O sons of Jacob*" *(Malachi 3:6, NKJV)*.

Israel was chosen to be His people, not because of any goodness on the part of the people but because of His sovereign will. Thus, His promise to them is not dependent on their good or bad behavior but simply on the integrity of His word *(Deuteronomy 7:6–8)*.

11:30–31 ***[30]In the past, you disobeyed God. But now God has been merciful to you because of the disobedience of the Jewish people. [31]In the same way, the Jewish people have also disobeyed so that God may be merciful to them as he was to you.***

Before the good news was proclaimed to them, Gentile believers were as disobedient as God's chosen people. However, that did not prevent God from moving through the rejection of His covenant people in such a way that salvation and restoration were offered to the Gentiles. This means that God can also be merciful to the Jews in the same way.

Paul also affirmed this principle in his letter to the Ephesians:

> *[12]At that time you were without Christ. You were excluded from citizenship in Israel, and the pledges God made in his promise were foreign to you. You had no hope and were in the world without God. [13]But now through Christ Jesus you, who were once far away, have been brought near by the blood of Christ. (Ephesians 2:12–13)*

In Christ, all believers, both Gentile and Jew, are restored to God and comprise His church, having been purchased by His precious blood on Calvary. All believers are first-class citizens in God's kingdom and members of His family. We are all a necessary part of God's house, built on the foundation of the apostles and the prophets, with Christ as the cornerstone.

> *[19]That is why you are no longer foreigners and outsiders but citizens together with God's people and members of God's family. [20]You are built on the foundation of the apostles and prophets. Christ Jesus himself is the cornerstone. [21]In him all the parts of the building fit together and grow into a holy temple in the Lord. (Ephesians 2:19–21)*

11:32 ***God has placed all people into the prison of their own disobedience so that he could be merciful to all people.***

Everyone, Jews and Gentiles, are and always have been disobedient before holy God. From birth to death, humanity has consistently pursued its own purposes, avoided its Creator, disobeyed His precepts, and ignored any consideration of His goodness and compassion. No one is exempt from this sin-directed activity.

> [10]*As Scripture says, "Not one person has God's approval.* [11]*No one understands. No one searches for God."* (Romans 3:10–11)

> *Scripture states that the whole world is controlled by the power of sin. Therefore, a promise based on faith in Jesus Christ could be given to those who believe.* (Galatians 3:22)

By affirming the disobedience of all people everywhere, Paul likewise asserted God's mercy bestowed on all people everywhere. God's goodness is demonstrated by the death of His Son Jesus and expressed in His drawing us to Himself. Adam and Eve hid from God in the garden, and He sought them and showed His mercy (Genesis 3:15–21). We have been running from God ever since, but He seeks us out to save us. "*We have all strayed like sheep. Each one of us has turned to go his own way, and the LORD has laid all our sins on him*" (Isaiah 53:6).

11:33 *God's riches, wisdom, and knowledge are so deep that it is impossible to explain his decisions or to understand his ways.*

Chapters nine through eleven end with a doxology of praise to God for His infinite being. The depth and the richness of His wisdom and knowledge are beyond human comprehension. Why did God call Abraham and his descendants, Israel, as His chosen nation? Why were they then blinded and the Gentiles given the good news? Why are they to be restored? God Almighty is the sovereign Creator and Sustainer, and we cannot begin to understand His thoughts.

This theme is expressed often in Scripture. "*He does great things that we cannot understand and miracles that we cannot count*" (Job 5:9). His ways are dynamic, far beyond the wisest, smartest, and most intelligent people. "[7]*Can you discover God's hidden secrets,* or *are you able to find the Almighty's limits?* [8]*God's wisdom is higher than heaven. What can you do? It is deeper than the depths of hell. What can you know?* [9]*It is longer than the earth and wider than the sea*" (Job 11:7–9).

Our Lord is awesome. He works in ways that our minds cannot conceive. "*How spectacular are your works, O LORD! How very deep are your thoughts!*" *(Psalm 92:5)*. His decisions are incomprehensible. We can never arrive at a full understanding of the scope of His greatness, especially as it is expressed in His limitless mercy.

> *O LORD, your mercy reaches to the heavens, your faithfulness to the skies. (Psalm 36:5)*
>
> *You have done many miraculous things, O LORD my God. You have made many wonderful plans for us. No one compares to you! I will tell others about your miracles, which are more than I can count. (Psalm 40:5)*

11:34–35 ***[34]"Who knows how the Lord thinks? Who can become his adviser?" [35]Who gave the Lord something which the Lord must pay back?***

Paul asked these three rhetorical questions that express how unthinkable it is for us to consider that we could ever understand how He thinks or suppose that He needs our advice. Paul posed the same question in 1 Corinthians 2:16: "Who has known the mind of the Lord so that he can teach him?" Also, this quote from Isaiah forty asks several probing questions about humanity's credentials before God: "[13]Who has directed the Spirit of the LORD or instructed him as his adviser? [14]Whom did he consult? Who gave him understanding? Who taught him the right way? Who taught him knowledge? Who informed him about the way to understanding?" *(Isaiah 40:13–14)*. Isaiah replied with graphic clarity and included two fascinating statements. Regarding the collective power of humanity, he said, "The nations are like a drop in a bucket and are considered to be like dust on a scale" *(Isaiah 40:15)*. Regarding people, he said, "God is enthroned above the earth, and those who live on it are like grasshoppers" *(Isaiah 40:22)*.

God is the great I Am. He existed before time was created. He owns everything, so no one can offer Him anything that he does not already have. "[10]*Every creature in the forest, even the cattle on a thousand hills, is mine.* [11]*I know every bird in the mountains. Everything that moves in the fields is mine.* [12]*If I were hungry, I would not tell you, because the world and all that it contains are mine*" (Psalm 50:10–12). Our Lord is indebted to no one because He is sovereign over all. By Him, all things exist. He answers to no other being or power in the universe.

11:36 ***Everything is from him and by him and for him. Glory belongs to him forever! Amen!***

All that God does is accomplished for His glory. Barnhouse explains:

> In this brief passage, Paul smashes a number of philosophical idols. Matter is not eternal, because it is created; thus materialism is questioned. God created all things; thus mechanical evolution is put to rest. He sustains all things; thus purposeless evolution is set aside along with any other system that would deny that the world is held together by the active intervention of a transcendent, immanent God. All things are for Him; thus to hold the idea of a purposeless universe is shattered.[5]

Notes/Applications

In one of the great doxologies of Scripture, Paul concluded this chapter by directing the attention to two profound precepts that we must recognize. First, he asserted our limitations that prevent us from comprehending the nature and attributes of God. Second, he unabashedly extolled the glory and majesty of a sovereign God Who is without equal and Who authored and sustains His creation.

One day, His promise will be reality—we will join Him in a kingdom where we will praise Jesus Christ His Son for all eternity. Like Job, we must put our hands over our mouths in awe as we stand before the magnificence of His majesty *(Job 40:4)*. We must bow before Him in endless worship and praise, rejoicing that we live both now and forever in the light of His matchless presence. "[5]*Glory and power forever and ever belong to the one who loves us and has freed us from our sins by his blood* [6]*and has made us a kingdom, priests for God his Father. Amen" (Revelation 1:5–6)*.

ROMANS 12

Romans 12:1–8

***12:1** Brothers and sisters, in view of all we have just shared about God's compassion, I encourage you to offer your bodies as living sacrifices, dedicated to God and pleasing to him. This kind of worship is appropriate for you.*

Chapters nine through eleven revealed Paul's pausing to focus on God's provision for the apostle's Jewish kinsmen. In this chapter, he returned to the main thrust of his epistle, one that had reached a high point with the declaration that nothing can separate us from God's love in Christ *(Romans 8:38–39)*. Paul then began to apply powerfully the precepts portrayed in these earlier chapters to believer's lives.

Having laid the foundation of God's compassion in giving His only Son to die for sin, Paul encouraged believers to offer their bodies as living sacrifices, dedicated and pleasing to Him. *Encourage* is a Greek word that means "to ask for something earnestly and with propriety (earnestly)."[1] Paul did not simply encourage believers; he appealed to them intensely to present every aspect of their existence as a sacrifice to God. There can be no greater motivation to give God our whole lives than the great love and mercy we have received (*2 Corinthians 5:14–15*).

Offering our bodies as living sacrifices is received by God as an act of worship. This kind of response does not come naturally for anyone. Nevertheless, this was the thrust of Paul's appeal—that we should offer our most precious and coveted possession, which is ourselves. Christ's unique sacrifice on the cross covers all of our sins. Since He gave Himself to us so completely in dying for us and thereby eradicating sin's penalty, the only reasonable sacrifice that we can offer in response is to give Him ourselves completely—our time, our talents, our treasure, and so forth.

12:2 *Don't become like the people of this world. Instead, change the way you think. Then you will always be able to determine what God really wants—what is good, pleasing, and perfect.*

The world influences us to think and act like the world thinks and acts. The Greek word for this "squeezing process" conveys a resolve not to "conform to, or fashion [ourselves] according to" the ways of the world.[2] In fact, our word *scheme* comes from this Greek word, so we are warned not to follow the world's schemes. Kenneth S. Wuest, in his *Word Studies in the Greek New Testament,* has this helpful comment: "Stop assuming an outward expression which is patterned after this world, an expression which does not come from, nor is it representative of what you are in your inner being as a regenerated child of God."[3]

The antidote to this worldly influence is to "change the way you think," or as the New Living Translation states, "let God transform you into a new person by changing the way you think." This action is expressed in the passive tense, meaning that believers are the recipients of God's action in their lives. The Holy Spirit works in believers' lives to reflect the change from the old nature to the new one. "[22]*You were taught to change the way you were living. The person you used to be will ruin you through desires that deceive you.* [23]*However, you were taught to have a new attitude. [24]You were also taught to become a new person created to be like God, truly righteous and holy" (Ephesians 4:22–24).*

The wonderful result of this transformed lifestyle is that we are doing what God wants, those things that are "good, pleasing, and perfect."

12:3 *Because of the kindness that God has shown me, I ask you not to think of yourselves more highly than you should. Instead, your thoughts should lead you to use good judgment based on what God has given each of you as believers.*

As we grow in Christ, we are to be humble with an honest self-image. Our salvation is by God's grace alone. Our spiritual growth is also by grace as God enables us to serve Him. There is no room for human pride before the Lord. Paul acknowledged this in his letter to the Corinthian church: "But God's kindness made me what I am, and that kindness was not wasted on me. Instead, I worked harder than all the others. It was not I who did it, but God's kindness was with me" *(1 Corinthians 15:10).*

However, notice that this says "more highly *than you should.*" We should respect ourselves because we are made in God's image, and in Christ, we are restored to wholeness, but we are not to be prideful. Instead of pride, we are to "use good judgment" based on what God has given each of us. The idea here is to be of sound mind. The Lord Jesus Christ is our prime example of the right attitude. This attitude and the resultant actions prepare us to live effectively in this present age.

> *[God's saving kindness] trains us to avoid ungodly lives filled with worldly desires so that we can live self-controlled, moral, and godly lives in this present world. (Titus 2:12)*
>
> *Keep your mind clear, and be alert. Your opponent the devil is prowling around like a roaring lion as he looks for someone to devour. (1 Peter 5:8)*

12:4–5 ***[4]Our bodies have many parts, but these parts don't all do the same thing. [5]In the same way, even though we are many individuals, Christ makes us one body and individuals who are connected to each other.***

Paul asked believers to recognize who they are in Christ, acknowledging that no one is better than anyone else. In addition, no one lives in Christ simply as a unique individual who stands alone. Instead, each believer is a part of the body of Christ, living together within the context of a redeemed community. To demonstrate his point, Paul explained that even though our bodies are complex with numerous parts, the various parts fit together into one living being. This is a beautiful picture of the church, the body of Christ. "*[12]The body is one unit and yet has many parts. As all the parts form one body, so it is with Christ. [13]By one Spirit we were all baptized into one body. Whether we are Jewish or Greek, slave or free, God gave all of us one Spirit to drink*" (*1 Corinthians 12:12–13*). The church is thus portrayed as one unified body, not a loose association of believers with Christ as the head of the body directing all members to fulfill their function. "*[15]As we lovingly speak the truth, we will grow up completely in our relationship to Christ, who is the head. [16]He makes the whole body fit together and unites it through the support of every joint. As each and every part does its job, he makes the body grow so that it builds itself up in love*" (*Ephesians 4:15–16*).

12:6–7 ***[6]God in his kindness gave each of us different gifts. If your gift is speaking God's word, make sure what you say agrees with the Christian faith. [7]If your gift is serving, then devote yourself to serving. If it is teaching, devote yourself to teaching.***

God graciously endows His people with varied gifts that are all for the benefit of His body, given for building up the church. No spiritual gifts are deserved or earned; all are bestowed by our wise, generous Lord. As we understand our spiritual gifts, we must accept them with gratitude and humility and exercise them for the good of the whole body. Each person will be judged for faithfulness in the stewardship of his or her gifts.

The first spiritual gift listed here is "speaking God's word," which is literally translated as *prophecy* but is also interpreted as "preaching God's Word." The primary meaning is "to speak for God" and is used in Scripture both for foretelling (telling the future) and forthtelling (telling the truth).[4] All speech must come from God and never contradict Holy Scripture. The Old Testament test of a prophet revealed how to tell whether a prophet was speaking truth from God. Those who did not speak God's truth received the death penalty *(Deuteronomy 13:1–2, 5)*. Clearly, God takes the speaking of His words very seriously. Those who speak for God must be certain that they know God's Word and understand their faith.

The second spiritual gift is *serving,* which is transliterated "deacon," the church office dedicated to meeting people's needs.[5] This is a gift of seeing the needs of the believers, enlisting the necessary resources, and making sure that the body of Christ is properly cared for. Many times such service is performed behind the scenes without concern for personal credit or what people may say. Although the gift of serving is given to some, all believers are to embrace a servant spirit like the one portrayed by Jesus when He washed His disciples' feet shortly before He died on the cross. "[13]*You call me teacher and Lord, and you're right because that's what I am.* [14]*So if I, your Lord and teacher, have washed your feet, you must wash each other's feet*" *(John 13:13–14)*.

The third spiritual gift is *teaching.* True teachers are knowledgeable in their fields of study and committed to guiding others to a better comprehension of their particular areas of knowledge. For Christian teachers, all knowledge must be measured by the truth of the Word of God, teaching God's truth as fundamental to the growth of Christ's body. God's gifted teachers rejoice in and teach the accuracy of God's Scriptures, relishing the search and research that affirms God's truth. In the hands of faithful teachers, God's Word will never be twisted to fit information or knowledge provided by humans. Faithful teachers welcome the discernment of others who share in the study of God's Word, measuring all comments against the inerrancy of the Scriptures.

12:8 ***If it is encouraging others, devote yourself to giving encouragement. If it is sharing, be generous. If it is leadership, lead enthusiastically. If it is helping people in need, help them cheerfully.***

The fourth spiritual gift is "encouraging others." Those with this gift have the special ability to apply the Word of God, to meet people where they are, and to provide the encouragement and comfort that are vital to understanding our service to a sovereign God Who loves and cares for His children. This gift of encouragement is desperately needed at a time when Christians are caught up in their busy lives, facing challenges and hazards every day. We are all urged to care for one another in the effort of maintaining our steadfastness with Christ in a hostile world. "[24]*We must also consider how to encourage each other to show love and to do good things.* [25]*We should not stop gathering together with other believers, as some of you are doing. Instead, we must continue to encourage each other even more as we see the day of the Lord coming" (Hebrews 10:24–25).*

The fifth spiritual gift in this list is *sharing*. This begins with who we are and is fulfilled by what we give. Those endowed by God with this special gift of sharing are enabled to give in unusual measure for the good of Christ's body. The Scriptures have always advocated the care for others.

> [8]*Be generous to these poor people, and freely lend them as much as they need. Never be hard-hearted and tight-fisted with them . . .* [14]*Generously give them provisions—sheep from your flocks, grain from your threshing floor, and wine from your winepress. Be as generous to them as the* LORD *your God has been to you. (Deuteronomy 15:8, 14)*

Those who practice this gift do so quietly and with discernment. They take great pleasure in seeing God provide for others through their generosity. Most importantly, they do not seek recognition for their giving but only desire God's approval.

The sixth spiritual gift listed is *leadership*. Those gifted in leadership are to supervise with enthusiasm. People respect leaders who know the way, are decisive, and move forward confidently. "[12]*Brothers and sisters, we ask you to show your appreciation for those leaders who work among you and instruct you.* [13]*We ask you to love them and think very highly of them because of the work they are doing. Live in peace with each other" (1 Thessalonians 5:12–13)*. These gifted leaders must not only be enthusiastic but humble as well *(1 Peter 5:1–3)*.

The seventh spiritual gift is "helping people in need," which demonstrates a heart of compassion and an eagerness to extend mercy.[6] Those who show mercy treat people with kindness even to those who may not deserve it. Genuine mercy is usually in short supply because we are naturally self-centered and judgmental. However, it is natural to God, Who is rich in mercy. Jesus included mercy among His list of the characteristics displayed by the citizens of God's kingdom *(Matthew 5:7)*. Believers who demonstrate this gift are simply reflecting the mercy they have received through Christ. They deal kindly and gently with others who are undergoing periods of deep distress, confusion, and uncertainty.

Notes/Applications

Romans 12:1–2 may well be the highest expression of how Christians should respond to God's abundant mercies in our Lord Jesus Christ. Paul issued a compelling challenge to all believers to freely present their bodies as living sacrifices that God will use for His glory. Chapter 12:1–2 and 13:11–14 represent two mountain peaks of God's grace. The verses between show how this great aspiration to serve Christ is fulfilled in the valley where we all live. It is most heartening to know that this seemingly unattainable challenge to service is lived out in our mundane, day-to-day experiences and empowered by the Holy Spirit.

Verses three through eight exhort us to honest thinking and living. As Christians, we are members of the body of Christ, dependent on the Holy Spirit and interdependent on each other to fulfill His great commission. Although we are one body, we have different gifts for enabling this body to serve Christ, our living head.

In two other epistles, First Corinthians and Ephesians, Paul also wrote about spiritual gifts. These letters seem to emphasize the gifts of church leaders—including prophets, missionaries, pastors, and teachers—given to prepare the believers for the work of the ministry. Therefore, the church is not the building where we gather for worship, teaching, and fellowship, but the dispersion of gifted and enabled believers throughout the community.

Romans 12:9–15

12:9 Love sincerely. Hate evil. Hold on to what is good.

Having described the special gifts through which God blesses the body of Christ, Paul exhorted all believers to godly deeds through which God nurtures His people. The apostle admonished, "Love sincerely," which means to love without hypocrisy. What is true love? It is unselfish, other-minded, and giving.

> *[4]Love is patient. Love is kind. Love isn't jealous. It doesn't sing its own praises. It isn't arrogant. [5]It isn't rude. It doesn't think about itself. It isn't irritable. It doesn't keep track of wrongs. [6]It isn't happy when injustice is done, but it is happy with the truth. [7]Love never stops being patient, never stops believing, never stops hoping, never gives up. [8]Love never comes to an end… (1 Corinthians 13:4–8)*

Love is the primary characteristic of Christianity; all we do and say should be done in the love of Christ *(1 Peter 1:22)*. As we submit ourselves to the Lord, He fills us with His love, enabling us to love others as He has loved us. *"Above all, love each other warmly, because love covers many sins" (1 Peter 4:8). "Dear children, we must show love through actions that are sincere, not through empty words" (1 John 3:18).*

In displaying the love of God given to us, we must also hate evil. As God abhors evil, so should we; as He loves sinners, so should we. In exemplifying Christ's love in all we do, we demonstrate our desire to "hold on to what is good."

12:10 Be devoted to each other like a loving family. Excel in showing respect for each other.

As believers, we are to express our love for each other in word and deed. Godly love always demonstrates itself in devotion to our brothers and sisters in Christ. This should even be a deeper relationship than we have with our own families since Christ's love holds eternal effect. As God's dear children, we are members of a loving family that surpasses our own family relationships. Sadly, this is not evident in many local churches or among many Christians. Nevertheless, Paul stated that we are united by the love of Christ, giving us the example and incentive to love one another.

> [1]*I, a prisoner in the Lord, encourage you to live the kind of life which proves that God has called you.* [2]*Be humble and gentle in every way. Be patient with each other and lovingly accept each other.* [3]*Through the peace that ties you together, do your best to maintain the unity that the Spirit gives. (Ephesians 4:1–3)*

In a world filled with alienation and distress because of sin, the testimony of Christians loving one another should have a profound effect. In fact, our witness to the truth is greatly enhanced if it is spoken in love.

So how can we "excel in showing respect for each other"? In a "me first" world, our great opportunity and challenge is to put others first. This addresses the attitudes of our hearts which determine our actions. Paul applied this through our great example, the Lord Jesus Christ, in Philippians 2:3–5:

> [3]*Don't act out of selfish ambition or be conceited. Instead, humbly think of others as being better than yourselves.* [4]*Don't be concerned only about your own interests, but also be concerned about the interests of others.* [5]*Have the same attitude that Christ Jesus had.*

If we would humbly think of others as being better than ourselves, we would again turn the world upside down (*Acts 17:6*), for this kind of perspective far surpasses the world's ideal of equality.

Even believers who have experienced the regenerating work of the Holy Spirit have great difficulty putting others first and suppressing the will of self. Nevertheless, Paul asserted that this is the objective toward which all Christians should aspire. Success in this venture can only be attained as believers mature along their faith journey with the indwelling Holy Spirit and follow the example of the Lord in obedience to His commands.

12:11 *Don't be lazy in showing your devotion. Use your energy to serve the Lord.*

Believers must not succumb to the temptation of laziness in whatever God has called them to do. Laziness is a great waste of time and energy. "*Whoever is lazy in his work is related to a vandal*" (*Proverbs 18:9*). As believers, we have been commanded to take care of what we have been given here on earth. We must use our energy in fulfilling the work God has given us. The King James Version translates this "fervent in spirit; serving the Lord." The Greek says more specifically "in the Spirit," indicating that the source of this power is the Holy Spirit and not our own determination. We are to radiate the Holy Spirit dwelling in us to do Christ's work.

Every Christian is called to "full-time Christian service," although not in the jargon of our day but in the truth of Scripture. Whether we are mowing the lawn or preaching a sermon, we are doing the Lord's work. All should be done in the power of the Holy Spirit without any hint of laziness. "[23]*Whatever you do, do it wholeheartedly as though you were working for your real master and not merely for humans.* [24]*You know that your real master will give you an inheritance as your reward. It is Christ, your real master, whom you are serving*" (Colossians *3:23–24*). This includes everything we do, and such an attitude of obedience will transform our lives. "*Whatever presents itself for you to do, do it with all your might*" (Ecclesiastes *9:10*).

12:12 *Be happy in your confidence, be patient in trouble, and pray continually.*

The core essence of faith is confidence in the Lord. This is often translated and defined as the Christian's hope, a term that stems from a certainty based upon God's integrity and trustworthiness. The Scriptures are filled with this truth:

> *Keep in mind that the LORD your God is the only God. He is a faithful God, who keeps his promise and is merciful to thousands of generations of those who love him and obey his commands. (Deuteronomy 7:9)*

> [24]*My soul can say, "The LORD is my lot in life. That is why I find hope in him."* [25]*The LORD is good to those who wait for him, to anyone who seeks help from him.* [26]*It is good to continue to hope and wait silently for the LORD to save us. (Lamentations 3:24–26)*

> *In the presence of our God and Father, we never forget that your faith is active, your love is working hard, and your confidence in our Lord Jesus Christ is enduring. (1Thessalonians 1:3)*

Every believer may truly rejoice in this confidence. We have hope because God always keeps His promises. Our confidence does not depend upon our works, obedience, or feelings but rests on the steadfastness and faithfulness of our Savior, Jesus Christ. "*God wanted his people throughout the world to know the glorious riches of this mystery—which is Christ living in you, giving you the hope of glory*" *(Colossians 1:27)*.

What does "be patient in trouble" mean? The Greek import of the word *patient* conveys endurance despite difficulty and suffering.[7] In everyday language, it means "don't give in—stick it out." Life is difficult, with many trials, temptations, and tribulations. In everything, Christ is with us, giving us the patience and courage to endure. "*I waited patiently for the LORD. He turned to me and heard my cry for help*" *(Psalm 40:1)*. "*We ask him to strengthen you by his glorious might with all the power you need to patiently endure everything with joy*" *(Colossians 1:11)*.

Then, we are told to "pray continually"—always remaining in touch with our Lord. This is not an action whereby we bow our heads in petition to the Lord but rather a constant attitude of being in touch with God at all times, maintaining an open line of communication. Our lives are to be so profoundly interwoven with our

Lord that we should literally walk through life in an ongoing companionship that expresses itself moment by moment in continual communication *(John 15:4–5)*.

True prayer releases Christ's supernatural endurance and assurance in the life of the believer *(Ephesians 6:18 and Philippians 4:6)*. What an awesome privilege and responsibility to be in communion with Almighty God, the Creator of the universe!

12:13 *Share what you have with God's people who are in need. Be hospitable.*

Sharing is love in action, fulfilling the command to "love your neighbor as you love yourself" *(Mark 12:31)*. Christians are to apply this expression of love to all people but especially to fellow believers. *"Whenever we have the opportunity, we have to do what is good for everyone, especially for the family of believers"* (Galatians 6:10). This expression of love was vital to the life of the early church, and it is just as important today. In all ages, when one part of the body is hurting or in need, the rest of the body responds to the need. We are to give of ourselves—our money, time, and talents. In this sense, we really are "our brother's keeper" and must care for each other.

The second exhortation, "be hospitable," continues to be very important in our time. The phrase is actually derived from a Greek word that combines two words, *love* and *stranger*.[8] Our word *xenophobia* means "fear or dislike of foreigners," which is the very opposite of this word for hospitality. Instead, *philoxenia* means that believers are to receive and show hospitality, not only to well-known friends but to strangers (that is, people who are not regarded as a member of the extended family or a close friend). *"Don't forget to show hospitality to believers you don't know. By doing this some believers have shown hospitality to angels without being aware of it"* *(Hebrews 13:2)*.

R. C. Sproul gives a helpful perspective on this: "In the Old Testament, hospitality was an extremely important virtue. In fact, it still is in the Middle East. One of the great reasons for this was that, in the ancient world, travel was exceedingly difficult and dangerous.

We are to make sure that the needs of the visitor in our gates are taken care of."[9]

Today, Christians facing persecution know how greatly hospitality is needed for fellow believers who are traveling or perhaps even fleeing for their lives. Our homes are to be open to one another. "*Welcome each other as guests without complaining*" *(1 Peter 4:9)*.

12:14 *Bless those who persecute you. Bless them, and don't curse them.*

This command can be extremely difficult to follow. Jesus set this standard in His Sermon on the Mount: "[43]You have heard that it was said, 'Love your neighbor, and hate your enemy.' [44]But I tell you this: Love your enemies, and pray for those who persecute you" *(Matthew 5:43–44)*. Then Jesus set a great example on the cross when He prayed, "Father, forgive them. They don't know what they're doing" *(Luke 23:34)*. To love our enemies means to show active love for them. We are to bless those who persecute us. This seems impossible until we realize that this is exactly what God did for us. He loved us and saved us when we were His enemies *(Romans 5:8–10)*. Christ's followers are expected to reflect their Lord's attitude toward their enemies. This teaching is unique to Christianity.

What happens when we pray for our persecutors? We will not hate them but rather will desire their salvation. When we love them, we will not permit hatred and bitterness to enter our hearts. Then we can be sure of the blessing promised by Jesus: "Blessed are you when people insult you, persecute you, lie, and say all kinds of evil things about you because of me" *(Matthew 5:11)*.

To obey this extremely difficult command, we must look to Jesus as our great example and enabler.

> [21]*God called you to endure suffering because Christ suffered for you. He left you an example so that you could follow in his footsteps.* [22]*Christ never committed any sin. He never spoke deceitfully.* [23]*Christ never verbally abused those who verbally abused him.*

When he suffered, he didn't make any threats but left everything to the one who judges fairly. (1 Peter 2:21–23)

12:15 *Be happy with those who are happy. Be sad with those who are sad.*

As believers, we are to be happy with those who are happy and share in their happiness. We are to rejoice genuinely in another's successes or joys. We should also "be sad with those who are sad." When other Christians face a health crisis or the death of someone close to them, we should be cognizant of their circumstances and sensitive to the disruptions that have entered their lives. Even though we are people of God's eternal kingdom, we are still flesh and blood and are mightily grieved by tragic events. As we share in the lives of other believers, the true character of God is displayed through us.

Paul emphasized the fact that although individually called to salvation in Jesus Christ we are still part of the body of believers. The parts of the body are tightly linked to each other through the bonding of the Holy Spirit; therefore, it is impossible for any one individual to be affected without impacting all the others. Paul had already discussed this with the Romans (*verses four and five*), and he also used this metaphor in a letter to the Corinthian church:

> [25]*God's purpose was that the body should not be divided but rather that all of its parts should feel the same concern for each other.* [26]*If one part of the body suffers, all the other parts share its suffering. If one part is praised, all the others share in its happiness.* [27]*You are Christ's body and each of you is an individual part of it. (1 Corinthians 12:25–27)*

Notes/Applications

This passage of Romans is a collage of practical applications that grow in the hearts of believers. It shows the reasonable outpouring of labor and energy that Christians expend on behalf of others, both believers and unbelievers, as they present their bodies as living sacrifices to the Lord Who has so graciously bestowed His love upon them.

Firmly grounded in the salvation Christ has purchased by His own blood, believers embark on a journey of discovery and growth in their relationship with Jesus through the work of the Holy Spirit. In this journey, the Word of God becomes their guiding light, shining on their pathway through good times and bad, through successes and failures, and through moments of unrestrained joy and profound sorrow. Our relationship to Christ becomes the one reliable constant in a world that is constantly changing, bringing us to such a level of continual communication that it can safely be said that we are always praying.

As our relationship with our Lord deepens, we discover that we find much joy as we share our personal journey with others who have been redeemed. In fact, it is this outpouring of love and service to others that best expresses the genuineness of our relationship with Jesus Christ. We simply enjoy giving to those around us, sharing both the happy times and the hard times, offering encouragement, and sharing the exhortations of the Scriptures.

In the final analysis, we affirm our relationship with Christ through the vehicle of selfless service. As with Peter and John, any observer can easily determine that we are the children of God, the redeemed of the Lord, and the body of Christ on earth. *"After they found out that Peter and John had no education or special training, they were surprised to see how boldly they spoke. They realized that these men had been with Jesus"* (Acts 4:13).

If we have been redeemed by Jesus Christ, do our lives reflect the fact that we have been with Him? Are our homes aglow with the Spirit of Christ Who dwells in our midst? This should be the fervent prayer of every believer. Let us present ourselves to Jesus Christ without hesitation or doubt, rejoicing in the salvation that has been so freely given to us. Then, let us immerse ourselves in the work of Christ's kingdom, serving one another as the Lord has served us.

Romans 12:16–21

12:16 *Live in harmony with each other. Don't be arrogant, but be friendly to humble people. Don't think that you are smarter than you really are.*

Paul frequently exhorted the redeemed community to live in harmony with each other *(Philippians 2:2)*. True harmony comes from the Holy Spirit filling us with His love, joy, and peace. In so doing, the Spirit demonstrates that we are ultimately one in Christ.

Pride and arrogance, however, disrupt the harmony of believers. We are all inclined to human pride, so Paul suggested befriending humble people as a practical antidote. This attitude is not the result of obedience to some religious "requirement" but the outgrowth of a genuine change in heart.

Many people, even Christian people, have trouble with the problem of arrogance. When an argument heats up, ego gets in the way. It is difficult to admit our own mistakes. The book of Proverbs exposes the folly of those who think they are wiser than everyone else: "Have you met a person who thinks he is wise? There is more hope for a fool than for him" *(Proverbs 26:12)*. How ironic that such people expose their own folly! God's judgment is on such people. "*How horrible it will be for those who think they are wise and consider themselves to be clever*" *(Isaiah 5:21)*. Paul warned us in 1 Corinthians 8:2, "Those who think they know something still have a lot to learn."

12:17 *Don't pay people back with evil for the evil they do to you. Focus your thoughts on those things that are considered noble.*

Jesus made it clear in the Sermon on the Mount that the law "an eye for an eye" was not the guiding principle for the citizens of His kingdom. "[38]*You have heard that it was said, 'An eye for an eye and a tooth for a tooth.'* [39]*But I tell you not to oppose an evil person*" *(Matthew 5:38–39)*. Our human nature is to get even because as sinners we are always inclined to avenge the wrong with an even greater evil.

Christians, however, do not have this option. "*Make sure that no one ever pays back one wrong with another wrong. Instead, always try to do what is good for each other and everyone else*" *(1 Thessalonians 5:15)*.

God's antidote to evil is doing good things. Goodness is much more powerful than evil, primarily because it reflects the goodness of God that has been imparted into the life of the believer *(1 Peter 3:9)*. This is honoring to the Lord and has the effect of disarming our enemies by communicating Christ's love *(1 Peter 2:12)*. What a marvelous witness of godliness in a world filled with bitterness and vengeance.

12:18 *As much as it is possible, live in peace with everyone.*

As Christians, we are to be peacemakers *(Matthew 5:9)*. Even though we do not live in a peaceful world, we are to pursue peace but without compromising the demands of our indwelling Savior. Peace should not be maintained at the expense of the Lord's holy name.

Our desire as believers should be to live in peace with everyone. "*Let Christ's peace control you. God has called you into this peace by bringing you into one body. Be thankful*" *(Colossians 3:15)*. Such peace is one aspect of the fruit of the Spirit *(Galatians 5:22–23)* and a powerful force in time of conflict. Peacemaking does not come naturally to the human spirit. By nature, we are self-centered and, therefore, very protective of our positions and our possessions. That makes everyone else a possible threat to our security, but once we have been redeemed and the Holy Spirit has entered our lives, our natural inclinations are gradually supplanted by the Prince of Peace. As we mature in our faith, we find that we are the recipients of Christ's peace, and we have become lovers of peace among our Christian family and among the warring factions of a lost world.

Jesus provided this metaphor as He taught His disciples: "Salt is good. But if salt loses its taste, how will you restore its flavor? Have salt within you, and live in peace with one another" *(Mark 9:50)*. Here, having the flavoring influence of Christ within, peace is related to salt. What does salt do? It preserves, heals, and causes thirst. Peace preserves by keeping people from rotting in their selfish desires. Peace heals by bringing our hurts into the open so they can be restored. Peace causes thirst by making us long for living water. Jesus calls us "the salt of the earth," and our "saltiness" should give birth to a peaceful environment around us.

12:19 ***Don't take revenge, dear friends. Instead, let God's anger take care of it. After all, Scripture says, "I alone have the right to take revenge. I will pay back, says the Lord."***

All of us have been wronged at some time in our lives, but we are not to seek revenge. Almighty God sees all, and He will take care of injustices. This was established in the law. "*I will take revenge and be satisfied. In due time their foot will slip, because their day of disaster is near. Their doom is coming quickly*" *(Deuteronomy 32:35)*.

Paul was not saying that justice is not forthcoming but that the dispensing of justice falls under the prerogative of the Lord and not of people. If we take things into our own hands, we are responsible for the outcome and thus defy the Lord's final authority. If we learn to forgive as God has forgiven us, we leave the vindication of transgressions in His hands. God alone is sovereign and knows the hearts of all people, and therefore, He is the only One Who can dispense justice in perfect truth and righteousness.

12:20 ***But, "If your enemy is hungry, feed him. If he is thirsty, give him a drink. If you do this, you will make him feel guilty and ashamed."***

This is an astounding challenge: our ultimate revenge upon our enemy is to show kindness! Long ago, Israel was commanded to care for its enemies. "[4]*Whenever you come across your enemy's ox or donkey wandering loose, be sure to take it back to him.* [5]*Whenever you see that the donkey of someone who hates you has collapsed under its load, don't leave it there. Be sure to help him with his animal*" *(Exodus 23:4–5)*. This verse in Romans is directly quoted from Proverbs 25:21–22, "[21]If your enemy is hungry, give him some food to eat, and if he is thirsty, give him some water to drink. [22]In this way you will make him feel guilty and ashamed, and the LORD will reward you."

12:21 Don't let evil conquer you, but conquer evil with good.

Evil is an insidious and persistent force trying to overthrow us. Satan himself roams about like a roaring lion, seeking to devour us *(1 Peter 5:8)*. This final verse urges us not to let evil conquer us but to conquer evil with good. James encouraged us to resist the devil so that he would run away from us *(James 4:7)*. Paul urged Timothy to pursue what has God's approval, to fight the good fight for the Christian faith, and to stay away from the lusts of youth *(1 Timothy 6:11–12; 2 Timothy 2:22)*.

There is little doubt that we are engaged in conflict from birth to the grave. As believers, that warfare is focused on obedience to the Lord, fighting on His side against the forces of darkness. "*This is not a wrestling match against a human opponent. We are wrestling with rulers, authorities, the powers who govern this world of darkness, and spiritual forces that control evil in the heavenly world*" *(Ephesians 6:12)*. In chapter seven, Paul said that only through Christ are we victorious in this epic struggle.

Paul stated that believers are not passively engaged in this battle but must take an offensive stance by overcoming evil with good. Essentially, to return evil for evil is evil; to return good for good is human; to return good for evil is godly *(Luke 6:32–36)*. Thus, we are urged to live godly lives, behaving in a way that is otherwise unknown in this world. It is the way of Christ and the command of His Word. Living in this way we express the love of Christ within us, demonstrating the hope that our actions will break the cycle of violence and challenge the offender to examine the claims of Christ.

These words are filled with hope because of the sovereign God we serve. We must not underestimate the enemy or the power of evil within us, but neither must we shrink in fear. The apostle John gave this wonderful assurance in 1 John 4:4: "Dear children, you belong to God. So you have won the victory over these people, because the one who is in you is greater than the one who is in the world."

Notes/Applications

This passage presents the law of Christ. It is strikingly similar to Moses' teachings because both come from the same Lawgiver. They are not just "suggestions" that will make our lives happier and more fulfilling. They are the commands of the Lord and are to be obeyed out of love *(John 15:10)*. Even Jesus was submissive to the Father's will. Believers are greatly blessed when they likewise submit to the law of Christ. Because of our obedience, many people benefit—not just those in the body of Christ but strangers in need as well and even our enemies.

We do not need to make a list of good deeds; God has already given us clear instruction on how to offer our bodies as living sacrifices, "dedicated to God and pleasing to him." This teaches us why obedience to the law of Christ is considered our appropriate kind of worship—it fulfills the will of God.

ROMANS 13

Romans 13:1–6

13:1 ***Every person should obey the government in power. No government would exist if it hadn't been established by God. The governments which exist have been put in place by God.***

As Paul closed chapter twelve, he encouraged believers to "conquer evil with good" *(Romans 12:21)*. Then, here in chapter thirteen, he affirmed that government is an integral part of God's plan to maintain an orderly society, assisting God's purposes to punish those who do evil and reward those who do right. Therefore, everyone should submit to civil authorities because these leaders have been established by God. This includes national and local authorities that are empowered to maintain order and administer justice within society. It makes no difference if the authority is good or evil. Early Christianity faced severe opposition from civil authorities. Jesus Himself was executed by the Roman authorities in Jerusalem at the demand of the Jewish leadership. Nevertheless, Peter, the leader of Jesus' disciples, affirmed this position on submission to the government in power despite the possible miscarriage of justice that sometimes occurs *(1 Peter 2:13–17)*.

13:2 ***Therefore, whoever resists the government opposes what God has established. Those who resist will bring punishment on themselves.***

Unless government directives violate a direct command of God's Word, people who disobey civil authorities are really disobeying the instructions of the Lord. Paul also instructed Titus to remind his fellow believers to obey civil authorities. "*Remind believers to willingly place themselves under the authority of government officials. Believers should obey them and be ready to help them with every good thing they do*" *(Titus 3:1)*.

Whoever disobeys will be punished by the authorities for breaking the law. The punishment for insubordination may come from the government directly or through the government by God Himself. If a person is falsely accused because of his Christian witness, he will earn the praise of his Lord. "[15]*If you suffer, you shouldn't suffer for being a murderer, thief, criminal or troublemaker.* [16]*If you suffer for being a Christian, don't feel ashamed, but praise God for being called that name*" *(1 Peter 4:15–16)*.

13:3 ***People who do what is right don't have to be afraid of the government. But people who do what is wrong should be afraid of it. Would you like to live without being afraid of the government? Do what is right, and it will praise you.***

Law keepers generally have no fear of the authorities, but lawbreakers do. Even dictators and despots are usually known for keeping law and order, even though they may brutally mistreat people. All government leaders are placed in position by God so that civil order is maintained. Although Christians in Paul's day were not lawbreakers, from time to time they were persecuted by Jewish and Roman authorities. Regardless of these injustices, both Paul and Peter taught obedience to civil authorities, providing a clear conscience and genuine peace of mind. "[13]*Who will harm you if you are devoted to doing what is good?* [14]*But even if you suffer for doing what God approves, you are blessed. Don't be afraid of those who want to harm you*" *(1 Peter 3:13–14)*. Christians must always live obediently, trusting God even in times of testing and adversity.

As Christians, we should do everything in a way that honors the Lord. One additional blessing of righteous living is that it usually brings approval even from the civil authorities.

13:4 ***The government is God's servant working for your good. But if you do what is wrong, you should be afraid. The government has the right to carry out the death sentence. It is God's servant, an avenger to execute God's anger on anyone who does what is wrong.***

God instituted human government for our well being. Every ruler has been placed in his or her position by God to administer justice. However, Psalm two warns the kings of the earth not to rule at their own discretion but instead to serve as God's administrators of justice *(Psalm 2:10–11)*. Nevertheless, we are very much aware that rulers do not always acknowledge God's supremacy in the administration of their duties.

Paul addressed believers and advised them to recognize that God is in charge even in this aspect of their earthly lives. As such, they are to respond to earthly authority appropriately. If a person does not honor that God-ordained authority, then he should be fearful for he defies not only the earthly authority but the Lord Who has determined its leadership. In order to maintain order and administer justice, government has the right to punish evildoers; it even has the right to impose the death penalty if the offense is determined to be extreme enough. John Calvin commented on this verse:

> It is another part of the office of magistrates, that they ought forcibly to repress the waywardness of evil men, who do not willingly suffer themselves to be governed by laws, and to inflict such punishment on their offences as God's judgment

> requires; for he expressly declares, that they are armed with the sword, not for an empty show, but that they may smite evil-doers.[1]

13:5 ***Therefore, it is necessary for you to obey, not only because you're afraid of God's anger but also because of your own conscience.***

Christians are further admonished to have an *attitude* of obedience to the governing authorities. Obeying those who rule enables believers to live in freedom within the boundaries of the law. These attitudes and actions seem strange to many today because obedience appears to impose restrictions we do not like. Nevertheless, this is God's Word to us through Paul, and we should endeavor to follow these directions.

Paul not only advocated obedience out of fear of both political authority and God's sovereign design, but he also introduced the governing characteristics of mankind's own conscience. When we obey because of our conscience, we experience true freedom from the guilt of disobedience. *Conscience* is defined as "one's own conduct, intentions, or character together with a feeling of obligation to do right or be good."[2] If we disobey the law and no human sees us, we still carry a sense of guilt. God still sees and knows all, and we are guilty before Him. However, believers should recognize that the governing institution is God's instrument as He ultimately rules in human affairs. Fundamentally, if we obey God in these matters, we have a clear conscience as we submit to the rule of these governing authorities.

13:6 ***That is also why you pay your taxes. People in the government are God's servants while they do the work he has given them.***

Taxes pay for the services the government provides. This verse identifies government workers as "God's servants" performing His appointed tasks by keeping order in society. Jesus also paid taxes.

When asked about this, He gave the following response: "[24]'Show me a coin. Whose face and name is this?' They answered, 'The emperor's.' [25]He said to them, 'Well, then give the emperor what belongs to the emperor, and give God what belongs to God'" *(Luke 20:24–25)*. Paying taxes is good and honorable. It is not something we should resent because the money helps to provide for the government that God has established.

Notes/Applications

Since government is ordained by God, we must not take the law into our own hands. Our attitude toward the authorities over us should be respectful, even when they are not honoring God's authority.

A great example of this in Scripture is when David, although anointed to be king, was harassed by the current king, Saul. When David's men urged him to seize power by force, he replied: "It would be unthinkable for me to raise my hand against His Majesty, the LORD's anointed king, since he is the LORD's anointed" *(1 Samuel 24:6)*. David realized that to kill the reigning king, even though David also knew that he would one day have the throne, would set a dangerous precedent for the men in his command. He did not want them to think that assassination would be an option. He wanted them to know that he would rely on God. Eventually, in God's time and way, David became Israel's reigning king and ruled for forty years.

Two other wonderful examples of men who obeyed God's commands were Joseph and Daniel. Joseph was mistreated by his brothers, sold as a slave in Egypt, and imprisoned unjustly before becoming second in command in that great land. Even in difficult and unfair circumstances, Joseph submitted himself to the authorities God had placed over him. As for Daniel, soon after being taken into exile in Babylon as a young man, he took a stand against the command of the king in order to obey God, and God honored his courage. Yet, even as he took that stand, he worked through the authority set directly over him to negotiate his position. "*Daniel made up his mind not to harm himself by eating the king's rich food and drinking the king's wine. So he asked the chief-of-staff for permission not to harm himself in this way" (Daniel 1:8)*. Daniel became a mighty leader under the kings Nebuchadnezzar and Belshazzar, and survived the overthrow of Babylon by the Persians to serve under the next king, Cyrus.

Obeying authority does not come naturally. Since the time of Adam and Eve, God's authority has been questioned *(Genesis 3:1)*. The supreme example of obedience, however, is Jesus Christ. He not only submitted willingly to the Father's commands but was subject to the authorities who eventually executed Him in the ultimate miscarriage of justice. Ironically, even during the authorities' illegitimate use of their God-given power, our sovereign Lord was still in control. *"By using men who don't acknowledge Moses' Teachings, you crucified Jesus, who was given over to death by a plan that God had determined in advance" (Acts 2:23)*.

May God grant us the faithfulness to honor our leaders as we should and yet to be discerning and courageous when we must stand for our faith.

Romans 13:7–14

13:7 ***Pay everyone whatever you owe them. If you owe taxes, pay them. If you owe tolls, pay them. If you owe someone respect, respect that person. If you owe someone honor, honor that person.***

Since all civil authority is put in place by God, we are to pay whatever we owe. Of all people, Christians should be the best citizens, leading exemplary lives of hard work, willing service to the community, and respectful obedience to the governing authorities.

Christian citizens should pay their *taxes* and *tolls*, which refer to any legal assessment determined by the government.[3] It is just as important that believers pay all their just debts, living without indebtedness to anyone.

Believers also owe a debt of respect to those in authority. We should be law-abiding and inoffensive. When we realize the power the government has to execute justice, then we have a sense of fearful respect. Peter even included respect for those in authority as a teaching for a culture in which slaves were a major segment of the society. *"Slaves, place yourselves under the authority of your owners and show them complete respect. Obey not only those owners who are good and kind, but also those who are unfair" (1 Peter 2:18).*

Finally, believers are to honor those who occupy positions of importance in our lives. This would include employers, pastors, teachers, and others in similar positions as well as civil agencies. We should respect our elders, those who bring a greater measure of experience to every situation. If we respect an office, then we will respect the person who occupies that office, not necessarily on the basis of that person's personal behavior but on the basis of the office that he or she holds. Treating people with honor and respect is ultimately pleasing to God.

13:8 ***Pay your debts as they come due. However, one debt you can never finish paying is the debt of love that you owe each other. The one who loves another person has fulfilled Moses' Teachings.***

Christians should not only pay their taxes, but they should also pay their debts on time. As good stewards of God's gifts, we are to keep all accounts clear. "[27]*Do not withhold good from those to whom it is due, when it is in the power of your hand to do so.* [28]*Do not say to your neighbor, 'Go, and come back, and tomorrow I will give it,' when you have it with you*" *(Proverbs 3:27–28,* NKJV*)*. Debt causes a kind of bondage that hinders the freedom we have received in Christ. In contrast, freedom from debt enables us to help out with other needs that may arise in the fellowship of believers.

There is, however, one debt that we can never pay off: our debt of love to each other. This is agape love, the kind of love that the Bible uses to describe the unselfish love God gives through the Holy Spirit. This is the godly love expressed in Jesus' great commandment:

> "[37]*Love the Lord your God with all your heart, with all your soul, and with all your mind."* [38]*This is the greatest and most important commandment.* [39]*The second is like it: "Love your neighbor as you love yourself."* [40]*All of Moses' Teachings and the Prophets depend on these two commandments. (Matthew 22:37–40)*

Loving one another is the ultimate objective of God's believing community. "*My goal in giving you this order is for love to flow from a pure heart, from a clear conscience, and from a sincere faith*" *(1 Timothy 1:5)*. There is no greater law than the law of love, and as this love flows from the Spirit through us, we are showing God's love to a needy world. "*You are doing right if you obey this law from the highest authority: 'Love your neighbor as you love yourself'*" *(James 2:8)*.

***13:9** The commandments, "Never commit adultery; never murder; never steal; never have wrong desires," and every other commandment are summed up in this statement: "Love your neighbor as you love yourself."*

In the Ten Commandments given by God through Moses, God provided directives by which His people should live *(Exodus 20:1–17)*.

Each of these commands regulates the conduct of believers with respect to their neighbors and to God. The first four direct the believers' unadulterated commitment to God, and the last six specifically direct the believers' conduct in community. We are to respect the life, spouse, property, honor, and possessions of our neighbors. These commands are succinctly summarized in the phrase, "love God and love your neighbors as yourselves." If we disobey in any point, we not only personally breach our neighbor's confidence, but we also dishonor God and reject both His word and gifts to us.

To obey these commands, we must first experience God's love given to us through Jesus Christ. If we truly love Him as our personal Lord and Savior, then His love flows through us to those around us. The witness of God's love among God's people is the defining characteristic that most greatly influences those who observe believers' conduct. *"Everyone will know that you are my disciples because of your love for each other" (John 13:35).*

13:10 *Love never does anything that is harmful to a neighbor. Therefore, love fulfills Moses' Teachings.*

Living under the authority of Christ's love fulfills the law, keeping us from harming our neighbor in any way. This is genuine love, expressed in the lives of believers through the presence of the Holy Spirit in them. This love leads to forgiveness rather than vengeance, to freedom rather than bondage.

Even as First Corinthians thirteen is the "love chapter," First John is the "love letter." It reminds us that true love comes from God, enabling us to fulfill His commandments:

> [19]*We love because God loved us first.* [20]*Whoever says, "I love God," but hates another believer is a liar. People who don't love other believers, whom they have seen, can't love God, whom they have not seen.* [21]*Christ has given us this commandment: The person who loves God must also love other believers. (1 John 4:19–21)*

13:11 ***You know the times in which we are living. It's time for you to wake up. Our salvation is nearer now than when we first became believers.***

Paul delivered a rousing alarm, issuing an urgent call for believers to wake up and be aware of the critical hour in which they live. Their Lord has called them to live as His redeemed community in a hostile world that is doomed to receive judgment. Therefore, they should understand the situation and see it as an opportunity to be witnesses in the midst of confusion and rebellion. Paul urged Christians to conduct themselves appropriately as good citizens of their countries, supporting the community of believers in love, and professing the faithful testimony of His saving grace.

Even as believers live faithfully in the present, they are very much aware that every moment brings the day of redemption closer. No one is even guaranteed the next moment. Every hour and day we have now counts for all eternity. We will live with Christ forever in the new heaven and the new earth, so we should live in the present moment with an eternal perspective. This is our Christian hope, pointing us forward to that day when we will see Jesus face-to-face. Christians should not look backward, grieving over a past that cannot be changed, but they should look forward to that day when they will stand in God's glorious presence. While waiting for that moment, we are to live in the reality of our redeemed present.

13:12 ***The night is almost over, and the day is near. So we should get rid of the things that belong to the dark and take up the weapons that belong to the light.***

Paul was stating that this world, or the believer's place in this world, is really like nighttime and darkness because of sin. The day is on the horizon when we will be brought into the blinding light of Christ's glory.

As Christians, we no longer live in the darkness of the night that surrounds us. We must rid ourselves of the works of darkness that define this world's culture and, for whatever time is left, prepare ourselves for the battle that confronts us every day. We must arm ourselves with the armor that God has provided:

> *[13]For this reason, take up all the armor that God supplies. Then you will be able to take a stand during these evil days. Once you have overcome all obstacles, you will be able to stand your ground. [14]So then, take your stand! Fasten truth around your waist like a belt. Put on God's approval as your breastplate. [15]Put on your shoes so that you are ready to spread the Good News that gives peace. [16]In addition to all these, take the Christian faith as your shield. With it you can put out all the flaming arrows of the evil one. [17]Also take salvation as your helmet and the word of God as the sword that the Spirit supplies. (Ephesians 6:13–17)*

13:13 ***We should live decently, as people who live in the light of day. Wild parties, drunkenness, sexual immorality, promiscuity, rivalry, and jealousy cannot be part of our lives.***

As children of God's redemption and light, our lives are to reflect Jesus, the Light of the World, and not the rulers of the darkness of the age.

> *So I advise you to live according to your new life in the Holy Spirit. Then you won't be doing what your sinful nature craves. (Galatians 5:16, NLT)*

> *[1]Imitate God, since you are the children he loves. [2]Live in love as Christ also loved us. He gave his life for us as an offering and sacrifice, a soothing aroma to God. (Ephesians 5:1–2)*

The ways of our old nature no longer have a hold on our lives. Instead, we are held firmly in the Lord's hands, and He now influences our attitudes, our decisions, and our actions *(1 Corinthians 6:9–11)*. Having been sanctified by the Holy Spirit, we are to live according to our new nature *(1 Peter 2:1–3)*.

13:14 ***Instead, live like the Lord Jesus Christ did, and forget about satisfying the desires of your sinful nature.***

This is the rationale for all that has been said earlier: Believers are to follow all of the outlined exhortations so that they can live like Christ, fulfilling the will of the Father and looking forward to the glory that He received when He returned to the Father.

Literally, this verse says that believers are to "put on the Lord Jesus Christ," meaning they are to clothe themselves with Christ.[4] This is the same word used in Galatians 3:27: "All of you who were baptized in Christ's name have clothed yourselves with Christ." When the Christian puts on Christ, he clothes his soul in the moral disposition and habits of Christ.[5] All who belong to Jesus through faith are *in Him*, assured of His salvation. In Christ, they are completely clothed in the presence of the holy God, for Christ is their righteousness, He is their truth, He is their peace, He is their salvation, and He is the living word.

In effect then, we are to live like the Lord Jesus Christ. This is more than just following His example; it is the way children grow up to become like their parents. Not only do they follow their example, but they have their genes. When we are in Christ, He enables us to live more and more like Him.

Further, we are not to make any provisions for the lusts of the flesh. Although as believers we are new creatures in Christ, we still have our old nature in us luring us to sin *(Romans 7)*. We must, nevertheless, daily subjugate our selfish desires and live for Christ *(Colossians 3:5–10)*.

When we obey this command to live for Christ and die to self, Christ continues to clothe us in His righteousness, and we become more like Him, having the attitude expressed by John the Baptist: "He must increase in importance, while I must decrease in importance" *(John 3:30)*.

Notes/Applications

The heart of this passage is love for God and for our neighbors. All we do should be based on Christ's command to love. *"I'm giving you a new commandment: Love each other in the same way that I have loved you" (John 13:34)*. This agape love comes only from God and reflects His love for us.

Verses seven through ten complete the commandments to all Christians under the "law of Christ." This law is basically a fulfillment of the Ten Commandments given by God through Moses. The emphasis here is on the *spirit of the law* that is constructed on the firm foundation of God's love. In the midst of this, Paul challenged us with this penetrating statement: "One debt you can never finish paying is the debt of love that you owe each other." Our supreme example of this is the Lord Jesus. He said, "The greatest love that you can show is to give your life for your friends" *(John 15:13)*, and then, "You are my friends if you obey my commandments" *(John 15:14)*.

The final paragraph (*verses 11–14*) is the high point of chapters twelve and thirteen. It is as if life were a great football or soccer field with verses 12:1–2 representing one goal and 13:11–14 the other goal. All of the scoring is done at these goals while the game is played on the field. How we play the game on the field in everyday challenges will determine the final outcome.

In order to compete in the game, we need both a strong offense and a tough defense. We must not underestimate our opponents—the world, the flesh, and the devil—but more importantly, we must not underestimate God's power that enables us to achieve final victory. *"Thank God that he gives us the victory through our Lord Jesus Christ" (1 Corinthians 15:57)*.

These final four verses are a wakeup call for Christians everywhere. We are in a real-life struggle against evil within and without, but God has fully equipped and prepared us for each encounter. May the words of this passage call many from darkness to light and stir

God's people to a firm resolution to engage in spiritual conflict in accordance with His commands.

ROMANS 14

Romans 14:1–9

14:1 ***Welcome people who are weak in faith, but don't get into an argument over differences of opinion.***

Those who are mature in the Christian faith are to embrace unconditionally those who are weak or immature in the faith. Christ is our example. Just as Christ received us in our weakness, so we should receive others. This weaker brother or sister may be a new believer or an older believer who has not matured in the faith.

The new Christian is a joy to receive, being naturally eager to grow in grace and knowledge of the Lord *(1 Peter 2:2)*. The older Christian who has failed to mature is a greater challenge *(Hebrews 5:12–14)*. Like a human baby that does not mature normally, this immature Christian can be difficult to handle. Nevertheless, the mature believer is to receive all who are weak in faith.

Also, we are to avoid disputes over issues that may be questionable but are not consequential to the faith. These kinds of arguments may lead to divisions among the body of believers, thus hurting our witness to the community surrounding us.

However, such acceptance does not imply that the stronger believer accepts the immature believer's poorly defined positions or undeveloped doctrines as if they were true. Instead, Paul was referring to loving consideration of the person; all believers need to remember that they were at one time young in the faith themselves. Older believers have an ongoing responsibility to help nurture younger believers, endeavoring by the grace of God to help them grow in the grace and knowledge of Jesus Christ *(Acts 18:24–28)*.

14:2 *Some people believe that they can eat all kinds of food. Other people with weak faith believe that they can eat only vegetables.*

Christian maturity is not defined by a simple list of what to do and what not to do, but by being in Christ and growing in His grace and knowledge through the Word of God *(Hebrews 13:9)*. Mature believers know the freedom they have in Christ is by God's grace through faith and not because of any works. New Christians may not yet understand their freedom in Christ in relationship to the necessity of obeying His commands. The older immature Christian may also lack understanding and, in some cases, may be caught up in legalism. The example of mature Christians is vital in helping both kinds of weak faith to grow spiritually.

The issue of food was extremely important in the ancient world. Certain foods were associated with previous religious or cultural practices, and thus, people of weak faith often did not feel comfortable eating them. In some cases, they may have been influenced by other immature believers who had an inadequate understanding of the Bible. It was important for mature Christians to exercise love in addressing this topic by not offending the immature believers while at the same time not resorting to legalism in order to coddle their incorrect notions. "*Be careful that by using your freedom you don't somehow make a believer who is weak in faith fall into sin*" *(1 Corinthians 8:9)*. Essentially, Paul was advising mature Christians that arguing over such issues was not beneficial to the body of believers. In fact, useless arguments over such minor concerns may defeat the believer's understanding of the doctrines that *are* essential to the Christian faith.

14:3 ***People who eat all foods should not despise people who eat only vegetables. In the same way, the vegetarians should not criticize people who eat all foods, because God has accepted those people.***

Eating or not eating certain foods does not make anyone more or less spiritual. The point is that Christians should be concerned for younger believers' growth in the faith; they must refrain from treating each other with judgmental attitudes. All Christians should learn to extend to each other the same grace and mercy that God has given them.

The focus here is on attitude. Believers are not to sit in judgment of one another for what they will or will not eat. *Despise* in the Greek language conveys a strong word that means to "look down on, count as nothing, or to reject."[1] The implication is that one set of believers actually rejects those of another persuasion on the basis of what they eat, not on what they believe about the person and work of Jesus Christ. If we obey this command not to despise fellow believers, God will change our attitude. The initiative should be with the mature believer, but all are commanded to accept one another since God has accepted us.

The issue in Paul's day centered on eating meat that might have been offered to idols. He dealt with this in detail in his first letter to the Corinthian church *(1 Corinthians 8:4–9)*. This was difficult both for Jewish Christians who found it hard to understand their new freedom from the Jewish ceremonial laws and for Gentile Christians who had been involved in idol worship. The apostle Peter's experience with Cornelius in Acts ten shows the depth of the problem of legalism. Romans fourteen and First Corinthians eight show the similar problems of those who came out of pagan religions. Thus, Paul encouraged those who are strong in the faith—those who have themselves been nurtured in the doctrines of the faith—to determine carefully those issues that are essential and those that have less importance.

14:4 ***Who are you to criticize someone else's servant? The Lord will determine whether his servant has been successful. The servant will be successful because the Lord makes him successful.***

Paul outlined another issue that was potentially harmful to a community of believers. In a world where slaves and slave owners were a prevalent aspect of the Roman culture, slaves were surely compared by their masters. By using this illustration, Paul drew a distinct parallel between the way that believers should behave toward each other. As the servant is responsible to his master, so the believer is responsible to the Lord. As the master deals with his servant, so the Lord deals with his people.

Paul was essentially advising believers to avoid being critical and meddling in others' affairs. While it is absolutely imperative that the mature believer overlooks the welfare of weaker believers, it is a waste of time to indulge in debating less important issues. In fact, God will deal faithfully with each of His children, and we must be willing to allow God the time and direction to make His own corrections without our unnecessary intrusions.

14:5 ***One person decides that one day is holier than another. Another person decides that all days are the same. Every person must make his own decision.***

Paul introduced another nonessential issue that tended to divide the early church. It was perfectly acceptable to observe special days like Jewish believers did. It was also perfectly acceptable to observe every day in the same way as the Gentiles did.[2]

At the council in Jerusalem in Acts fifteen, these ceremonial issues were hotly debated. The conclusion of that council was that such issues should not divide believers; they were not important enough to split the body of Christ. Therefore, Paul indicated that the keeping of certain days as holier than others was neither right nor wrong but a matter for individual conscience.

The principle taught here gives us guidelines for dealing with current practices among Christians of various cultures, ethnic backgrounds, and church denominations. We need to discern these carefully and examine them according to the Word of God. Our Christian relationships must be committed to the clear truth of Scripture and motivated by genuine love for one another. There is plenty of room for various opinions on the nonessentials of the faith. We are not to make others conform to our particular practices, but we are to receive all believers in love.

14:6 ***When people observe a special day, they observe it to honor the Lord. When people eat all kinds of foods, they honor the Lord as they eat, since they give thanks to God. Vegetarians also honor the Lord when they eat, and they, too, give thanks to God.***

The liberty that believers receive in Christ Jesus should rise above minor issues that might otherwise divide them. In the end, our attitude toward one another will display our maturity in the faith by demonstrating that these issues have no effect upon our acceptance of one another. In fact, they become the source of great rejoicing because the Lord has crossed the lines of all cultural histories to bring His salvation to the nations. In emulating the love of Christ for people of all languages, cultures, and persuasions, we honor Christ's work among the peoples of the world. As long as these believers are doing everything in thanksgiving to God, then we have no right to impose our practices on them. "*So, whether you eat or drink, or whatever you do, do everything to the glory of God*" (1 Corinthians 10:31). "*Everything you say or do should be done in the name of the Lord Jesus, giving thanks to God the Father through him*" (Colossians 3:17).

14:7–8 ***[7]It's clear that we don't live to honor ourselves, and we don't die to honor ourselves. [8]If we live, we honor the Lord, and if we die, we honor the Lord. So whether we live or die, we belong to the Lord.***

Paul encouraged believers to use this perspective. From the moment that Christ's salvation is imparted to us, we belong to the Lord. We no longer run our lives according to our self-directed perspectives but according to the will of Christ Who redeemed us. We belong to God because of the sacrificial death of God's Son, the Lord Jesus Christ. "*[19]Don't you know that your body is a temple that belongs to the Holy Spirit? The Holy Spirit, whom you received from God, lives in you. You don't belong to yourselves. [20]You were bought for a price. So bring glory to God in the way you use your body*" *(1 Corinthians 6:19–20)*.

As Christians, we are the possessions of our Redeemer. His possession of us is all-encompassing in that it affects everything that we are in this life and in the life to come. Never again will we be left on our own in our decisions, joys, adversities, sufferings, and victories. All are a part of God's plan for us. He has bound Himself to us in the promise of His Word, and we are secure in the faith He has given to us.

Abiding in the sacred covenant the Lord has bestowed on us, we bring honor to Him. "*He died for us so that, whether we are awake in this life or asleep in death, we will live together with him*" *(1 Thessalonians 5:10)*. Like Paul, we can exclaim, "[20]I eagerly expect and hope that I will have nothing to be ashamed of. I will speak very boldly and honor Christ in my body, now as always, whether I live or die. [21]Christ means everything to me in this life, and when I die I'll have even more" *(Philippians 1:20–21)*.

14:9 ***For this reason Christ died and came back to life so that he would be the Lord of both the living and the dead.***

Our relationship to Jesus Christ is the fundamental criterion that affects everything we do. The purpose for Christ's incarnation was to redeem a people for Himself out of all tongues and nations. In His sacrificial death and His resurrection, He became the Lord of both the living and the dead. He is Lord over all creation, and in His redeeming work, He is Lord over all those whom He has purchased with His blood. All of the other "issues" are secondary to this. In fact, they are less than secondary; they are immaterial.

The Lord Jesus is alive and possesses the keys to death and hell *(Revelation 1:18)*. He is the judge of the living and the dead *(Acts 10:42)*. He is the Christ, God's Messiah, the Son of God. He is able to keep those He has redeemed both in this life and throughout eternity.

Notes/Applications

Christians today have different opinions about right and wrong. Should we use cosmetics, dance, go to movies, keep certain holy days, eat or drink certain foods? The list goes on. These subjects are divisive but truly secondary according to this passage.

More important is our commitment to the Lord, our desire to please Him, and our attitude of love and concern for others. Our primary focus must be upon our Lord Jesus Christ, seeking His guidance through the Scriptures, asking forgiveness for our sins, and desiring to lead others to know and serve Him. We are to keep His commands out of love, but a list of what and what not to do that goes beyond Scripture leads to a legalism that thwarts our liberty in Christ. The task assigned to mature believers is to guide and substantiate weaker believers in the central issue of Christ's place in their lives, admonishing them to avoid worrying about or arguing over secondary issues that are really insignificant.

In Christ, we are free to be the people He wants us to be. This is what we should desire for our Christian brothers and sisters.

> [23]*We must continue to hold firmly to our declaration of faith. The one who made the promise is faithful.* [24]*We must also consider how to encourage each other to show love and to do good things.* [25]*We should not stop gathering together with other believers, as some of you are doing. Instead, we must continue to encourage each other even more as we see the day of the Lord coming. (Hebrews 10:23–25)*

In all that we do and say, with thanksgiving, we honor and praise the Lord Who has ushered us into the glory of His presence. We worship Him both individually and corporately, encouraging each other and strengthening our mutual faith. In this sacred environment of praise, we acknowledge that Christ is Lord over all, the supreme Sovereign of all that we are and the Master of all our circumstances.

Romans 14:10–15

14:10 Why do you criticize or despise other Christians? Everyone will stand in front of God to be judged.

In the earlier passage, we concluded that Christ is Lord over all aspects of believers' lives. If we agree on that conclusion and accept it as the truth of God's Word, then Paul was quite correct when he asked, "Why do you criticize or despise other Christians?" Paul obviously was not satisfied to bring believers to this conclusion without probing deeply into their behavior. The two verbs literally mean "judge" and "look down on." We are not qualified to do either. "[1]*Stop judging so that you will not be judged.* [2]*Otherwise, you will be judged by the same standard you use to judge others. The standards you use for others will be applied to you*" *(Matthew 7:1–2)*. These words from Jesus' Sermon on the Mount reveal that we habitually violate this command. How ironic that we will be convicted even by the standards we impose upon others, a standard far below God's standard!

When we are critical of other believers, we show contempt for the Redeemer Who is working out His perfect will in their lives. This is antithetical to the exhortation in Philippians 2:3 to "humbly think of others as being better than yourselves." In our flesh, we tend to look for things that are wrong (rather than right) with other people. The apostle James addressed this forcefully: "Brothers and sisters, stop slandering each other. Those who slander and judge other believers slander and judge God's teachings. If you judge God's teachings, you are no longer following them. Instead, you are judging them" *(James 4:11)*. Instead of judging and criticizing, we are to love and instruct our brothers and sisters in the Lord.

14:11 Scripture says, "As certainly as I live, says the Lord, everyone will worship me, and everyone will praise God."

This quote from the prophet Isaiah assured the people of Paul's day that the Lord, the only true God, sovereignly controlled the activities on the earth and was the source of their salvation:

> [22]*Turn to me and be saved, all who live at the ends of the earth,*
> *because I am God, and there is no other.*
> [23]*I have bound myself with an oath.*
> *A word has gone out from my righteous mouth that will not be recalled,*
> *"Every knee will bow to me*
> *and every tongue will swear allegiance."*
> [24]*It will be said of me,*
> *"Certainly, righteousness and strength are found in the* LORD *alone."*
> *All who are angry with him will come to him and be ashamed.*
> [25]*All the descendants of Israel will be declared righteous,*
> *and they will praise the* LORD. *(Isaiah 45:22–25)*

This prophecy is wonderfully fulfilled in our Lord Jesus Christ *(Philippians 2:9–11)*. On the integrity of His own name, God attests that everyone will one day worship Him. There is no longer any debate about His sovereign lordship. It is immutably established by God Himself. In light of all that Paul explained throughout this chapter, believers should recognize that, even as they wrongly judge the behavior of other Christians, God will one day rightly judge everyone. In fact, God's declaration is so sweeping in its scope that unbelievers will one day also be included in the worship of God. No longer will people argue about what choices they have made. God has already determined that they, too, will bow their knees and acknowledge that He is Lord over all.

14:12 *All of us will have to give an account of ourselves to God.*

There is much in the Bible about accountability. Paul forcibly asserted that believers are primarily accountable to God, Who sees all things. However, we tend to obey authorities only when they are visible while God sees us all the time. However, the Scripture confirms that God will judge the works of every person, including believers. This provides a strong hedge to guard believers from taking their salvation or their gifts in a casual manner.

14:13 ***So let's stop criticizing each other. Instead, you should decide never to do anything that would make other Christians have doubts or lose their faith.***

Paul spoke bluntly. Apparently such "criticizing" was common practice. But to be honest, this is still true today—to our shame! How many Christians are hurt and churches damaged because of this very sin?

This is not meant to exclude church discipline that follows biblical guidelines. Nothing in this chapter is to be interpreted as saying that we are to tolerate all behavior or differences of opinion. We are under God's law as revealed in the Ten Commandments and fulfilled in the law of Christ. The Word of God is our standard for Christian living:

> [1]*Brothers and sisters, if a person gets trapped by wrongdoing, those of you who are spiritual should help that person turn away from doing wrong. Do it in a gentle way. At the same time watch yourself so that you also are not tempted.* [2]*Help carry each other's burdens. In this way you will follow Christ's teachings.* (Galatians 6:1–2)

This instructs us regarding both our attitudes and our actions. If followed, it brings great blessing to Christ's body.

In cases of personal offense, we are not only permitted but are actually directed to confront our brothers and sisters, as set forth in Matthew eighteen:

> [15]*If your brother sins against you, go and tell him his fault between you and him alone. If he hears you, you have gained your brother.* [16]*But if he will not hear, take with you one or two more, that "by the mouth of two or three witnesses every word may be established."* [17]*And if he refuses to hear them, tell it to the church. But if he*

> *refuses even to hear the church, let him be to you like a heathen and a tax collector. (Matthew 18:15–17,* NKJV*)*

This biblical remedy for dealing with sin, when followed in reliance on the Lord, will result in reconciliation or necessary discipline in the church. To our great detriment, this is all too rare in recent times.

Notwithstanding, believers should make every effort possible not to be offensive to fellow believers *(1 Corinthians 10:32)*. As mature Christians, we need to be good examples of godly living, constantly trying to edify others in the faith. The law of love will enable us to benefit fellow Christians. "*Those who love other believers live in the light. Nothing will destroy the faith of those who live in the light*" *(1 John 2:10)*.

14:14 ***The Lord Jesus has given me the knowledge and conviction that no food is unacceptable in and of itself. But it is unacceptable to a person who thinks it is.***

In his affirmation that everyone will eventually face Christ as judge, Paul again urged Christians to refrain from being critical of those whose practices may differ. Paul erased the grounds for such baseless criticisms, asserting that no food is intrinsically unacceptable. However, for the person who believes that certain foods may be unacceptable, eating them could be considered a great offense. If there is no explicit command or clear inference from a command, we have freedom in the Lord. Paul developed this truth more fully in 1 Corinthians 10:23–26:

> *[23]Someone may say, "I'm allowed to do anything," but not everything is helpful. I'm allowed to do anything, but not everything encourages growth. [24]People should be concerned about others and not just about themselves. [25]Eat anything that is sold in the market without letting your conscience trouble you. [26]Certainly, "The earth is the Lord's and everything it contains is his."*

14:15 So if what you eat hurts another Christian, you are no longer living by love. Don't destroy anyone by what you eat. Christ died for that person.

In exercising our freedom in Christ, we must be respectful and considerate of one another. We are to be more concerned for others than ourselves. "[8]*Food will not affect our relationship with God. We are no worse off if we eat that food and no better off if we don't.* [9]*But be careful that by using your freedom you don't somehow make a believer who is weak in faith fall into sin*" *(1 Corinthians 8:8–9)*.

If eating or drinking certain foods offends a fellow believer, we should not do it. We have liberty in Christ to eat anything. That same liberty in Christ gives us the freedom *not* to eat anything that would offend our Christian friends. Paul forcefully stated the application of this principle: "Therefore, if eating food offered to false gods causes other believers to lose their faith, I will never eat that kind of food so that I won't make other believers lose their faith" (*1 Corinthians 8:13*).

In Christ, we have great freedom but few rights. Our most important right is to be called children of God. "*He gave the right to become God's children to everyone who believed in him*" *(John 1:12)*. Many things are lawful in Christ but may not be beneficial if they cause others to sin. "*When you sin against other believers in this way and harm their weak consciences, you are sinning against Christ*" *(1 Corinthians 8:12)*. We have been given liberty in Christ, but we must not abuse this liberty. "*You were indeed called to be free, brothers and sisters. Don't turn this freedom into an excuse for your corrupt nature to express itself*" *(Galatians 5:13)*.

Notes/Applications

In Christ, we have great freedom in all areas not commanded in Scripture. Nevertheless, we are not to judge others about such matters. At the same time, we must not cause other believers to stumble by insisting on freedom in areas that would offend them. The law of love should rule our lives in relationship to fellow believers. If there is an offense between believers, God's Word provides a remedy to put such issues to rest, thereby insuring the tranquility of the body of Christ *(Matthew 18:15–18)*.

May the love of our Lord so command our normal inclinations that we will not be stumbling blocks to anyone. *"Whenever we have the opportunity, we have to do what is good for everyone, especially for the family of believers"* (*Galatians 6:10*).

The Lord Jesus, the Christ, will one day judge all matters. He will judge the motives of all our hearts and bring to light all of our thoughts, words, and actions. One day everything will be brought into His true light. Therefore, we should refrain from being judgmental of other believers over matters of small importance. Instead, we should encourage the liberty and freedom of others, finding joy and satisfaction as they mature in their relationship to Jesus Christ.

Romans 14:16–23

14:16 Don't allow anyone to say that what you consider good is evil.

The early verses of chapter fourteen established this basic principle: We are to welcome people who are weak in faith but not to dispute over differences concerning matters not specified in the Scriptures. Those who eat certain foods are not to despise those who do not eat them, and those who do not eat those foods are not to despise those who do. Therefore, Paul reminded everyone not to sin by improperly judging others.

If we make major issues out of insignificant preferences, our liberty in Christ will be misinterpreted and our witness will be greatly diminished. Further, the goodness of God could be considered a burden imposed on others rather than the release from sin that God has promised. What God has meant for good might be determined by outside observers to be evil.

Nevertheless, we are to seek a good conscience before God as we seek His conviction of us on such matters:

> [29]*I'm not talking about your conscience but the other person's conscience. Why should my freedom be judged by someone else's conscience?* [30]*If I give thanks to God for the food I eat, why am I condemned for that?* [31]*So, whether you eat or drink, or whatever you do, do everything to the glory of God. (1 Corinthians 10:29–31)*

All Christians are enjoined to love one another and seek the unity of the Spirit:

> [14]*We encourage you, brothers and sisters, to instruct those who are not living right, cheer up those who are discouraged, help the weak, and be patient with everyone.* [15]*Make sure that no one ever pays back one wrong with another wrong. Instead, always try to*

do what is good for each other and everyone else. (1 Thessalonians 5:14–15)

14:17 *God's kingdom does not consist of what a person eats or drinks. Rather, God's kingdom consists of God's approval and peace, as well as the joy that the Holy Spirit gives.*

The kingdom of God does not consist of a set of regulations established by the preferences imposed by one group of believers on another group of believers. After all, we all became citizens of God's kingdom by the work of the Spirit imparting to us sinners the truth of His Word, revealing the work of Christ as the Savior of the world. Once adopted as children of the King, we embark on a journey of faith, learning to love and obey our King. That journey begins in the joy of the Holy Spirit as the burden of sin is removed; the journey ends in a song of praise when we meet our Savior face-to-face. All other issues pale in the light of His presence.

God's kingdom is essentially composed of His righteousness, peace, and joy—all given by the Holy Spirit. This is the very antithesis of the kingdoms of this world that are ruled by the prince of darkness. They are full of injustice, hate, conflict, and empty promises of pleasure. The Scriptures portray this contrast in many ways: life and death, light and darkness, love and hate, works of the flesh and fruit of the Spirit.

God's kingdom is within each believer individually by the Holy Spirit and in the body of Christ corporately by the same Spirit *(Galatians 5:22–23)*. This great promise to each believer is secured by Jesus' death, resurrection, and ascension to His Father.

14:18 *The person who serves Christ with this in mind is pleasing to God and respected by people.*

When the Spirit lives within people who have been adopted into God's kingdom, their perspectives change, and their minds and hearts are focused on Christ and on the work that He has accomplished on their behalf. Having been forgiven of their sins and living in the peace and joy that the Spirit imparts, they no longer regard the minor issues as important. Instead, their full devotion to the Lord consumes every waking moment as they seek to find ways to help others in their walk. In this service, they welcome the help that others give to them as they journey with the rest of the body of believers. Thus, as Christ served the Father, we serve Christ.

Such an example testifies to the change that God has wrought in our lives. Even unbelievers are impressed by Christians who walk among them with honesty and integrity, avoiding religious pretenses and critical analysis of anything and everything around them. In this way, the Christian is assured of God's approval and the respect of those who have never bowed their knee to Him. In fact, the world cannot help but admire such genuine Christians. They are real people, not religious hypocrites.

14:19 *So let's pursue those things which bring peace and which are good for each other.*

Even though Paul had directed his readers to the kingdom of God and the peace and joy that the Holy Spirit gives, there are very practical applications that grow out of these lofty doctrines. Those practical applications create the atmosphere in which believers should live and serve. The thoughts of every individual should be directed toward the welfare of every other individual and the well being of the body of Christ as a whole.

First, Paul urged Christians to pursue those things that establish peace among believers. Differences of opinion have many solutions. Stronger believers should always consider the opinions of others to be more important than their own. We do not have to compromise the truth of God's Word, but many times, the issues are not important enough to warrant a continuing debate. Instead, we should always search for the most peaceful means of bringing resolution to such situations.

When Paul urged us to "pursue those things which bring peace," he implied that we must work against our natural inclinations and desires. We must suppress the sinful nature in order to seek the peace that God bestows. *"Become complete. Be of good comfort, be of one mind, live in peace; and the God of love and peace will be with you" (2 Corinthians 13:11,* NKJV*).*

We need to continually help our fellow believers grow, rejoicing as they mature in faith. We should guard our words and restrain the selfishness that wants to come out of our mouths. We should avoid anything that tears the body of Christ apart. Instead, we should always seek to do what is helpful and constructive *(Ephesians 4:29).* This peace that we are to pursue is not for a few "super saints" but for all of God's people *(Colossians 3:12–15).*

14:20–21 ***[20]Don't ruin God's work because of what you eat. All food is acceptable, but it's wrong for a person to eat something if it causes someone else to have doubts. [21]The right thing to do is to avoid eating meat, drinking wine, or doing anything else that causes another Christian to have doubts.***

In view of God's wonderful gifts to His people, the issue of Christian liberty is a minor pursuit. We who are strong must not exercise our freedom at the expense of a weaker brother. The real issue is not eating and drinking but attitude. In view of everything we have in Christ, should we not willingly give up something that might negatively impact the faith of another Christian?

God is working in all of our lives. As we help each other, we must not allow our preferences to hinder the growth of others. Rather, we must set a godly example and take every opportunity to instruct and guide those who are weaker, including new believers and immature Christians.

If eating certain foods and drinking wine offends a fellow believer, Paul made it clear that we are not to insist on our freedom. Our love for God and for them must be the determining factor from which our actions develop. Our freedom does not give us the right to do anything, for we have been bought with a price and Christ owns us. We are free in Christ to love as He loved. If we are Christ-centered, we will not be focused on ourselves but on others.

14:22 ***So whatever you believe about these things, keep it between yourself and God. The person who does what he knows is right shouldn't feel guilty. He is blessed.***

Paul's strongest advice for Christians was to keep their mouths shut about their positions on these minor issues. If the issue is unimportant, let it go. We should not beat others over the head with our personal preferences. That does not prevent us from doing what is right. We need to have the courage of our convictions before the Lord. However, creating an atmosphere of contention for the sake of one's personal preference is not worthy of our calling before Jesus Christ. When we succumb to peer pressure at any age or do something simply because another Christian is doing it, we are on shaky ground. There may be things others do that we should not do or things we do that they should not do. A mark of Christian maturity is having the discernment to understand the difference.

We all should do what we know is right. However, this is not about salvation or moral conduct. Instead, Paul was speaking about the insignificant issues—eating meat or giving special importance to one day over another. In such matters, we can do what we believe is right without feeling guilty. One person can refrain from eating certain foods because this is a personal conviction; another person may eat those same foods and do so with absolutely no guilt. Both are right! It's between the individual and God.

Knowing in our hearts that we are doing what God wants results in contentment because we are living in the Father's will. "*Keep your conscience clear. Then those who treat the good Christian life you live with contempt will feel ashamed that they have ridiculed you*" (1 Peter 3:16).

14:23 ***But if a person has doubts and still eats, he is condemned because he didn't act in faith. Anything that is not done in faith is sin.***

The Amplified Bible says it this way:

> *But the man who has doubts (misgivings, an uneasy conscience) about eating, and then eats [perhaps because of you], stands condemned [before God], because he is not true to his convictions and he does not act from faith. For whatever does not originate and proceed from faith is sin [whatever is done without a conviction of its approval by God is sinful].*

Throughout this chapter, Paul emphasized the responsibility of stronger Christians toward the weaker and less mature ones. It is imperative that stronger believers never do anything that would cause weaker believers to stumble, to question their faith, or to doubt God's faithfulness. However, in this verse Paul also placed responsibility on the weaker Christians. If they indiscriminately follow the advice of stronger Christians without being convinced of the rightness of the action, they are accountable. If they falter in this matter, then they have offended their own convictions and have fallen into sin not because they have really done anything wrong but because they have not acted out of faith.

No matter whether we are stronger or weaker believers, all our actions should be taken out of the strong position of our faith. If stronger believers deliberately mislead weaker believers on some minor matter, they are committing sin. If weaker believers follow the stronger simply because they are stronger but are going against their own consciences in doing so, they are committing sin. Both will one day stand before the judgment seat of Christ and give account for their actions. This should motivate both stronger and weaker Christians to pause and consider any and all actions before acting on or following ideas of which they have not yet been fully convinced by the Holy Spirit.

Notes/Applications

Our God is a dynamic God. He holds the constellations in the palms of His hands. He also directs the paths of each of His children as they walk in the faith that He has given them. In the diversity of our different lives, He determines the directions that His children take. We should marvel at the miracle that God has created in all of us through the indwelling Christ. We should appreciate and rejoice that not all people are like us. God has directed a wide diversity of people to receive the gift of His salvation.

Throughout these verses, Paul consistently and repeatedly reminds us that we should recognize the greatness of the Lord and, in the light of this recognition, forget the numerous petty issues that might keep us from enjoying the fellowship of others just because they have differing opinions about nonessential issues. We should be mature enough to allow for differences. We should also be willing to submit to others so that we do not offend weaker believers. Instead, we should do everything we can to help them grow even if that means giving up something we perceive as a personal right.

In the end, Christians have been set free. Jesus said, "If the Son sets you free, you will be absolutely free" *(John 8:36)*. Still, that freedom does not give us license to sin, and neither does it give us license to flaunt that freedom if doing so could cause another believer to stumble.

ROMANS 15

Romans 15:1–7

15:1 ***So those of us who have a strong faith must be patient with the weaknesses of those whose faith is not so strong. We must not think only of ourselves.***

Paul's encouragement toward stronger Christians continued here from the previous chapter: all strong Christians should help weaker believers. The strong have matured in the faith to the point where belief has grown into conviction. The faith of the weak has been hindered by doubts about what they can do as Christians. Their faith is genuine but fragile. Those who are strong need to encourage the weak in the knowledge of God's Word so that their consciences can become strong, trusting the Lord rather than depending on others.

We are not to do what pleases ourselves but, rather, seek the welfare of those around us. Doing so strengthens our own faith and builds us into potent believers who are able to help others grow in their faith in Christ. "[1]*My child, find your source of strength in the kindness of Christ Jesus.* [2]*You've heard my message, and it's been confirmed by many witnesses. Entrust this message to faithful individuals who will be competent to teach others" (2 Timothy 2:1–2).*

15:2 *We should all be concerned about our neighbor and the good things that will build his faith.*

Our thoughts should be toward the welfare of others with the objective of building their faith. Being centered in Christ, we must subject our personal goals to the good of weaker brothers and sisters, thus edifying the whole body of Christ *(1 Corinthians 10:24, 33).*

This will lead to healthy growth in the Christian life and in the Christian community. Each member of Christ's body who is strengthened helps build the whole body as a strong witness to the world. When these weaker members become strong in the faith, they are motivated and enabled to reach out to others who are in need. This produces a church that serves God and honors Christ.

15:3 *Christ did not think only of himself. Rather, as Scripture says, "The insults of those who insult you have fallen on me."*

As he did so many times before, Paul pointed to Jesus Christ as the supreme example of what we are to do as mature believers. The eternal Son of God became the perfect man, enduring the reproach of the people that He came to save.

Paul quoted from Psalm 69:7, referred to as a messianic psalm: "Indeed, for your sake I have endured insults. Humiliation has covered my face." Jesus bore sins, insults, and injustices in the world for the sake of His Father so that we might be exalted. Christ obeyed, and believers are the recipients of redemption as a result of His obedience and humiliation. He purchased salvation with His shed blood. He endured scourging, mocking, hatred, and scorn to please God, leaving us a legacy of love that is unmatched in history. Paul reminded us of Christ's selflessness, which serves as the example of the selflessness with which we should uphold one another, supporting and strengthening the faith of others. Barnhouse has captured the fine distinctions that this verse presents to the believer:

> So, quietly, knowingly, trustfully, the Lord Jesus took everything that the world could say or do to Him. The mocking, the scourging, the reviling, the spitting, the death—He took it all because He loved the Father. And we shall become like Him as we know Him better and love Him more, and are willing to stand in His place in this world, not only in what we let Him do through us in love and grace to others, but in what we let the world do to us because of His dear name's sake.[1]

15:4 *Everything written long ago was written to teach us so that we would have confidence through the endurance and encouragement which the Scriptures give us.*

The Old Testament Scriptures were written for our instruction. The history of the creation, the fall, and redemption are revealed to give us truth, knowledge, and wisdom in serving God. Without exception, the books of Moses, the histories, the psalms, and the prophecies urge us to live in submission to the one and only living God. "[6]*These things have become examples for us so that we won't desire what is evil, as they did…* [11]*These things happened to make them an example for others. These things were written down as a warning for us who are living in the closing days of history*" (1Corinthians 10:6, 11).

God's written Word has been given to us by our heavenly Father to instruct us on how to live. "[16]*Every Scripture passage is inspired by God. All of them are useful for teaching, pointing out errors, correcting people, and training them for a life that has God's approval.* [17]*They equip God's servants so that they are completely prepared to do good things*" (2 Timothy 3:16–17).

As we read, study, and meditate upon all of Scripture, we are to study diligently and adopt the Lord's teachings. This endurance brings encouragement and hope.

> [4]*Through his glory and integrity he has given us his promises that are of the highest value. Through these promises you will share in the divine nature because you have escaped the corruption that*

> *sinful desires cause in the world.* [5]*Because of this, make every effort to add integrity to your faith; and to integrity add knowledge;* [6]*to knowledge add self-control; to self-control add endurance; to endurance add godliness;* [7]*to godliness add Christian affection; and to Christian affection add love.* [8]*If you have these qualities and they are increasing, it demonstrates that your knowledge about our Lord Jesus Christ is living and productive.* (2 Peter 1:4–8)

15:5 ***May God, who gives you this endurance and encouragement, allow you to live in harmony with each other by following the example of Christ Jesus.***

This kind of endurance and encouragement comes from God alone, Who faithfully leads us through His written Word to see His Son, the living Word. Jesus' life of obedience to the will of His Father sets a perfect example of joyful submission. "*We must focus on Jesus, the source and goal of our faith. He saw the joy ahead of him, so he endured death on the cross and ignored the disgrace it brought him. Then he received the highest position in heaven, the one next to the throne of God*" (*Hebrews 12:2*).

Following Jesus' example not only produces endurance and encouragement, but it brings harmony among believers. This harmony was experienced fully in the early church soon after the Holy Spirit came upon the believers at Pentecost:

> [46]*The believers had a single purpose and went to the temple every day. They were joyful and humble as they ate at each other's homes and shared their food.* [47]*At the same time, they praised God and had the good will of all the people. Every day the Lord saved people, and they were added to the group.* (Acts 2:46–47)

15:6 ***Then, having the same goal, you will praise the God and Father of our Lord Jesus Christ.***

This like-mindedness can only be experienced as believers focus on the work that Jesus Christ is doing within them. As believers observe God's faithfulness in all situations, they cannot help but join together in praise to God.

***15:7** Therefore, accept each other in the same way that Christ accepted you. He did this to bring glory to God.*

Joyful acceptance of one another is the embodiment of gratitude for God's acceptance of us. Paul was telling believers that the only way they could live in harmony was to accept each other in the context of Christ's acceptance. While there is no real comparison since He died for us while we were still His enemies, believers should be the first to extend their hand in friendship to others. In the end, the purpose of our mutual respect and harmonious fellowship is to bring glory to the God Who has so graciously redeemed us. We can only accomplish this by His grace.

Notes/Applications

Fellowship and relationships within our faith family are vital to our Christian walk. We *are* our brothers' keepers and our sisters' keepers as well! All believers are members of the body of Christ, and each member needs the encouragement, intercession, and teaching of the others. As God's dear children, we need Christlike respect and mutual concern for one another, forgiving each other as our Father has forgiven us. This is not some sort of warm, fuzzy feeling but God's instrument by which His church is nurtured, strengthened, and equipped for the ministry to which He has called it *(Ephesians 4:12–16)*.

Let us help our brothers and sisters to grow, help them up if they fall, and help them if they have not grown in the faith as much as we have. We all are weak from time to time and need the help of one another. Let us show grace and mercy rather than criticism to our weaker brothers and sisters. In so doing, we will fulfill Paul's admonition, our calling in Christ, and our witness to the unsaved community around us. May the Father be glorified in our lives and in our churches.

Romans 15:8–13

***15:8* Let me explain. Christ became a servant for the Jewish people to reveal God's truth. As a result, he fulfilled God's promise to the ancestors of the Jewish people.**

Christ, God's Messiah, fulfilled the Lord's promise to Abraham: "Through your descendant all the nations of the earth will be blessed, because you have obeyed me" *(Genesis 22:18)*. In his letter to the Galatians, Paul emphatically declared that this referred to the Messiah. "*The promises were spoken to Abraham and to his descendant. Scripture doesn't say, 'descendants,' referring to many, but 'your descendant,' referring to one. That descendant is Christ*" *(Galatians 3:16)*.

Jesus Himself affirmed that the purpose of His incarnation was to serve His Father. "*The Son of Man . . . didn't come so that others could serve him. He came to serve and to give his life as a ransom for many people*" *(Matthew 20:28)*. Accordingly, in fulfilling the Father's will, Christ fulfilled God's promise to Israel:

> *[1]In the past God spoke to our ancestors at many different times and in many different ways through the prophets. [2]In these last days he has spoken to us through his Son. God made his Son responsible for everything. His Son is the one through whom God made the universe. [3]His Son is the reflection of God's glory and the exact likeness of God's being. He holds everything together through his powerful words. After he had cleansed people from their sins, he received the highest position, the one next to the Father in heaven. (Hebrews 1:1–3)*

***15:9* People who are not Jewish praise God for his mercy as well. This is what the Scriptures say, "That is why I will give thanks to you among the nations and I will sing praises to your name."**

The entire world is blessed through Israel. Through Abraham's "descendant," salvation came to all people, including the Gentiles. The verse quoted is from Psalm eighteen where King David speaks of the nations and also refers to "his descendant forever." "[49]*That is why I will give thanks to you, O LORD, among the nations and make music to praise your name.* [50]*He gives great victories to his king. He shows mercy to his anointed, to David, and to his descendant forever" (Psalm 18:49–50)*.

The magnificent scene in Revelation chapter five depicts the broad scope of the people who will eventually sing the praises of God's anointed one. People from every corner of the globe—Jews and Gentiles—will join their voices in a song of praise to the Lamb of God that has no end.

> [9]*Then they sang a new song, "You deserve to take the scroll and open the seals on it, because you were slaughtered. You bought people with your blood to be God's own. They are from every tribe, language, people, and nation.* [10]*You made them a kingdom and priests for our God. They will rule as kings on the earth." (Revelation 5:9–10)*

15:10–11 [10]***And Scripture says again, "You nations, be happy together with his people!"*** [11]***And again, "Praise the Lord, all you nations! Praise him, all you people of the world!"***

Paul encouraged everyone to live with an attitude of praise because of God's salvation. Those Gentiles who were saved were to rejoice alongside those believers who were Jewish, further shattering the misconception that salvation was for the Jews only. That God's redemption is available to all was not a new idea, but one that resounds throughout the Old Testament.

> [2]*Then your ways will be known on earth, your salvation throughout all nations.* [3]*Let everyone give thanks to you, O God. Let everyone give thanks to you.* [4]*Let the nations be glad and sing joyfully because you judge everyone with justice and guide the nations on the earth. (Psalm 67:2–4)*.

> [1]*Praise the* L*ORD, all you nations! Praise him, all you people of the world!* [2]*His mercy toward us is powerful. The* L*ORD's faithfulness endures forever. Hallelujah! (Psalm 117:1–2)*

All people were created to worship God, but only by His grace can we praise Him as His redeemed people.

15:12 Again, Isaiah says, "There will be a root from Jesse. He will rise to rule the nations, and he will give the nations hope."

Isaiah chapter eleven traces the Messiah's root to Jesse, the father of King David *(Isaiah 11:1–5, 10)*. Jesus' lineage in Matthew chapter one and Luke chapter three clearly affirmed Isaiah's prophecy given seven hundred years earlier. Jesse was the grandson of Ruth, Boaz's wife, whose story is told in the Old Testament book of Ruth. Jesse was the father of David, the second king of Israel. David was of the tribe of Judah, from which the Messiah was to come. Finally, Jesus Himself affirmed His human genealogy in John's revelation: "I am the root and descendant of David. I am the bright morning star" *(Revelation 22:16)*. Thus, the birth of Jesus Christ was the fulfillment of these prophecies.

"He will rise to rule the nations" refers to a coming day when the Lord Jesus Christ will rule the whole world. At that time all injustice will be dealt with. Jews and Gentiles alike will rejoice in their king, Jesus.

> [27]*All the ends of the earth will remember and return to the* L*ORD. All the families from all the nations will worship you* [28]*because the kingdom belongs to the* L*ORD and he rules the nations. (Psalm 22:27–28)*

> *He was given power, honor, and a kingdom. People from every province, nation, and language were to serve him. His power is an eternal power that will not be taken away. His kingdom will never be destroyed. (Daniel 7:14)*

In stating that "he will give the nations hope," Paul attested that Isaiah foretold the very message that Paul had been impressing upon them—namely, that salvation is available to all, both Jews and Gentiles, through faith in Christ alone.

15:13 ***May God, the source of hope, fill you with joy and peace through your faith in him. Then you will overflow with hope by the power of the Holy Spirit.***

The prophetic evidence of the Old Testament is another means by which Paul asserted the truth of God's Word fulfilled in the person of Jesus Christ. When we fully recognize that Christ is all that the Scriptures have thoroughly revealed, then we can receive the benediction that Paul expressed here. He again affirmed that God is the only source of hope for all things present and those to come. This hope is an unwavering, unfailing reality established in the peace of Christ and affirmed by the power of the Holy Spirit. This hope is only a bud, the flowering of which is still in the future. Barnhouse comments:

> Thus God is not only our help in time of trouble (Psalm 46:1), our present strength and support, our advocate and comforter; he is also the God who will bring to full brightness that future day which will know no sunset. Our future is as bright as the promises of God, which are as certain as God Himself. Patrick Henry said, "I know of no way of judging the future but by the past," and therein lies the hopelessness of man's life. But the believer judges the future by the promises of God who has bound Himself by oath to do all that He has promised.[2]

Notes/Applications

God's truth is confirmed throughout the Scriptures with the Old Testament prophecies being fulfilled in the New Testament revelation of Jesus Christ. God has been faithful to His promise, imparting the righteousness of Christ on undeserving sinners. From the moment of our new birth in Christ, we exalt the name of Jesus Christ, bowing in worship and praise to Him Who has shed His own blood to remove from us the eternal punishment of our sin.

Most people quickly acknowledge those prophecies that speak of God's anointed one as the agent by which all wrongs are made right, evil is destroyed, righteousness established, and blessing granted to the nations. These prophecies were extolled by the Jews, believing that God would again restore the kingdom to Israel and drive out its enemies. In fact, they so fully adopted the rabbinic interpretations of the Scriptures that they never recognized their Messiah when He came to them.

However, other prophecies speak of a Messiah who would suffer for His people. God's anointed one would be broken for the sins of the world. These are the prophecies that Paul emphasized here, affirming that the glory of God's salvation would come upon humankind through a cross, not a crown, and through suffering, not victory.

The crown was given to God's Messiah after He had purchased our redemption on the cross. The victory was conferred on God's suffering servant when He rose from the grave. This is the victorious Lord we praise. This is the redeeming Lord we worship in this life and for eternity. To be received into the family of God is an immeasurable gift. Truly, to be clothed in the righteousness of Christ is an inestimable treasure and the only hope of a lost world desperately in need of a Savior.

Romans 15:14–21

15:14 ***I'm convinced, brothers and sisters, that you, too, are filled with goodness. I'm also convinced that you have all the knowledge you need and that you are able to instruct each other.***

Paul embarked on his extended personal conclusion to this letter with high commendation to the Roman believers. He had opened his letter with this encouraging word: "First, I thank my God through Jesus Christ for every one of you because the news of your faith is spreading throughout the whole world" *(Romans 1:8)*. These believers were mature in Christ, full of goodness and knowledge. This is particularly interesting since they had not been taught by any of Christ's apostles. Instead, the goodness that they possessed was derived from the Savior Who possessed them. The knowledge that they gained had been implanted by the Holy Spirit.

This goodness and knowledge qualified them to instruct one another. When we study God's Word, it is not simply to learn His truth, but also to be immersed in the Spirit Who leads us into God's truth. The Roman believers achieved a level of mutual instruction that few churches achieve. They heard, accepted, and adopted the instruction of the Spirit and kept each other attuned to their holy calling in Christ Jesus.

15:15–16 ***[15]However, I've written you a letter, parts of which are rather bold, as a reminder to you. I'm doing this because God gave me the gift [16]to be a servant of Christ Jesus to people who are not Jewish. I serve as a priest by spreading the Good News of God. I do this in order that I might bring the nations to God as an acceptable offering, made holy by the Holy Spirit.***

Because of their maturity in Christ, Paul was more forceful in his presentation of the gospel in this letter. He spoke sternly about the aspects of the gospel that affected both his own people, the Jews, and the other nations of the world. Through the guidance of the Holy Spirit, these Christians had grown strong and mature in the faith.

Verse sixteen presents a surprising twist to the normally conceived idea of a servant. Paul used the word *priest*, a term used in secular life of a public minister or a servant of the state, and in sacred things of the priests of the Jerusalem temple.[3] Paul considered his service to the Gentile people to be similar to the office of the temple priesthood. Paul described his calling as an apostle to the Gentiles not in the usual terms of preaching and teaching but in the imagery of the Jewish liturgy. Paul said that he was appointed by God to bring the Gentile nations to God as an offering, acceptable and sanctified by the Holy Spirit. This in no way contradicts or diminishes his apostolic office as preacher and teacher, but rather enriches our understanding of the gospel as encompassing the prophetic *and* priestly offices of the Old Testament.

15:17–19 ***[17]So Christ Jesus gives me the right to brag about what I'm doing for God. [18]I'm bold enough to tell you only what Christ has done through me to bring people who are not Jewish to obedience. By what I have said and done, [19]by the power of miraculous and amazing signs, and by the power of God's Spirit, I have finished spreading the Good News about Christ from Jerusalem to Illyricum.***

These are not the words of a proud, self-centered evangelist. In other letters, Paul described himself as "the least of the apostles" *(1 Corinthians 15:9)* and "the foremost sinner" *(1 Timothy 1:15)*. He declared in Galatians 6:14, "It's unthinkable that I could ever brag about anything except the cross of our Lord Jesus Christ. By his cross my relationship to the world and its relationship to me have been crucified." Rather, Paul was speaking here of "bragging in Christ Jesus" about what Christ had done through him to bring the Gentiles to faith and obedience.

Paul's "bragging rights" were not in his own knowledge and skills but in God's calling and grace that both assigned and equipped him to proclaim the good news. He was ordained to teach and apply the truth to establish the Gentiles in the faith. Paul confessed that the power he possessed did not come from his own inner resources but rather from the unlimited resource of God's Spirit working through him. "[5]*By ourselves we are not qualified in any way to claim that we can do anything. Rather, God makes us qualified.* [6]*He has also qualified us to be ministers of a new promise, a spiritual promise, not a written one. Clearly, what was written brings death, but the Spirit brings life"* *(2 Corinthians 3:5–6)*. Paul's ministry was authenticated by supernatural signs and wonders by the Holy Spirit. "*God worked unusual miracles through Paul*" (Acts 19:11).

15:20 ***My goal was to spread the Good News where the name of Christ was not known. I didn't want to build on a foundation which others had laid.***

Paul had the spirit of a pioneer. His passion was to reach people who had never heard the good news. This desire was planted in him from the time of his conversion. When God sent him to Ananias for instructions, God told Ananias in Acts 9:15–16: "[15]Go! I've chosen this man to bring my name to nations, to kings, and to the people of Israel. [16]I'll show him how much he has to suffer for the sake of my name." In his second letter to the Corinthians, Paul again expressed his personal goal of "spreading the Good News in the regions far beyond you" *(2 Corinthians 10:16)*.

In his first letter to the Corinthian church, Paul very carefully outlined the way that God's building, His church, should be constructed.

> [9]*We are God's coworkers. You are God's field. You are God's building.* [10]*As a skilled and experienced builder, I used the gift that God gave me to lay the foundation for that building. However, someone else is building on it. Each person must be careful how he builds on it.* [11]*After all, no one can lay any other foundation than the one that is already laid, and that foundation is Jesus Christ.*
> *(1 Corinthians 3:9–11)*

15:21 ***As Scripture says, "Those who were never told about him will see, and those who never heard will understand."***

This is quoted from Isaiah. "*He will cleanse many nations with his blood. Kings will shut their mouths because of him. They will see things that they had never been told. They will understand things that they had never heard*" *(Isaiah 52:15)*. This reference is found in the great messianic prophecies in chapters fifty-two through fifty-four of Isaiah. The fulfillment of these words in the life and death of Jesus also included Paul's mission to spread God's word to the Gentiles.

The Messiah was to come to earth through God's chosen people, Israel. They were expecting Him, even though most people were unaware of the full impact of these prophecies. Now Christ, God's anointed one, had come, and Paul was spreading the good news to the Jews first and then to the Gentiles that they might share in the blessings of God's kingdom.

Notes/Application

Paul was an outstanding witness for his Lord Jesus Christ because of his own unusual salvation experience. God had been preparing him from birth for this special assignment. He was a fiery Hebrew who took his religious convictions seriously. Thus, he faced his previous life squarely without hesitation and confessed the errors of what had been misguided theology *(1 Timothy 1:12–14)*.

All Christians are saved in the same way that Paul was—by God's grace through faith. Obviously, Paul had no merit in his religiously zealous life that would warrant his salvation. In fact, he admitted that he had persecuted Christ's church. Nevertheless, Paul's special calling and conversion were unique. No one in his day would have considered him a candidate to become the greatest apostle.

In a similar fashion, each believer has a unique path by which Christ leads him or her to the cross. Each believer has a path of service for which God has saved him or her, a unique position in the kingdom that only he or she can fill. This reminds us of our dependence upon God, not only for our redemption but also for direction in the path that our redeemed life should take. Our Lord promises that He has saved us and will use us for His glory.

Romans 15:22–27

15:22 *This is what has so often kept me from visiting you.*

In chapter one, Paul said that he had often planned to visit the believers in Rome but was hindered from doing so *(Romans 1:13)*. He stated that Satan sometimes hindered his travel plans *(1 Thessalonians 2:18)*. Other times, Christ prevented Paul from going into some area *(Acts 16:7)*. Whatever the reasons, Paul's life had been extremely busy, filled with the obligation to teach and disciple believing Christians in the eastern section of the Roman empire. More importantly, Paul's life was under the direction of God's sovereign oversight, and he would go to Rome only when God permitted and in the manner that God directed.

15:23–24 *[23]But now I have no new opportunities for work in this region. For many years I have wanted to visit you. [24]Now I am on my way to Spain, so I hope to see you when I come your way. After I have enjoyed your company for a while, I hope that you will support my trip to Spain.*

Now that his work in the eastern section of the Roman empire was finished, Paul planned to visit Spain and hoped to stop in Rome on the way. God's timing is always right, and evidently Paul's extensive ministry from Jerusalem to Illyricum had been fulfilled. He had enjoyed a unique long distance relationship with the healthy church in Rome, but longed to see them in person *(Romans 1:9–12)*.

Certainly, Rome was not an afterthought, for Paul even suggested they might want to support his trip to Spain. This would make sense in view of their evident spiritual vitality and maturity. It would certainly include support in both prayer and finances but also include the possibility of some of them accompanying Paul in his travels.

Paul's aspiration to visit Spain showed his profound commitment to spreading the good news and his interest in reaching people for Christ. Reaching Spain, at the far western end of the empire, presented monumental challenges to even the most ambitious traveler.

Some believe Paul actually fulfilled this goal, but there is no biblical record of such a visit.

In the last chapter of Acts, Paul finally arrived in Rome as a prisoner in chains. Although this was likely not the way he had envisioned himself arriving in Rome, he was able to minister among the Roman believers for two years.

15:25–26 ***[25]Right now I'm going to Jerusalem to bring help to the Christians there. [26]Because the believers in Macedonia and Greece owe a debt to the Christians in Jerusalem, they have decided to take up a collection for the poor among the Christians in Jerusalem.***

This proposed visit to Jerusalem was likely a part of Paul's third missionary journey *(Acts 18:23–21:16)*. *"After all these things had happened, Paul decided to go to Jerusalem by traveling through Macedonia and Greece. He said, 'After I have been there, I must see Rome'" (Acts 19:21)*.

Notice that Paul's main mission in Jerusalem was to minister to the believers. He was a true "servant-leader" in his whole ministry to people. This focus on meeting their physical needs was not inconsistent with his calling to preach the good news. In fact, it was part of that calling, as Jesus had demonstrated in His ministry. Even though Paul considered himself to be the Apostle to the Gentiles, his intention to take the contribution to Jerusalem revealed his intense love for Jewish believers.

Out of gratitude to God and the believers in Jerusalem, the Christians in Macedonia and Greece had taken up generous collections to send to the church in Jerusalem, which was suffering greatly. Following the model of the early believers, they helped one another.

15:27 ***These Macedonians and Greeks have shared the spiritual wealth of the Christians in Jerusalem. So they are obligated to use their earthly wealth to help them.***

In keeping with the context of his letter, Paul asserted that the Macedonians and Greeks were the recipients of the spiritual wealth that came to them through the Jews. Because the church in Jerusalem was by that time so severely oppressed by both the Roman authorities and their Jewish leaders, Paul felt the Macedonians and Greeks were obligated to help the church in Jerusalem by giving from their material resources.

The spiritual principles of godly giving that characterized the Macedonians and Greeks are applicable to all but sadly have rarely been practiced among believers throughout history. These Christians were not impoverished by their lavish generosity, but rather, they experienced great joy and delight in their giving. While the example of their giving is good and commendable, it was also their duty. *"If we have planted the spiritual seed that has been of benefit to you, is it too much if we receive part of the harvest from your earthly goods?" (1 Corinthians 9:11).*

Obligation is a worthy motivator to our giving, but gratitude is much greater. Generous giving among Christians is contagious; it begins an endless cycle of giving and receiving around the world. Most important, it honors our Lord.

DIG DEEPER: ***Godly Giving***

The church in Macedonia is a wonderful example of godly giving. Although they had never met their fellow believers from Jerusalem, they shared willingly and lavishly, far beyond any expectations. The classic passage on Christian giving is found in chapters eight and nine of Paul's second letter to the Corinthians *(2 Corinthians 8:1–5* and *2 Corinthians 9:1, 5–11).*

Notes/Applications

Paul expressed his deep desire to visit the Roman believers at the beginning of this letter and again in the closing paragraphs. Although his life's ministry was primarily to the Gentiles of Asia Minor and the immediate surrounding regions, he felt that it was important to visit the capital city of the Roman empire and affirm the faith of the believers there. The reports that came from Rome verified that these believers were extraordinarily mature in their faith, even though it appeared that they had received no apostolic visits. To realize his dreams, Paul laid out plans to visit Spain and to visit Rome on the way, eliciting the prayers and the support of the believers there.

However, in the past this visit had been diverted by other concerns. Sometimes, Paul was deliberately redirected by the Holy Spirit. Paul made his plans, but God's direction prevailed, overriding Paul's personal desires. This is another example of Paul's clearly defined expectation to take the gospel to Spain, but according to available resources, he likely never achieved this objective. His plans to go to Rome, however, were realized, but not in the way that he expected. Instead of traveling as a free citizen, he was arrested in Jerusalem. He took advantage of his Roman citizenship and appealed to Caesar. Thus, he arrived in Rome in chains as a prisoner for the sake of the gospel.

Most believers can identify with Paul. Who hasn't made plans, big ones and little ones, only to find that they are changed or even canceled because of some conflicting information or sudden change in circumstances? Unfortunately, many times we react with grumbling, irritated that our hard work was for nothing. If we take a closer look at the reversals in Paul's plans, we discover that he never begrudged these changes but accepted them as the intervention of the Lord. Can we do the same?

We should understand beyond any shadow of a doubt that God is in charge of all aspects of our lives. God's interruptions are corrections for our lives, nudging us in a different direction than we had originally planned. Instead of responding in frustration, we should accept these "interruptions" as evidence of God's continued care for us. Paul's recurring theme throughout this letter has been to affirm without hesitation the sovereignty of God. This was true for the Jewish people, the Gentile nations, and was true for Paul himself.

This is still true for every person who has been redeemed by Christ. And so, regardless of the circumstances, believers should rejoice that God keeps them in the center of His gracious will, protecting them, guiding them, and bringing honor to His holy name.

Romans 15:28–33

15:28–29 ***[28]When the collection is completed and I have officially turned the money over to the Christians in Jerusalem, I will visit you on my way to Spain. [29]I know that when I come to you I will bring the full blessing of Christ.***

Paul's priority was clear: to finish the collection from the Greeks and Macedonians and to deliver it safely to the Jerusalem believers. Then he planned to fulfill his long-time desire to visit Rome on his way to Spain. Duty must always have priority over desire, and Paul had learned to "put first things first."

"Officially turned the money over" is translated in the King James Version as "sealed to them this fruit."[4] This is interesting in that the term "fruit" designates this offering as pleasing to God. John Calvin comments aptly: "The word *fruit* seems to designate the produce, which he had before said returned to the Jews from the propagation of the gospel, in a way similar to the land, which by bringing forth fruit supports its cultivator."[5] Calvin also suggests that Paul was attesting to his own integrity with the word *sealed.* For certain, he took his financial responsibility most seriously, a shining example to all trustees of God's gifts.

When this mission was accomplished, Paul reaffirmed his intention to visit the believers in Rome. As already mentioned, although we have no record that Paul ever made it to Spain, he did have a providential delivery to Rome. Likewise, we are advised to plan ahead under the guidance of the Holy Spirit but always in submission to God's will:

> *[13]Pay attention to this! You're saying, "Today or tomorrow we will go into some city, stay there a year, conduct business, and make money." [14]You don't know what will happen tomorrow. What is life? You are a mist that is seen for a moment and then disappears. [15]Instead, you should say, "If the Lord wants us to, we will live and carry out our plans." (James 4:13–15)*

Paul knew that if and when he finally arrived in Rome, it would be with the full blessing of the Lord Jesus Christ. He would have much to share with them about his many ministry experiences. Most important, he would bring with him a special blessing from God, just as rich as the material blessings he carried to the Jerusalem believers.

15:30–31 ***[30]Brothers and sisters, I encourage you through our Lord Jesus Christ and by the love that the Spirit creates, to join me in my struggle. Pray to God for me [31]that I will be rescued from those people in Judea who refuse to believe. Pray that God's people in Jerusalem will accept the help I bring.***

As he concluded the body of this letter, Paul asked the Roman believers to be his prayer warriors in the name of the Lord and in the love imparted by the Holy Spirit. Throughout the years of his ministry, Paul often faced opposition that sometimes resulted in beatings, stoning, and imprisonment. His struggle for Christ was extremely strenuous and filled with many anxious moments. Here, he asked fellow believers to share in his ministry by praying for him in these struggles.

In this urgent plea, Paul anticipated that his return to Jerusalem could be treacherous since he had been warned of specific threats on his life if he went there. When the prophet Agabus warned that he would be harmed, Paul replied, "I'm ready not only to be tied up in Jerusalem but also to die there for the sake of the Lord, the one named Jesus" *(Acts 21:13)*. Therefore, Paul's urgent request was based on a warning. He asked the Roman believers to pray that the Lord would deliver him from these enemies of the gospel. Paul, the grand leader especially of Gentile Christians, was on their "most wanted—dead or alive" list.

Paul showed tremendous courage and faith in determining to go to Jerusalem in spite of grave danger.

> *[22]I am determined to go to Jerusalem now. I don't know what will happen to me there. [23]However, the Holy Spirit warns me in every city that imprisonment and suffering are waiting for me. [24]But I don't place any value on my own life. I want to finish the race I'm running. I want to carry out the mission I received from the Lord Jesus—the mission of testifying to the Good News of God's kindness.* (Acts 20:22–24)

His second prayer request was just as important to him: that he would be received well by the church of Jerusalem and that his gift from the churches of Greece and Macedonia would be acceptable to them. In the Council of Jerusalem *(Acts 15)*, his testimony had been received, and he was commended in his ministry to the Gentiles. Nevertheless, there were many Jewish Christians who, for various reasons, were not fully satisfied with his ministry. This was an important moment in the history of the Jerusalem church, and Paul's great desire was that they would receive the generous gift of fellow believers who were primarily Greeks.

15:32 *Also pray that by the will of God I may come to you with joy and be refreshed when I am with you.*

His third and final prayer request was to visit Rome in the joy of the Lord so that he might be energized by sharing with them. The most joyous place in the world is to be in the center of God's will. Since Paul was convinced that God was leading him to Jerusalem, he rejoiced in that assurance despite the risks. Paul was completely committed to his Lord, so his joy did not depend on his circumstances.

Nothing compares with the certainty of our salvation and the fellowship with other believers. Together, we are invigorated by His holy Word, corporate worship, prayer, and sharing God's gifts.

15:33 *May the God of peace be with you all. Amen.*

The body of Paul's long letter to the Romans ends with a short benediction. The words are filled with meaning for all Christians. God alone has the authority and power to give meaning and order to the lives of believers. He alone can demand our obedience. He alone deserves our praise. To confer the blessing of this sovereign being as the God of peace is a source of great encouragement and comfort. Just as those whom Paul was addressing, we have peace with God *(Romans 5:1)*, the peace of God *(Philippians 4:7)*, and the God of peace *(Hebrews 13:20)*. What a powerful conclusion to this magnificent letter!

Notes/Applications

Paul's letters are filled with prayers and references to prayer. In 1 Thessalonians 5:17, he exhorted believers to "never stop praying." In Ephesians chapter six, prayer was one of the two offensive weapons God provided for spiritual warfare. After mentioning the Word of God as the sword of the Spirit, he said the following: "[18]Pray in the Spirit in every situation. Use every kind of prayer and request there is. Use every kind of effort and make every kind of request for all of God's people. [19]Also pray that God will give me the right words to say" *(Ephesians 6:18–19)*.

In our busy lives, we must rediscover the vital importance of moment-by-moment prayer. There is a critical need for Christians around the world to pray for one another. Paul set a wonderful example of a praying Christian, but our Lord Jesus is our greatest model for prayer. The eternal Son of God depended upon His Father for daily bread, but His primary petition was "Let your kingdom come. Let your will be done on earth as it is done in heaven" *(Matthew 6:10)*.

May we follow the example of Christ and humbly bow before our faithful Lord in praise and gratitude for His unending faithfulness. May we also intercede faithfully for the spiritual welfare of our Christian brothers and sisters.

ROMANS 16

Romans 16:1–16

***16:1** With this letter I'm introducing Phoebe to you. She is our sister in the Christian faith and a deacon of the church in the city of Cenchrea.*

This long letter to the Christians in Rome was being delivered by Phoebe; therefore, Paul included this commendation so that the readers would know that the letter was authentic. Phoebe was identified as a sister in the faith and a deacon of the church in Cenchrea. Deacons are described as those who, by virtue of the office assigned to them by the church, "care for the poor and have charge of and distribute the money collected for their use."[1]

Cenchrea was Corinth's seaport that looked toward Asia. It was situated on the Saronic Gulf.[2] We can assume that Paul knew Phoebe from his visits to Corinth. This is the only mention of her in the Bible.

16:2 ***Give her a Christian welcome that shows you are God's holy people. Provide her with anything she may need, because she has provided help to many people, including me.***

Paul asked the believers in Rome to welcome Phoebe graciously, show her genuine hospitality, and minister to her needs. She was personally commissioned to carry Paul's letter to the Roman Christians, and he commended her for having served him and many others. In the early church, there was a special reason for hospitality and other acts of service among Christians. Many were poor and often in distress, sometimes suffering persecution. The example of believers caring for others is always a profound witness. "*Whenever we have the opportunity, we have to do what is good for everyone, especially for the family of believers*" *(Galatians 6:10)*.

16:3–4 ***[3]Greet Prisca and Aquila, my coworkers in the service of Christ Jesus. [4]They risked their lives to save me. I'm thankful to them and so are all the churches among the nations.***

Prisca and Aquila are the same people mentioned in Acts 18:1–2. In Acts, she is called Priscilla, the diminutive form of Prisca.[3] Priscilla and Aquila were a married couple, Paul's dear friends, and fellow servants in Christ. Paul had met them on his trip to Corinth *(Acts 18:2–3)*.

These coworkers were well-known for their teaching and ministry. When Apollos, an eloquent teacher of the Scriptures, came to Ephesus, it became clear that he needed more instruction in the faith. They "took him home with them and explained God's way to him more accurately" *(Acts 18:26)*. Priscilla and Aquila truly loved Paul and, in fact, at one time risked their lives to save him. No details about this event are known, but their faithful service as Jewish Christians, often at significant risk, greatly impressed the Gentile believers.

16:5 ***Also greet the church that meets in their house. Greet my dear friend Epaenetus. He was the first person in the province of Asia to become a believer in Christ.***

Priscilla and Aquila hosted a "house church," a common meeting place for first-century believers. Personal greetings from Paul would be appreciated since many undoubtedly knew him. Among these was his first convert in Asia, a man named Epaenetus, who is not mentioned elsewhere in the Scriptures. Asia was that region called Asia Minor, encompassing most of what is now the country of Turkey and perhaps some of the surrounding area.

16:6–7 ***[6]Greet Mary, who has worked very hard for you. [7]Greet Andronicus and Junia, who are Jewish by birth like me. They are prisoners like me and are prominent among the apostles. They also were Christians before I was.***

All we know about this Mary is her labor on behalf of the Roman believers. Andronicus and Junia, identified as fellow Jews, were imprisoned for their faith in Christ just as Paul had been. These two were well-known and respected by Jesus' apostles. They were not among Paul's converts because they had become believers before he had. Whatever their roles, they had an important role in establishing the church in Rome.

16:8–12 ***[8]Greet Ampliatus my dear friend in the service of the Lord. [9]Greet Urbanus our co-worker in the service of Christ, and my dear friend Stachys. [10]Greet Apelles, a true Christian. Greet those who belong to the family of Aristobulus. [11]Greet Herodion, who is Jewish by birth like me. Greet those Christians who belong to the family of Narcissus. [12]Greet Tryphaena and Tryphosa, who have worked hard for the Lord. Greet dear Persis, who has worked very hard for the Lord.***

In greeting these people, Paul showed great affection for them and appreciation for their faithful service and hard work for the Lord Jesus Christ. They were recognized for their witness as genuine

Christians among the family of faith and their communities at large. No information is given about how or when Paul knew them, but they likely met him in one or more of the cities he visited on his missionary journeys, prominent cities like Corinth, Athens, Ephesus, Philippi, or Thessalonica. There was a great deal of commercial travel to and from Rome, the capital of the empire. Like Priscilla and Aquila, some of these believers had probably lived in those cities. Two extended families, the households of Aristobulus and Narcissus, were mentioned.

16:13–15 ***[13]Greet Rufus, that outstanding Christian, and his mother, who has been a mother to me too. [14]Greet Asyncritus, Phlegon, Hermes, Patrobas, Hermas, and the brothers and sisters who are with them. [15]Greet Philologus and Julia, Nereus, and his sister, and Olympas, and all God's people who are with them.***

This reference to Rufus is intriguing, and we would probably all wish Paul had told us more about their relationship. Not only did Paul call him an "outstanding Christian" (literally "chosen of God"), but Rufus' mother received Paul's affectionate commendation for her important role in the apostle's life. We know nothing more of the others mentioned here, except that they were special to Paul, probably people he had met during his travels throughout Asia Minor. Whoever these people were, they are a part of God's Word and their names are recorded in acknowledgment of their significance in the work of Christ's kingdom. The term "God's people," used often in the New Testament letters, refers to God's people whom He has *set apart* for His service.

16:16 ***Greet each other with a holy kiss. All the churches of Christ greet you.***

The "holy kiss" was a common practice in that culture. Many of the letters that circulated among the early Christians encouraged this practice as a special expression of Christ's love. *"Greet each other with a holy kiss" (1 Corinthians 16:20). "Greet one another with a holy kiss" (2 Corinthians 13:12). "Greet each other with a kiss of love" (1 Peter 5:14).* This was an expression of deep love and affection among the Christian community. There was no deceit in this greeting; it expressed heartfelt, honest love of their brothers and sisters in Christ and was a powerful witness of their love for one another to the world. Jesus taught His disciples in John 13:35: "Everyone will know that you are my disciples because of your love for each other."

The greetings from "all the churches of Christ" could be given best by Paul. Through his apostleship commissioned by God, he had started churches in many of the cities that he visited. Throughout his three missionary journeys, many people came to Christ and became a part of God's family.

Notes/Applications

Most of these twenty-eight names, many hard to pronounce, are unfamiliar to us. Still, they were people well-known and dearly loved by Paul. Some had been with him in churches he had planted and nurtured. Many would have been known to other believers. Since Paul emphasized their service for Christ, they would be especially appreciated by fellow Christians. Finally, they would be notable servants of Christ, worthy of mention, like a contemporary *Who's Who in the Apostolic Churches*. Their presence in Paul's writings reflects his genuine appreciation of other people and his desire to see them become useful servants of the Lord Jesus Christ.

The challenge for every Christian is to care for others and to help develop them in the faith. Paul set the wonderful example of a mature servant-leader who cared deeply about people he had met throughout his frequent journeys. Their names were not forgotten but were recorded permanently in this letter, just as Christ Himself entered them in His Book of Life. Paul's love for them faithfully reflected the love that Christ had shown to him. All believers should endeavor with the help of God to follow Paul's example.

Romans 16:17–20

16:17 ***Brothers and sisters, I urge you to watch out for those people who create divisions and who make others fall away from the Christian faith by teaching doctrine that is not the same as you have learned. Stay away from them.***

While the church at Rome was strong and united, Paul urged the believers there to look for early signs of division and false teaching. Paul strongly warned them to avoid people who opposed the doctrine they had been taught. Falsehood frequently creeps in quietly, sowing seeds of dissension and heresy. "*It may be that some people will not listen to what we say in this letter. Take note of them and don't associate with them so that they will feel ashamed*" *(2 Thessalonians 3:14)*.

The first warning Paul gave was about those who cause divisions. He had personally witnessed the devastation that a divisive environment can produce. He had seen it happen in the church in Corinth. "*When you are jealous and quarrel among yourselves, aren't you influenced by your corrupt nature and living by human standards?*" *(1 Corinthians 3:3)*. Paul sharply rebuked the Corinthians for their divisions and rivalry and warned the Romans to beware of any early signs of divisiveness.

Then he warned against false teachers who led others astray from the Christian faith. This church was well established in the truth of the Scriptures, but no one is immune to false teaching. There are people who delight in distorting the truth, even in the guise of bringing greater understanding *(1 Timothy 6:3–5)*.

By the manner in which Paul warned them, it is evident that the Roman Christians were fully committed to the truth and their faith remained strong. However, all Christians, no matter how strong they suppose themselves to be, must be very aware of false doctrine and practices since they can be so easily enticed. Paul's strong advice was to stay away from people who do not teach the truth. "[10]*If anyone comes to you and doesn't bring these teachings, don't take him into your home or even greet him. [11]Whoever greets him shares the evil things he's doing" (2 John 10–11).*

16:18 ***People like these are not serving Christ our Lord. They are serving their own desires. By their smooth talk and flattering words they deceive unsuspecting people.***

The people identified in verse seventeen were self-centered, not Christ-centered. It is impossible to be both. The danger was that they appeared to be speaking good words. Their speech was filled with enough Bible references and familiar Christian expressions that they had the potential to deceive even believers.

Professing to be Christ's servants, they were enslaved by their inner appetites. Those who twisted the truth were already common then and have in every age preyed on believers *(Philippians 3:18–19)*.

Jesus likewise warned in Matthew 7:15–16: "[15]Beware of false prophets. They come to you disguised as sheep, but in their hearts they are vicious wolves. [16]You will know them by what they produce." We should not be surprised when they appear but must be alert for signs and be prepared to oppose them.

16:19 ***Everyone has heard about your obedience and this makes me happy for you. I want you to do what is good and to avoid what is evil.***

Having warned them of false teaching, Paul commended them for their obedience to the faith. In Romans 1:8, he had said: "First, I thank my God through Jesus Christ for every one of you because the news of your faith is spreading throughout the whole world." What a marvelous reputation! Throughout the centuries, there have always been churches that are well-known for their faithfulness to the Scriptures even though there is apostasy all around them. But sadly, through the years, some of these have succumbed to false teaching and eventually fallen away. These warnings are extremely important, admonishing believers to identify the early signs of heresy and deal with them decisively.

The apostle Paul was pleased with the church at Rome and their positive influence. His exhortation was simple: "I want you to do what is good and to avoid what is evil." The New International Version states it this way: "I want you to be *wise* in the good, and *innocent* in evil." Paul was urging the Roman believers to exercise skillful discernment of their Christian environment and to remain untainted by the world's evil, especially the deceptiveness of false teaching. Jesus sent out His disciples to serve with these instructions: "I'm sending you out like sheep among wolves. So be as cunning as snakes but as innocent as doves" *(Matthew 10:16)*. The believers in Rome were shining examples of genuinely mature Christians.

> *In the same way let your light shine in front of people. Then they will see the good that you do and praise your Father in heaven. (Matthew 5:16)*

> *Then you will be blameless and innocent. You will be God's children without any faults among people who are crooked and corrupt. You will shine like stars among them in the world. (Philippians 2:15)*

16:20 ***The God of peace will quickly crush Satan under your feet. May the good will of our Lord Jesus be with you!***

Only the sovereign God can be called "the God of peace." True peace comes only from God and does not originate in this world. Jesus promised His disciples in John 14:27: "I'm leaving you peace. I'm giving you my peace. I don't give you the kind of peace that the world gives. So don't be troubled or cowardly." This is a quality of peace that is foreign to the world.

What did Paul mean when he said that God's peace will crush Satan? To understand this, we must return to the garden of Eden in Genesis chapter three, right after Adam and Eve disobeyed God. At that time, God said to the serpent (Satan): "I will make you and the woman hostile toward each other. I will make your descendants and her descendant hostile toward each other. He will crush your head, and you will bruise his heel" *(Genesis 3:15)*.

In His mercy, God did not crush Adam and Eve but rather promised that Satan would one day be crushed. Then He covered their nakedness with animal skins, the first instance in which blood was shed to pay for sin. Finally, He drove them from the garden of Eden as a judgment for their disobedience. The spiritual warfare that began in the garden continues today but will end in God's certain victory.

Before Satan's head could be crushed, Christ had to fulfill His ultimate sacrifice. *"He was wounded for our rebellious acts. He was crushed for our sins" (Isaiah 53:5)*. The cross appeared to be Satan's final triumph, but it was not the end. Christ came back to life, and through His death and resurrection, Satan's head was crushed because he no longer had the power of sin and death. Satan is a defeated foe, but he is still able to inflict a great deal of adversity in the world as he faces his final defeat.

In concluding this section, Paul again pronounced the good will of God upon his readers. His letters are filled with expressions of hope and blessing upon his fellow believers.

Notes/Applications

This brief warning about false doctrines and unbelieving teachers reminds us that no church is immune from danger. Paul did not address this until the very end of his letter, probably because the church in Rome was remarkably strong and healthy. He actually urged them to watch out for small, early signs of divisiveness or heresy. These can be hard to detect and were often tolerated because they began in small and insignificant ways.

These verses are especially beneficial to churches and individual Christians who are united and healthy. The dangers of division or false teaching are great because they are so subtle. We need to be wary of little signs of error in doctrine, which often start with questions about the complete inspiration and authority of Scripture, the deity of Christ, or the sovereignty of God. If these or other basic doctrines are subject to human misunderstandings, we are in danger of denying God's authority as often seen in the Old Testament invocation of "This is what the LORD says." On the individual level, even small disobedience in this area will lead to a disruption of the believer's relationship to Jesus Christ. Therefore, we should make a conscious, determined effort to know the authors we read and those who teach, preach, and guide our Christian thinking:

> [28]*Pay attention to yourselves and to the entire flock in which the Holy Spirit has placed you as bishops to be shepherds for God's church which he acquired with his own blood.* [29]*I know that fierce wolves will come to you after I leave, and they won't spare the flock.* [30]*Some of your own men will come forward and say things that distort the truth. They will do this to lure disciples into following them.* [31]*So be alert! Remember that I instructed each of you for three years, day and night, at times with tears in my eyes.* [32]*I am now entrusting you to God and to his message that tells how kind he is. That message can help you grow and can give you the inheritance that is shared by all of God's holy people. (Acts 20:28–32)*

Romans 16:21–27

16:21–22 ***[21]Timothy my coworker greets you; so do Lucius, Jason, and Sosipater, who are Jewish by birth like me. [22]I, Tertius, who wrote this letter, send you Christian greetings.***

The letter ends with personal greetings from Paul's coworkers traveling with him. Timothy, Paul's faithful son in the faith, persevered with Paul to the end of his life. Timothy traveled with Paul and Silas on two missionary journeys, and Paul included him in the salutations of five of his epistles: 2 Corinthians, Philippians, Colossians, and both letters to the Thessalonians.

Lucius is sometimes mistaken for Luke, the beloved physician who accompanied Paul on his missionary journeys, but this Lucius was a Jew, like Paul, whereas Luke was probably born at Antioch in ancient Syria of a non-Jewish family. Jason might have been the one mentioned in Acts 17:5–9, and Sosipater in Acts 20:4. We do know that they were close companions of Paul.

Tertius was Paul's scribe, writing Paul's words as he dictated them. This was Paul's common practice, as it is evident that his eyesight was failing. He implied this condition in Galatians 6:11: "Look at how large the letters in these words are because I'm writing this myself." Whether in his own hand or by the hand of a scribe, Paul's letters displayed a great deal of personal warmth and friendliness.

16:23 ***Gaius greets you. He is host to me and the whole church. Erastus, the city treasurer, greets you. Quartus, our brother in the Christian faith, greets you.***

This verse provides evidence that this letter was written in Corinth shortly before Paul left for Jerusalem. He was staying in the home of Gaius, likely the one mentioned in 1 Corinthians 1:14 and one of very few people Paul had baptized. An Erastus is mentioned in Acts 19:22. Whether they were the same person is unknown. However, this Erastus was the city treasurer, demonstrating how the good news of Jesus Christ had reached the highest offices of civil government in Corinth. This is the only mention of the name Quartus.

Verse twenty-four, which GOD'S WORD® Translation and other later English translations omit in accordance with the early Greek manuscripts used in their translation process, reads, "May the good will of our Lord Jesus Christ be with all of you. Amen." Most of these translations include this benediction as a footnote. Nevertheless, its inclusion or exclusion is immaterial to the import of Paul's letter to the Romans. Certainly, it provides a benediction as the letter draws to a close. In this benediction, intercession is offered for the believers to abide always in Christ Jesus.

16:25–27 ***[25]God can strengthen you by the Good News and the message I tell about Jesus Christ. He can strengthen you by revealing the mystery that was kept in silence for a very long time [26]but now is publicly known. The everlasting God ordered that what the prophets wrote must be shown to the people of every nation to bring them to the obedience that is associated with faith. [27]God alone is wise. Glory belongs to him through Jesus Christ forever! Amen.***

Paul concluded his great epistle with this profound benediction. He focused on the good news about Jesus Christ, especially the revelation of the mystery that people from all nations were included in God's plan of redemption:

> *[6]This mystery is the Good News that people who are not Jewish have the same inheritance as Jewish people do. They belong to the same body and share the same promise that God made in Christ Jesus. [7]I became a servant of this Good News through God's kindness freely given to me when his power worked in me. (Ephesians 3:6–7)*

Paul made clear that this was not an afterthought of God but an integral ingredient of the prophets' message. God has always had only one plan established before the creation of the world by which humanity could be saved. Jesus disclosed this to His disciples after the resurrection *(Luke 24:44–47)*. At the end of his message to the house of Cornelius in Acts 10:43, the apostle Peter said: "All the prophets testify that people who believe in the one named Jesus receive forgiveness for their sins through him."

Paul's final statement was the grand finale: "God alone is wise. Glory belongs to him through Jesus Christ forever! Amen." In writing to his son in the faith, Timothy, Paul expressed a similar view of God. "*Worship and glory belong forever to the eternal king, the immortal, invisible, and only God. Amen" (1 Timothy 1:17)*. This expresses the deepest hope of every believer who is nurtured by God's Word, especially as expressed in Paul's letter to the Romans. "[5]*Glory and power forever and ever belong to the one who loves us and has freed us from our sins by his blood* [6]*and has made us a kingdom, priests for God his Father. Amen" (Revelation 1:5–6)*.

Notes/Applications

Paul concluded this great masterpiece of Christian doctrine with personal greetings from several coworkers and a glorious benediction of praise to Almighty God. Paul's stature as a man of God is greatly enhanced by his friends and associates and his commitment to selecting, training, and enabling his coworkers to fulfill Jesus' Great Commission.

This benediction, although not quoted as much as some of his others, has great character befitting the wisdom of the entire epistle. Paul rejoiced in God's magnificent plan of redemption for His people, both Jews and Gentiles from all nations. These final words of praise summarized the message of Romans in which God determined to tell His story of creation and its fall into sin and reveal its redemption through Christ to the entire world. They reveal God's overwhelming victory through His love in Christ, and they encourage our loving response in sacrificial service to Him and summarize a fitting highpoint to this masterpiece of divine grace.

In all things may the redeemed praise the name of God the almighty, creator of heaven and earth, Who demonstrated His love for us, not only in the sacred pages of His eternal Word, but in the gift of His Son, Jesus Christ, our Lord, Who was sent to earth to purchase our salvation by His blood. We praise Him for providing the means, the hope, by which people from all nations can be set free from the curse of sin. As the recipients of His limitless grace, we eagerly look forward to that day when we will lift our voices in song and praise in the glory of His eternal presence.

TEXT NOTES

Introduction

1. *The American Heritage Dictionary,* 3rd ed., s.v. "doctrine."
2. R. Jamieson, A. R. Fausset and D. Brown, "A Commentary, Critical and Explanatory on the Old and New Testaments," in *Logos Scholar's Library.* CD-ROM (Oak Harbor, WA: Logos Research Systems, 1997).
3. Henry Halley, *Halley's Bible Handbook* (Grand Rapids: Zondervan Publishing House, 1962), 584.
4. Ibid., 584.
5. Ibid., 585.

Chapter One

1. J. P. Louw and E. A. Nida, *Greek-English Lexicon of the New Testament: Based on Semantic Domains,* vol. 1 (New York: United Bible Societies, 1989), 740.

2. H. Liddell, "A Lexicon: Abridged from Liddell and Scott's Greek-English Lexicon," in *Logos Library System*. CD-ROM (Oak Harbor, WA: Logos Research Systems, 1997).
3. Donald Grey Barnhouse, *Man's Ruin*, in *Romans*, vol. 1 (Grand Rapids: Eerdmans Publishing Company, 1977), 46.
4. Louw and Nida, *Greek-English Lexicon*, 748.
5. B. M. Newman, *Concise Greek-English Dictionary of the New Testament* (Stuttgart, Germany: United Bible Societies, 1993), 2.
6. Barnhouse, *Romans,* 15.
7. Louw and Nida, *Greek-English Lexicon,* 726.
8. "Christian History: Martin Luther, Early Years," in *Logos Research Systems*. CD-ROM (Oak Harbor, WA: Logos Research Systems, 1997).
9. "A Mighty Fortress is Our God," words by Martin Luther, 1529. Public domain.
10. R. L. Thomas, *New American Standard Hebrew-Aramaic and Greek Dictionaries,* updated ed. (Anaheim: Foundation Publications, 1998), 1617.
11. James Strong, *The Exhaustive Concordance of the Bible: Greek Dictionary of the New Testament*, (Iowa Falls: World Bible Publishers, 1986), 61.
12. John Calvin, *Calvin's Commentaries: Romans,* vol. XIX (Grand Rapids: Baker Books, 1999), 82–83.

Chapter Two

1. James Strong, *The Exhaustive Concordance of the Bible: Greek Dictionary of the New Testament* (Iowa Falls: World Bible Publishers, 1986), 11.
2. John Calvin, *Calvin's Commentaries: Romans,* vol. XIX (Grand Rapids: Baker Books, 1999), 83.
3. J. P. Louw and E. A. Nida, *Greek-English Lexicon of the New Testament: Based on Semantic Domains,* vol. 1 (New York: United Bible Societies, 1989), 761.
4. Max Lucado, *In the Grip of Grace* (Nashville: W Publishing Group, 1996), 37.
5. Strong, *Exhaustive Concordance of the Bible,* 47.

6. "Come, Ye Souls by Sin Afflicted," words by Joseph Swain, 1792. Public domain.
7. Donald Grey Barnhouse, *God's Wrath*, in *Romans*, vol. 1 (Grand Rapids: Eerdmans Publishing Company, 1977), 116.

Chapter Three

1. J. P. Louw and E. A. Nida, *Greek-English Lexicon of the New Testament: Based on Semantic Domain*, vol. 1 (New York: United Bible Societies, 1989), 433.
2. John Calvin, *Calvin's Commentaries: Romans*, vol. XIX (Grand Rapids: Baker Books, 1999), 128.
3. James Strong, *The Exhaustive Concordance of the Bible: Greek Dictionary of the New Testament* (Iowa Falls: World Bible Publishers, 1986), 9.
4. Louw and Nida, *Greek-English Lexicon of the New Testament*, 357.
5. Ibid., 503.
6. K. S. Wuest, *Wuest's Word Studies from the Greek New Testament: For the English Reader* (Grand Rapids: Eerdmans Publishing Company, 1997), 59-60.
7. G. Kittel, G. W. Bromiley, and G. Friedrich, eds., *Theological Dictionary of the New Testament*, vol. 1 (Grand Rapids: Eerdmans Publishing Company, 1976), 359-360.
8. "When I Survey the Wondrous Cross," words by Isaac Watts, 1824. Public Domain.

Chapter Four

1. J. P. Louw and E. A. Nida, *Greek-English Lexicon of the New Testament: Based on Semantic Domains*, vol. 1 (New York: United Bible Societies, 1989), 757.
2. Ibid., 754.
3. Charles Hadden Spurgeon, *All of Grace: The Infinite Love of God* (Springdale, PA: Whitaker House, 1983), 27.
4. Ibid., 16.
5. Louw and Nida, *Greek-English Lexicon of the New Testament*, 59.
6. William Newell, *Romans: Verse-By-Verse* (Grand Rapids: Kregel Publications, 1994), 143.

7. G. Kittel, G. W. Bromiley, and G. Friedrich, eds., *Theological Dictionary of the New Testament,* vol. 1 (Grand Rapids: Eerdmans Publishing Company, 1976), 432.
8. "Amazing Grace," words by John Newton, 1779. Public Domain.

Chapter Five

1. Donald Grey Barnhouse, *God's River*, in *Romans*, vol. 2 (Grand Rapids: Eerdmans Publishing Company, 1977), 165.
2. Charles Haddon Spurgeon, *All of Grace: The Infinite Love of God* (Springdale, PA: Whitaker House, 1983), 76.
3. Ibid., 81.
4. "The Mercy of God Is an Ocean Divine," words by Albert B. Simpson, 1891. Public Domain.

Chapter Six

1. James Strong, *The Exhaustive Concordance of the Bible: Greek Dictionary of the New Testament* (Iowa Falls: World Bible Publishers, 1986), 21.
2. "And Can It Be," words by Charles Wesley, 1738. Public Domain.
3. J. P. Louw and E. A. Nida, *Greek-English Lexicon of the New Testament: Based on Semantic Domains,* vol. 1 (New York: United Bible Societies, 1989), 582.
4. *The Book of Confessions* (Louisville, KY: Office of the General Assembly, Presbyterian Church, U.S.A., 1985), 4.001.
5. William Ernest Henley, "Invictus," in *The Oxford Book of English Verse, 1250–1900,* ed. Sir Arthur Thomas Quiller-Couch (Clarendon: Oxford University Press, 1919), 841.
6. Louw and Nida, *Greek-English Lexicon of the New Testament*, 781.

Chapter Seven

1. Donald Grey Barnhouse, *God's Freedom*, in *Romans,* vol. 3 (Grand Rapids: Eerdmans Publishing Company, 1977), 179.
2. Douglas J. Moo, *The Epistle to the Romans* (Grand Rapids: Eerdmans Publishing Company, 1996), 465.

Chapter Eight

1. Douglas J. Moo, *The Epistle to the Romans* (Grand Rapids: Eerdmans Publishing Company, 1996), 495.
2. J. P. Louw and E. A. Nida, *Greek-English Lexicon of the New Testament: Based on Semantic Domains*, vol. 1 (New York: United Bible Societies, 1989), 463-464.
3. Donald Grey Barnhouse, *God's Heirs*, in *Romans*, vol. 3 (Grand Rapids: Eerdmans Publishing Company, 1977), 97.
4. John Calvin, *Calvin's Commentaries: Romans*, vol. 19 (Grand Rapids: Baker Books, 1999), 303.
5. Moo, *The Epistle to the Romans*, 515.
6. William Hendriksen, *Romans*, of *New Testament Commentary* (Grand Rapids: Baker Books, 1980), 283-284.

Chapter Nine

1. Douglas J. Moo, *The Epistle to the Romans* (Grand Rapids: Eerdmans Publishing Company, 1996), 587.
2. Anne Steele, *Poems on Subjects Chiefly Devotional*, 1760.
3. "Hail, Sovereign Love," words by Jehoida Brewer, in the *Gospel Magazine*, October 1776.

Chapter Ten

1. Donald Grey Barnhouse, *God's Covenants*, in *Romans*, vol. 4 (Grand Rapids: Eerdmans Publishing Company, 1977), 61.
2. R. C. Sproul, *The Gospel of God: An Exposition of Romans* (Scotland: Christian Focus Publications, 1999), 180-181.
3. Timothy Friberg, Barbara Friberg, and Neva Miller, *Analytical Lexicon of the Greek New Testament* (Grand Rapids: Baker Books, 2000), 71.

Chapter Eleven

1. J. P. Louw and E. A. Nida, *Greek-English Lexicon of the New Testament: Based on Semantic Domains*, vol. 1 (New York: United Bible Societies, 1989), 805.

2. James Strong, *The Exhaustive Concordance of the Bible: Greek Dictionary of the New Testament* (Iowa Falls: World Bible Publishers, 1986), 52.
3. R. C. Sproul, *The Gospel of God: An Exposition of Romans* (Great Britain: Christian Focus Publications, 1999), 186.
4. "Love Divine, All Loves Excelling," words by Charles Wesley, 1747. Public Domain.
5. Donald Grey Barnhouse, *God's Covenants*, in *Romans,* vol. 4 (Grand Rapids: Eerdmans Publishing Company, 1977), 168.

Chapter Twelve

1. J. P. Louw and E. A. Nida, *Greek-English Lexicon of the New Testament: Based on Semantic Domains,* vol. 1 (New York: United Bible Societies, 1989), 407.
2. James Strong, *The Exhaustive Concordance of the Bible: Greek Dictionary of the New Testament* (Iowa Falls: World Bible Publishers, 1986), 94.
3. K. S. Wuest. *Wuest's Word Studies from the Greek New Testament: For the English Reader,* vol.1 (Grand Rapids: Eerdmans Publishing Company, 1997), 206-207.
4. Strong, *The Exhaustive Concordance of the Bible*, 83.
5. Ibid., 27.
6. Louw and Nida, *Greek-English Lexicon of the New Testament,* 750.
7. Ibid., 307.
8. Ibid., 454.
9. R. C. Sproul, *The Gospel of God: An Exposition of Romans* (Great Britain: Christian Focus Publications, 1999), 203.

Chapter Thirteen

1. John Calvin, *Calvin's Commentaries: Romans,* vol. XIX (Grand Rapids: Baker Books, 1999), 481.
2. *Merriam-Webster Online Dictionary,* s. v. "conscience," http://www.merriam-webster.com (accessed 4 Aug. 2005).
3. J. P. Louw and E. A. Nida, *Greek-English Lexicon of the New Testament: Based on Semantic Domains*, vol. 1 (New York: United Bible Societies, 1989), 577.

4. G. Kittel, G. W. Bromiley, and G. Friedrich, *Theological Dictionary of the New Testament,* vol. 2 (Grand Rapids: Eerdmans Publishing Company, 1976), 320.
5. R. L. Thomas, *New American Standard Hebrew-Aramaic Greek Dictionaries*, updated ed. (Anaheim: Foundation Publications, 1998) 1648.

Chapter Fourteen

1. B. M. Newman, *Concise Greek-English Dictionary of the New Testament* (Stuttgart, Germany: United Bible Societies, 1993), 64.
2. R. C. Sproul, *The Gospel of God: An Exposition of Romans* (Great Britain: Christian Focus Publications, 1999), 234.

Chapter Fifteen

1. Donald Grey Barnhouse, *God's Glory*, in *Romans,* vol. 4 (Grand Rapids: Eerdmans Publishing Company, 1964), 44.
2. Ibid., 72.
3. K. S. Wuest, *Wuest's Word Studies from the Greek New Testament: For the English Reader,* vol.1 (Grand Rapids: Eerdmans Publishing Company, 1997), 249.
4. Wuest, *Word Studies from the Greek New Testament*, 253-254.
5. John Calvin, *Calvin's Commentaries: Romans*, vol. XIX (Grand Rapids: Baker Books, 1999), 537.

Chapter Sixteen

1. James Strong, *The Exhaustive Concordance of the Bible: Greek Dictionary of the New Testament* (Iowa Falls: World Bible Publishers, 1986), 27.
2. W. Hendriksen and S. J. Kistemaker, *Matthew*, of *New Testament Commentary* (Grand Rapids: Baker Book House, 2001), 499.
3. K. S. Wuest, *Wuest's Word Studies from the Greek New Testament: For the English Reader*, vol.1 (Grand Rapids: Eerdmans Publishing Company, 1997), 259.

Commentaries available from
PRACTICAL CHRISTIANITY FOUNDATION

DANIEL
In God I Trust

MARK
Jesus Christ, Love in Action

JOHN
The Word Made Flesh

ROMANS
Hope of the Nations

THE GENERAL EPISTLES
A Practical Faith

REVELATION
Tribulation and Triumph

For more information, please visit www.greenkeybooks.com